Singles now comprise approximately forty percent of the total adult population and yet remain one of the most misunderstood and ignored species of our social order. After suffering the indignities of divorce, we tend to dash out into this brand new experience called single life, with our emotional flies wide open, totally unprepared for the consequences. As a result, many end up bogged down in one of the classic traps.

The many acute changes in this new lifestyle, such as: new social standards, loneliness, financial problems, depression, new responsibilities, insecurities, rejection and new friends, often blend together to make this transition, a casserole of confusion. Add to this the sense of failure which often accompanies divorce and you have quite a problem. It's not as hopeless as it might seem. But it is not the emotional picnic that our media and many publications would lead us to believe either.

This extremely fun to read book is designed to present insights on new survival strategies in such a way as to let readers select their own mode of survival. Single's Survival is not just an extremely helpful book. It soon becomes an old friend, which one can sit down and laugh about single experiences with.

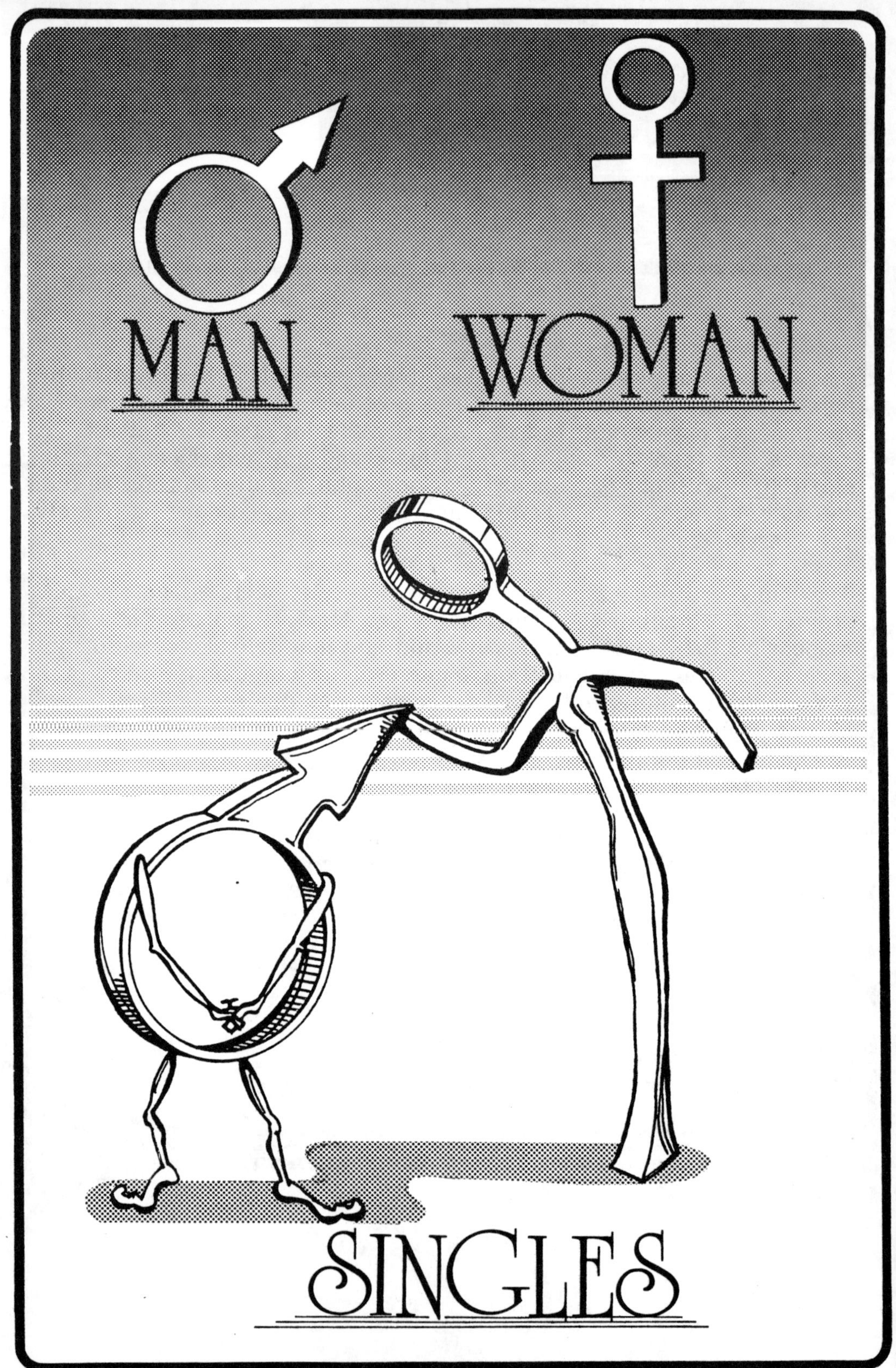

MAN
WOMAN
SINGLES

Written, Designed & Illustrated
by
Mort Buckley

EDITED BY
Boye De Mente

SINGLE'S pocket guide to SURVIVAL

PUBLISHED BY

5043 N. 20th AVE. PHOENIX, ARIZONA 85015

WRITTEN AND ILLUSTRATED BY MORT BUCKLEY
COPYRIGHT © 1983
ALL RIGHTS RESERVED

ISBN: 0-914067-00-1

First paperback edition, 1983

Library of Congress Catalog Card Number:83-90907

Printed in the U.S.A.

<u>*Dedication*</u>

I dedicate this book to

Tiffany and Brady, my kids

Who gave me, their father, life

after my wife died.

<u>Never underestimate the power of kids!</u>

<u>*Acknowledgements*</u>

To the many singles who knowingly

and unknowingly contributed to this book

and especially to those of you who encouraged me on

I am greatly indebted.

——————— ❋ ———————

To Boye DeMente

My editor, mentor and the only one

I would trust with an editing pen,

Thank You.

You took an "excellent" manuscript

and made it even "excellenter".

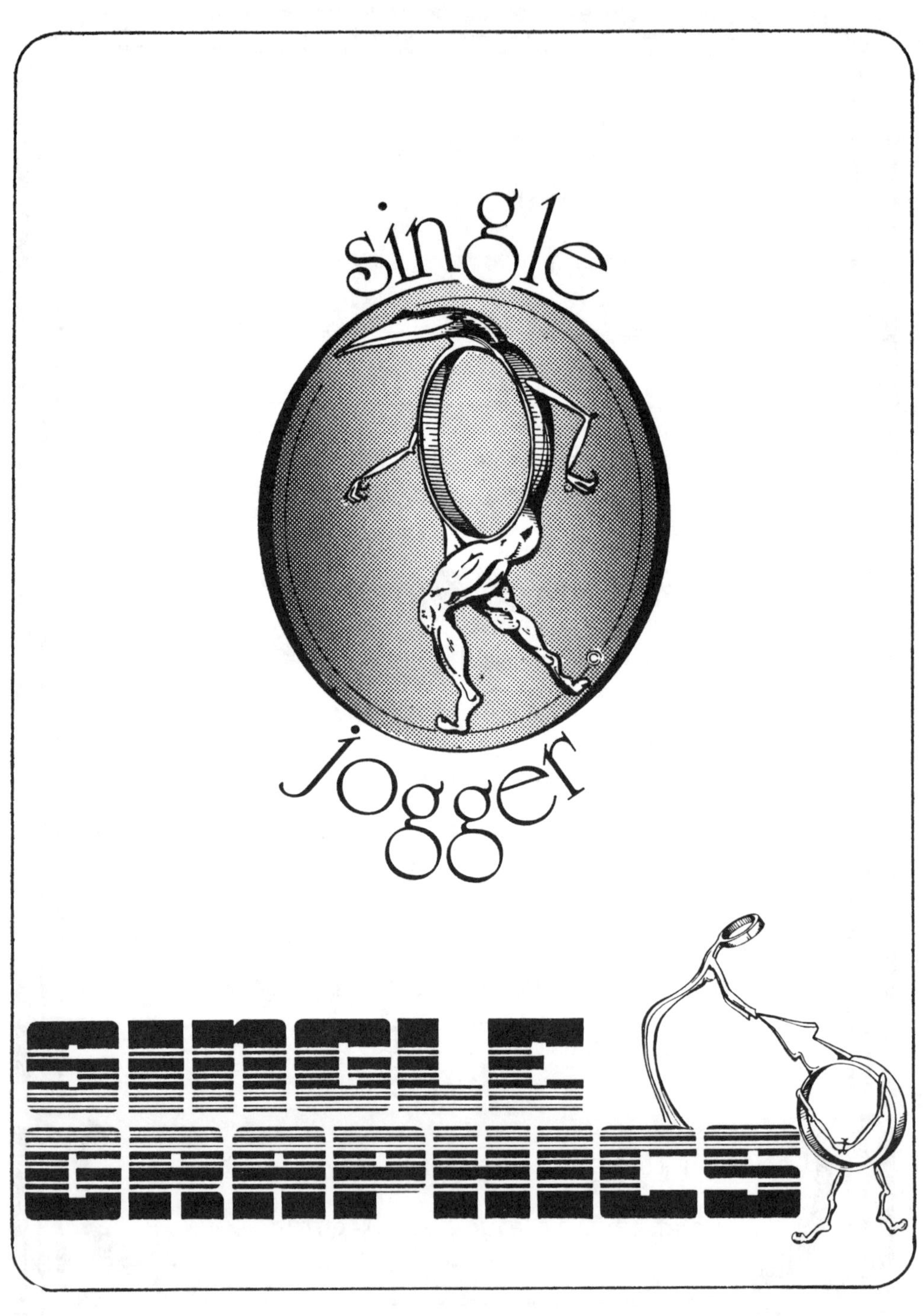

single
jogger
SINGLE
GRAPHICS

TABLE OF CONTENTS

INTRODUCTION

I emerged from my "singlization" very vulnerable, confused and grief stricken, mainly because I had no experience on which to base decisions governing my new single lifestyle.

I am basically a very calm, logical person and, as a result, I calmly flew into a blind state of mass hysteria.

"Here I am, thirty-five years old and starting all over again. The world is passing me by!"

A quick glance at the mirror assured me that at the rate my body was deteriorating, no one would want the remains if I waited much longer.

I calmly concluded that I had only a couple of days left in which to find another mate and make my place in this new dimension of confusion before it was too late. As a result, I dashed out into the single-world totally unprepared for the consequences, and then spent the next two years in the confirmed belief that I couldn't last one more day.

Singlehood was unlike anything I had imagined it to be, and my "free, easy," new lifestyle soon proved to be about as much fun as a dose of salts! I wanted desperately to join this new organization called "The Single World," but I couldn't find it. I looked everywhere, including the Yellow Pages. Singles were all around but everyone was busy doing their own thing without me!

Everyone seemed self-sufficient and no one seemed to need me as much as I needed them. In an attempt to show my sincerity, I would fling open my raincoat of despair and bare my innermost soul to them. As a result, the friends I had made refused to speak to me!

One evening, in an attempt to explode myself to death by overeating, I came to the realization that there must be an answer somewhere. As a result, I soon found myself embarking on a journey in search of truth and self fulfillment -- a journey that would ease the pangs of torment which I had been experiencing. I returned some time later with an armload of "How to Cope" books and a jumbo-pack of Alka-Seltzer.

The profound wisdom that I found within the pages of these

books did give me a few answers but little relief. I ended up spending the remains of my family fortune on books that were dedicated to the attributes of being single. The glittering propaganda pouring forth from these pages sounded so good and yet my single life was so bad!   By the time I finished the last one of these beauts, I was so emotional I had a tendency to cry at car wash dedications.   After a while, I managed to get my crying under control and started looking in the public library for answers, but was asked to leave because I kept gritting my teeth too loudly.

Married friends shunned me. My desperation frightened off prospective new friends and all of this rejection soon convinced me that I was not suitable company even for myself.

My hunger for answers regarding love, happiness and the single life became an obsession.   I continued reading everything on these subjects I could find.   I purchased one book titled "HOW TO HUG" and didn't realize until I got home that it was volume nine of the Encyclopedia Britannica.

At this point, I began to realize the need for a clear, concise book which would allow singles to laugh at their problems and yet offer good advice on how to cope and what to expect.   I realized that as a new single, I was going to have to learn from the mistakes of old singles, because I surely wouldn't survive long enough to make all the mistakes myself.

I started attending single's seminars, discussion groups, workshops, encounter groups and discussing issues with singles, in places ranging from bars to spiritual retreats.

This book is a product of the experiences, both good and bad, of these veteran singles. The following pages constitute a surprisingly accurate cross-section of the problems, attitudes, cures and emotional adjustments which the average single experiences. However, I have found that, for every single, there seems to be an individual set of rules.   Therefore, the advice and patterns set forth here represent the general opinion of the single society, not necessarily every single.

Parts of this book are dedicated to the new single, and even though they are sprinkled with "humor," they may appear mundane or depressing to those who are not experiencing the adjustment pangs of "singlization". This transition can be a most depressing time in the life of a new single and even those who "have the answers," can benefit from a better understanding of these problems.

I have found that areas of this book have a tendency to make certain people angry. After analyzing it though, we usually discover that this emotion is the result of hitting upon a truth which they subconsciously want to suppress. If <u>you get angry at different points in this book, take the time to analyze it and find out why.</u> This book is not designed to insult anyone or to change philosophies that are working for you.

Single Symbols ©

I have illustrated this book with a new concept that I call SINGLEGRAPHICS©; A twentieth century form of hieroglyphics, specifically taylored for...Today's Single. To acquaint you with this contemporary analogy of ancient hieroglyphics, I have included this short course in modern archeology.

First you take...

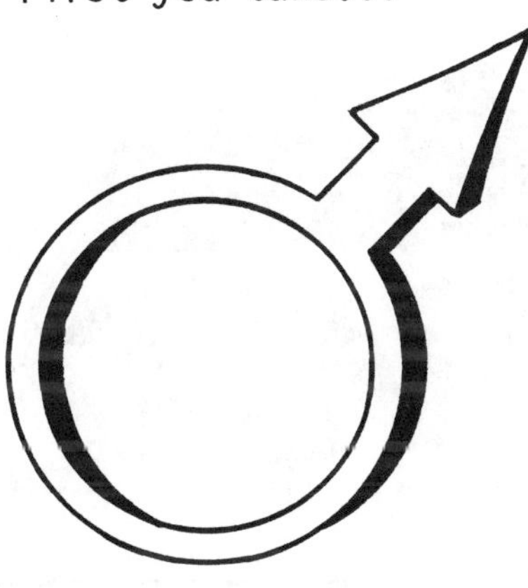

A MAN

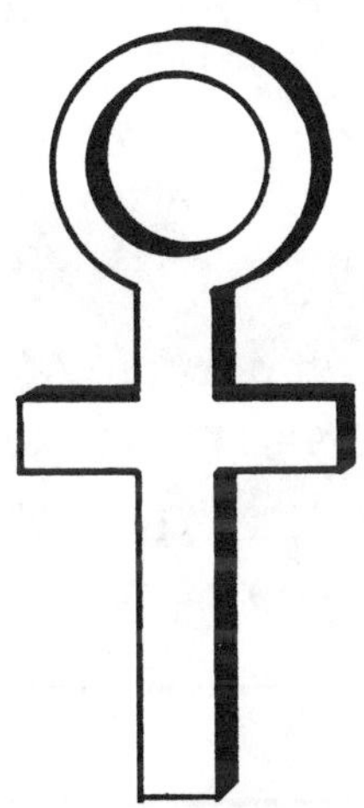

and   A WOMAN

Then you add...

and if you're not careful, you can come up with...

A MESS!

In order to get ourselves straightened out, many of us take part in a social ritual called...

Divorce gets us untangled but leaves us...

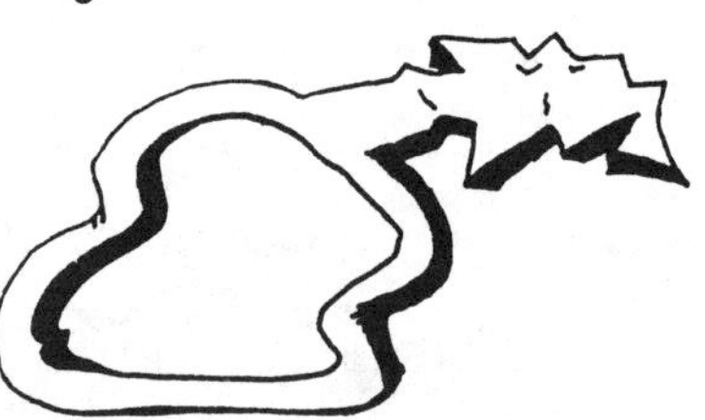

UNSTRAIGHTENED OUT

In order to get ourselves straightened out, we have to go through a thing called...

ADJUSTMENT

Now Adjustment is necessary
but it is painful, so we...

RUN FROM IT

When we finally run out of breath and Adjustment
does catch us, it creates a new kind of man and
woman called The Straightened Out...

SINGLE

Female ~ Male
SINGLE SYMBOLS

Now for some reason, most single men and women still retain
an unexplainable compulsion to get hopelessly wrapped up in
one another but it is controlled by an element called...

EXTREME FEAR

Once in a while, however, they each decide to make an emotional investment, go in together and build...

A RELATIONSHIP

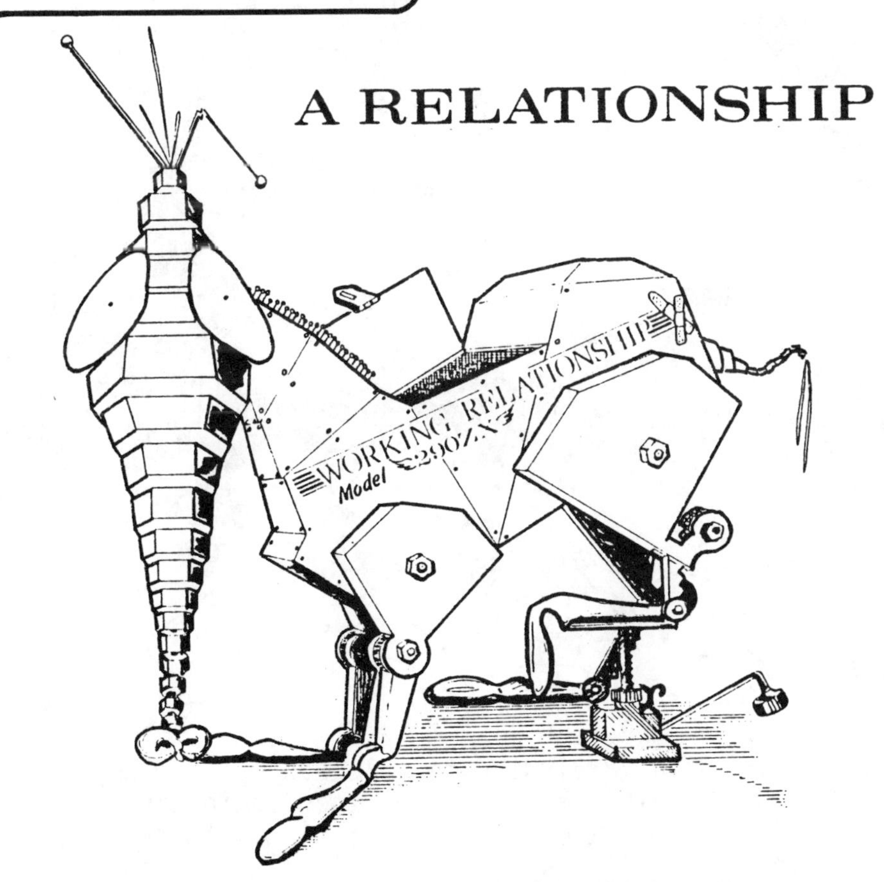

It takes two people to build one of these things and two
people to keep it working because, as you can see in the
last illustration, relationships tend to break down very
often. When they do work though, they are fantastic! You
can both climb on...put it into drive and ride under the
nearest rainbows to brave the storms of life together.

So in concluding this lesson on Single
Symbols, we will enter the fascinating
realm of motivation, starting with the
birth of a single; A process hereafter
referred to as...

CHAPTER 1
Singlization

Chapter 1

SINGLIZATION

Somewhere between the ecstasy of freedom and the desolation of loneliness, lies a dimension called The Single Life.

It is a composit of:

> The excitement of a new love
> and the agony of rejection.
> The pleasure of self awareness
> and the panic of insecurity.
> The freedom of choice
> and the confines of loneliness.
> The spice of variety
> and the fear of growing old, alone.

Single life has many different meanings for its many different participants, but we all enjoy its fruits and lament its pain.

For many, single life is fickle, promising fulfillment of fantasies but yielding loneliness. Or promising loneliness and yielding self-fulfillment.

Those who learn to be self-sufficient will improve in character and strength.   Those who cannot will suffocate in their own grief or remarry out of desperation rather than love.   Single life is not always comprised of the euphoric elements that "popular wisdom" depicts, and is, therefore, a profound disappointment to many of its recruits.

Single life is a little like Scotch.   It isn't easy to adjust to, nor easy to give up once you have.   Many "unsingles", bored with their lives, have felt that they could adjust to it reeaal easy.   A new sex partner every night, no responsibilities and no one to answer to!   As

(19)

a result, many have tried it, only to find themselves hopelessly bogged down within a year's time, with a new spouse and the same old problems.

Why is singlization so difficult to adjust to?   Well, one reason is that society has managed to place us all in sexist roles and provide guidelines for us to live by that are impossible even under the best of circumstances.   As an example, let us combine the pressures of adapting to a new single life with the frustration of trying to live up to society's blueprint of the ideal American Male or Female.   First, let's look at the ideal male image.

<u>The Ideal American Male</u>
He is a worldwise protector, a successful provider, a wise counselor, a fantastic lover, and one whose undying confidence gives him the capability of controlling any situation.   The problem is, at this particular time in his life, our worldwise protector is nothing more than a bowl of emotional mush that has been out of circulation for so long that the average ten-year old girl is more worldwise and in-tune than he is.   Current circumstances (divorce or loss of a spouse) may have left our successful provider with just enough money to buy a girl a cup of coffee provided she does not order a doughnut. He has definitely lost a great deal of self-confidence in the area of wise counseling.   His own state of affairs bears witness to that.

Now as our example of male machoism stands before the mirror, he notes that his machoism has settled somewhat into the middle to lower extremities, and that some of his hair went with it.   As he stands there, stripped by the scrutiny of his own reflection, he ponders the possibility of plastic surgery and hair transplants.   A barrage of memories drift between him and the bewildered stranger staring back from the mirror.   He recalls the stories which were confided to him by some of his single buddies, about today's liberal society, with its sexual diversions, subversions and perversions.   The stories were exciting six months ago but now....in a sheer panic, he decides that maybe he's just not ready for this.   To openly acknowledge his insecurities would be admitting that he was having trouble living up to society's image of manhood so he stands there hoping for a revelation of some kind.   Some of the solutions our male pillar of strength may consider at this point are the Foreign Legion, a monastery, and suicide.   Now let's look at society's image of the New American Female.

The Female's New Social Image

She is up, bright-eyed and bushy-tailed at 5:00 A.M. She fixes breakfast for the children and then takes a shower with a new kind of vitalizing soap. She brushes her perfect teeth to a blinding flash of white, combs her long, bouncy, shining hair into a flip on the top of her head, then slips her well-stacked and slender body into an $800 suit and a $100 pair of spikes.

She calls her attorney and banker out of bed to give them some last minute instructions or tips, and loads her kids into the Mercedes. After dropping the kids off she does the grocery shopping while the checkout boys all faint with ecstasy, and then returns home to complete her household chores.

Arriving at work precisely on time at 8:07, she bounces into the conference room where thirty-seven handsome executives await her instructions. Her day is full as she runs the business affairs at the office, visits the various construction sites in her color-coordinated hardhat to make sure the buildings are being built correctly, and then lunches with the tallest, handsomest millionaire in town aboard his private jet.

Later, she returns to her office to complete the fashion sketches for the Miss Universe contest and then on to the television studio for a personal interview. From there, she drives across town to keep a dinner engagement. As she bounces into the restaurant, finally letting her hair down and shaking it into a cascade of beautiful curls, the men all hungrily shout her name: "HI, FREDDIE"! She graciously flashes a flirtatious smile, but she really only has eyes for her date because she is a woman, and has definite plans for dessert!

As she seats herself, her Robert Redford lookalike date gently takes her hand and says, "Honey, you've come a long way."

The scene at the restaurant fades abruptly as our girl sits straight up in bed, awakened by the reality that somewhere between her "I do" and her "I don't", she went completely out of style.

As she passes the mirror on the way to the bathroom, she pauses. She isn't exactly bright-eyed but she is definitely bushy tailed. As a matter of fact, it seems to bush out all over the place. Her eyes drop a few inches and suddenly freeze, as she takes in the size of those thighs.

After locating the kitchen, she begins the ordeal of preparing breakfast. She opens the cupboard door and stares with glazed eyes, hoping that something tasty and easy will tumble out. As she sits at the table staring at her cereal box, she realizes that she has dedicated her entire life to fulfilling society's blueprint of the perfect, helpless, subservient woman, and just as she has become really good at it, society changes its mind. She doesn't know how overdrawn she is because the checkbook refuses to balance. The faucet leaks, the plumbing is stopped up, everyone tells her that she is unqualified for employment, and she couldn't drive to work anyway because the fuse that opens the garage door is blown. To make matters worse, socializing is out of the question because of her chronic thigh-problem and she just discovered a fly in her last box of cereal.

She quickly grabs a breakfast roll to ease her insecurities and woofs it down, as she ponders her fate. Some of the solutions that drift between her and the fly are: Going back to bed, Becoming a nun, and Suicide.

<u>Adjusting_</u>
At this point in time, neither Mr. or Ms. America's problems are even close to over. Obviously, one of the largest obstacles is the old dragon of insecurities, or "What does everyone else think of me?" neurosis. This neurosis is most prevalent among marrieds and people who only use others to bounce reflections of themselves off to see how they are.

It's a big, new kind of world out there and neither of them know exactly who they are, what to expect, or what is expected of them. They have spent the better part of their lives listening to someone else's criticisms, and being programmed to please a society whose entire existence hinges upon how many dead dinosaurs it can come up with.

For a time, Mr. and Mrs. America will probably each bury themselves completely in work, family or other forms of safe or not so safe escapism, and wait for fate to determine the course of their lives.

There are numerous other obstacles in the way of a girl's adjustment such as:

Black and blue fingernails caused by an inaccurate hammer. Singed off eyelashes from trying to fix the stupid furnace. Dislocated back from losing a fight with a heavy piece of furniture.

or

Finding that her front door is permanently closed after the Superglue dries on the weatherstripping she just installed.

Then there will be times when she goes out with a guy and right in the middle of the most extravagant cuisine she could find on the menu, he tells her that until a relationship matures past the point of friendship, he always goes dutch. Or she finds out that Mr. Wonderful is wearing leather leotards under his three piece suit!

Similarly, there are many obstacles between a guy and his ability to adjust like:

When he presses out his best slacks with the back of his only skillet (because his Ex kept the iron) and they mysteriously grow black stripes.

Or, when he starts to wash out the stripes in the kitchen sink and flips on the garbage disposal instead of the light switch. Then he gets his tie caught in this mechanical cannibal while trying to save his pants and suddenly realizes that the smoke is there because his skillet is changing state right there on his very own stove.

Or, the folding bed in his new apartment automatically folds up with him in it and his only course of escape is to tear through the mattress and climb out through the springs.

Or, he might spend $50 on his date's dinner only to find out that in order to keep her figure, she throws up after every meal.

Or, like when he takes his seventeen year old girl friend to church the first time, (introducing her as a long lost niece) and during the testimony she stands up and tells the congregation that he is the most sexually gratifying lover she has ever had!

Another problem they will experience is with the inconsistency of sexist roles. At this particular point in time, you just never know what to expect. When a guy opens a door for a girl he is fairly sure she will react in one of two ways. She will either say, "Thank you" and step through, or she will break his nose with a karate jab and call him a chauvinist pig!

Similarly, girls used to have an edge on the guys by misrepresentation--through the use of makeup, padded bras and false eyelashes. Now guys are using some makeup and woven hairpieces of their own, and some have been known to strap a small salami to an inside thigh before slipping into their tight pants. The latter is most prevalent at single's bars where "crotch watching," as it is called, is a favorite female pastime.

Generally, if you limit your socializing to the confines of your own generation, you will have less trouble adjusting to modern, sexist inconsistencies. The overall overhaul of American tradition has produced a much more liberal society.

If you can stand the pressures of adjustment, you will find that by sharing a majority of your spare time with yourself, you will get to know and respect yourself a great deal. This better understanding of yourself will enable you to correct your weaknesses and in time, if given the chance, single life can reveal the route to personal happiness and self-contentment. The rest is up to you--and it probably won't be easy!

CHAPTER 2
So You Want A Divorce

Chapter 2

So You Want A Divorce

It has been established that beyond any shadow of a doubt, the number one cause of divorce in this country is marriage.

The Cop-Out

The question we now have to ask is, "Why are there so many marriages?"   One reason, of course, is due to the sudden surge of remarriages from the resulting divorces.   However, our most thoughtful answer is two-fold:

1.   Considering the importance of a total lifetime commitment, the decision to marry can be very spontaneous and the requirements for marriage very simple.

2.   As a result of the new social attitude regarding divorce laws, most people enter marriage with the idea that if the going gets rough (as it definitely does from time to time), they can always get a divorce.   With this proverbial back door open, the decision to marry is much easier.   An interesting statistic to this fact is that the average marriage now lasts only six years.   Further, over one-third of all remarriages fail, and 40% of the resulting divorces occur within the first year.

In short, marriage and divorce are just too easy.   If filing for a divorce suddenly became punishable by death there would be a lot more successful marriages.   With this back door closed, locked and sealed, married couples not only would have a much greater incentive to get along and make it work, they would control the pangs of passion and give the whole idea of marriage a lot more thought before jumping in the first place.

The point I am trying to make is not that divorce and marriage laws should be changed to protect us from our own mistakes. I simply want to show that people often have a potential for making a marriage work _if they want it to._ If both had to make it work, they probably could. Since we don't have to make it work, we often take what appears to be the easy way out and scream about it all the way.

If a couple has problems that absolutely prevent any chance of reconciliation, and if professional help is out of the question, they might be wise to get out. On the other hand, if they are looking for the happiness that they can't seem to find in their present marriage, there is a very good chance that they will not find it through divorce or even a second marriage, either.

It's an unfortunate fact that most people never discover this until the adverse effects of divorce prove to them that their marital state or spouse cannot make them happy, particularly if they have made the choice, for some reason, to be unhappy. Only we can make that choice for ourselves. An outside influence like a spouse, tends only to fulfill our own personal attitude, which can be happiness if we want it to be. When we rely on others for our main source of happiness, we will be disappointed every time.

The Escape Artists

Problems are a basic ingredient for life as we know it. As a result, we all have a subconscious need for them which often takes form in the unhappy (or painful) attitude that we maintain in our lives. In short, we all have a tendency to beat ourselves up. If the Good Fairy came to you today and took away every problem you had, in a subconscious drive for survival you would, within a week or less, develop just as many new problems to support this need. We all hate the pain of our problems, and yet cherish and cling to them all the way.

Why do we do this? Because problems give us purpose! _Without problems, we would have no purpose_! As a result, we create problems, then we try and escape from them. If we succeed, we feel unimportant again! This quest for purpose can cause us to overdose on problems and the resulting frustration can cause us more pain. What do we often blame it on? The most influential element in our lives, of course, our marriage!

Most of us have a subconscious realization that we need problems, in order to build strength, character, wisdom and to give us purpose.   On the other hand, we try to escape them, and the resulting conflict, raging deep within our psyche, can become so frustrating and confusing we experience more pain than an arthritic centipede.

Remember, the <u>First</u> <u>Single's</u> <u>Law</u> <u>of</u> <u>Stress</u> states: "There is no problem on earth so small that it can't be blown completely out of proportion."

Our incessant desire to escape pain at any cost often results in bad decisions which usually just create more pain. Instead of experiencing the initial pain and learning from it, we jump right into a new set of pain-inducing problems. This is due largely to our inability to trust our own judgments. Why do so many of us have trouble in trusting our own judgments?   Mainly because we are in the habit of fooling ourselves into believing whatever we want to believe. As a result, we stop trusting ourselves just like we would stop trusting anyone who showed bad judgment or lied to us. (This profound theory of "truth decay" will be covered more extensively throughout the book.)

Pain continues to build as the result of our running, until we reach a threshold we can no longer endure.   This is the time when truths are often revealed because of our critical need for answers. Unfortunately many singles, in an attempt to escape the painful tempering process needed to reach this stage, remarry too soon and never make it.   Or they develop a thick layer of emotional callousing. Eventually, this results in an advanced stage of emotional rigor mortis and they stop feeling altogether! Our society, with its physical and emotional comforts, has developed a generation of escape artists which are so confused and miserable they don't know which way to turn.

There are a few singles who have reached their solitary state from having no other choice, and many enter the realm of single life simply to fulfill fantasies or to find a quick solution to their existing problems.   Life is complex and it holds few easy solutions, regardless of one's marital status.   Expectations are not fulfilled in reaching adulthood, so we marry.   Expectations are not fulfilled in marriage, so we divorce.   Expectations are not fulfilled in divorce so we jump back into marriage, always convinced that happiness lies just around the corner, in the arms of someone else.

It is true that married life can have a tendency to be boring.

When you start trying to remember the last time you made love in order to determine when you should do it next, you are definitely in a holding pattern. But then, flying solo is not necessarily the answer either. I honestly believe that somewhere, deep inside every unsingle, there is a single fighting to get free, and somewhere within every single, there is an unsingle wanting to get caught. This just testifies that no matter which side of matrimony many of us are on, it can be the wrong side.

The single soul often cries out for the old, down-home, rocking-chair comfort of a long past marital relationship. Now I'm not saying that all single life is not good. I'm merely saying that it is not exactly as many married people think. Before escaping permanently from your rocking chair you might be well-advised to consider the saddle sores associated so often with the "exciting life."

<u>Counselling</u>

Counselling is not the magic cure-all that many believe it is, but a good marital psychologist can be very helpful in determining the weak spots in a relationship and providing solutions to work with. The problem is that few people take advantage of this potential. The three basic reasons for their reluctance are:

1. <u>Finances.</u> As a rule this is a cop-out because if you are sincere about it, there are many organizations (usually church or community sponsored) which will charge only in relation to your income. Most churches can give you information on these services and will be happy to do so whether you are a member or not. In some areas, there are free community sponsored programs that can be located by contacting your local Information And Referral Service.

2. <u>Emotional Modesty.</u> There is some strange little inner voice that tells many of us we should know all the secrets to good emotional health ourselves, and that we should not bare our psyche to anyone. The need for emotional help can be as necessary as our need for medical help, but we sometimes fail to see this. We don't mind trusting someone with our bodies but baring our minds before someone would be just too embarrassing. After all, who wants to run around showing their bare psyche to complete strangers? The funny thing is, those who try it generally like it and often leave with fantastic new insights and realizations.

    3.   <u>Guilt</u>. When Spouse #1 doesn't come up to the expectations of Spouse #2, Spouse #2 often attempts to change Spouse # to fit their own desires. To do this, Spouse #2 needs to have control, and many use guilt as the manipulator. After a prolonged period of guilt programming, Spouse #1 realizes that the relationship is not working and feels very guilty about it. It's no small wonder that Spouse #1 is reluctant to go to a marriage counselor. The counselor will more than likely, just lay more guilt and impose impossible demands on old #1 to make #2 happy. A good marriage counselor, however, will immediately see the problem and might in fact, lay a small guilt trip on Spouse #2 for a change.

<u>Separate</u>

    A very significant majority of many divorced singles I have talked with regret their decision for divorce. This is particularly true of men. When their expectations of single life crash they try, unsuccessfully as a rule, to renew their marriage and end up grief stricken in their failure. Before agreeing on a divorce, at least try separating for awhile. If you can come to mutual terms, try an informal separation of at least five or six months with separate living quarters, support payments and visitation rights for the kids (if applicable). If you both like it, go for it. If not, talk it out.

<u>Detriments Of Divorce</u>

    Now let's take a look at a few of the problems that new singles encounter initially after divorce.

<u>Loss Of Friends</u>

    You will gradually have less and less in common with your married friends and you will often feel as necessary as a third glove when you are around them. A friend's spouse may consider you a threat to the marital stability of your friend. Your friend, on the other hand, might consider you a sexual threat to his or her spouse, and old memories will be uncomfortable to discuss. Another big problem is that friends' loyalties are often torn between the two divorced singles, resulting in emotional discomfort while in their presence. You may also find yourself harboring jealousy and resentment toward married friends.

Spousal Withdrawal

Most divorced people experience a heart-tearing loss of belonging that they may not have been aware of during marriage. Insecurities like loneliness, a sense of failure, uncertainty and the horrors of starting a new lifestyle are also adverse realities worthy of consideration.

Finances

Drastically lowered lifestyles and financial hardships are other factors which should not be overlooked. You may find that borrowed books and generic wine will occupy a good amount of your single fun-time. You may find yourself anxiously anticipating your once a week extravaganza, consisting of a brisk walk to your corner drug store to splurge recklessly on a package of gum.

Children

When applicable, children are one of the main considerations and are in fact, one of the chief reasons for many divorces. A great many wives seek a divorce mainly because the husband does not spend enough time with the family and the time that is spent is not of good quality. Following the divorce, for reasons that will become obvious, these mothers often find themselves in the same rut that their Ex was in. Most statistics show that children from single parent homes have a much greater tendency for delinquency and poor scholastic performance; however, severe marital problems within the family unit can also have a tremendous effect upon the kids.

Time And Workload

The additional workload experienced in accepting the responsibilities of both partners becomes critical when small children are present. There are domestic chores such as shopping, cooking, cleaning, washing, etc. as well as household repairs, car repairs, maintenance, gardening and so forth. If you have children with you, multiply the workload factor by at least two.

Attributes

Despite the many adverse considerations of divorce there are many positive attributes of being single, some of which are:

Independence; self-awareness; self-esteem; unlimited closet space---and freedom, which is the greatest asset of all.

The good and bad points of single life will be covered in detail later because divorce and single life are two completely separate entities and therefore must be considered separately.

If your final decision is divorce, you may be standing on the threshold of an exciting and challenging new experience so just hang in there and don't look back.

3
CHAPTER
Legalities of Divorce

Chapter 3

THE LEGALITIES OF DIVORCE

It has been said that the only uniformity in the laws governing divorce is their lack of uniformity. As a matter of fact, by the time you get through this chapter (if you're still awake) you may decide that it would be much simpler to just stay married.

It goes without saying that this should not be considered a do-it-yourself guide to divorce, and the services of a good attorney are recommended. The purpose of this chapter is to inform you of the important precautions and procedures to take prior to filing, and to also make those who are considering divorce a little more aware of what they are getting into.

Separations

There are several different types of separations. Basically, they all boil down to two main categories.

1. The Legal Separation
2. The "I am just getting the heck out" separation.

The legal separation may be expensive and is fairly binding. It is a basic contract between the husband and wife proportioning the family's material worth as well as the kids and dog. The husband usually pays support money to the wife (similar to alimony) as well as child support, and he usually retains visitor's rights. For all general purposes it's like a divorce except that both remain legally married even though they live separately.

The legal separation can be utilized when two married people want to split up for religious or other reasons, but do not want to divorce.   The legal separation is also very often used as a wedge by the woman in an effort to force the husband into a more lucrative divorce settlement later.   The husband is more apt to give in, after he realizes that he is paying as a divorced man with few of its benefits.

The second, simple separation may not be as simple as you think. You could be giving your spouse grounds for divorce on the basis of abandonment or desertion.   As a rule, however, the absence of one spouse against the will of the other has to be proven, and the period of time required to establish desertion is not usually less than six months.   In some states it is as high as three years.

If both parties agree to separate for a period of time, there is usually no grounds for desertion, but, the husband is often required to make an effort for reconciliation even though he may not be the one to have left.   If you and your spouse patch things up and live together for even one day (or night), the time period starts all over again.

Another problem with the simple separation is the tax advantage.   If in separating, you volunteer to pay support money to your spouse, it is not deductible unless it is required under a court order or a written separation agreement.   On the other hand, any support money paid to the wife is non-taxable to her.

Legal Grounds

Generally speaking, both parties in a divorce are at least to some degree at fault, right?   Wrong!   A great many court judgments are based upon the notion that one party takes all of the blame and the other party is completely innocent.   Incredible as it sounds, a divorce may not even be granted if both or neither party is at fault.

At this point, it may be advisable to sit down with your spouse-- the one that threw the cat at you after you screamed the obscenities and quietly discuss which one is going to be the bad guy.   Forget about the claw marks on your head, ask forgiveness for the profoundly accurate dirty names that you screamed and say, "It's my fault dear and I will take all the blame."

When you are desperate enough to do this, you are one small step closer to successfully achieving a divorce but this does not necessarily mean that you should be the bad guy!

There is a national trend toward no-fault divorce.   However, a large number of states still require substantial grounds.   Likewise, the general belief that incompatibility is grounds for divorce is pure science fiction in many states.   The only grounds recognized in every state is adultery, which is becoming harder and harder to prove and is used less and less.

Desertion is currently used as grounds in every state except North Carolina and Oregon.   In order to provide grounds by desertion (as we have learned), one party usually has to leave against the will of the other and cannot return to live, reconcile or have sex with the other for a period of six months to three years, depending upon the state in which you reside.   The average length of time is one year.

Generally, the law recognizes the husband as "the head of the household" and, therefore, he has the legal right to decide the place of residence.   If he decides to or is required to move and the wife refuses, the grounds for desertion would ordinarily be dismissed.   It is very difficult but sometimes possible for a husband to prove desertion on the wife's part if she refuses to relocate with him.

The term "Constructive Desertion" describes the act of one party forcing the other party to leave against their will.   The grounds are, of course, leveled against the one doing the forcing-- provided that the party which left does so out of genuine fear, physical compulsion and/or against their will.

The most commonly used grounds for divorce, at present, is "Mental Cruelty."   It is used in every state except Alabama, Washington, D.C., Maryland, Michigan, North Carolina, Vermont and Virginia.   Consistent with the inconsistencies of divorce laws, nobody really seems to know exactly what mental cruelty is and thousands of cases are dismissed each year as a result.   But many thousands more are granted on these grounds.

Everyone seems to agree that mental cruelty can be anything which "utterly destroys" a marriage through any "unjustifiable" type of conduct.   It is largely connected with physical abuse, threats of violence, severe mental anguish, denial of sexual duties and a series of smaller charges which can be shown to set a pattern of combined offenses over an extended period, including nagging, cursing, infidelity, intolerable hygiene, sexual perversion, etc..

Mental cruelty is used, to a large extent, as a substitute for more embarrassing charges such as adultery or impotency.

Other grounds for divorce used, to a lesser extent in a varied number of states, include bigamy, alcoholism, drug addiction, felony resulting in imprisonment, impotency, insanity and non-support.

It is not true that you are out of luck if a spouse refuses to sign the papers (as in "I love you, but my wife won't give me a divorce".) Divorce, in other than no-fault states, is very hard to get without proper grounds anyway, and the refusal of one party to cooperate does not add that much more of a burden. Anyway you look at it, there does have to be grounds showing that the marriage just could not work at all.

Why not go to a "no fault" state? Again, it is not that simple; especially if your spouse will not agree, as a no-fault divorce is based upon mutual consent. Also, most states have a residence period ranging from six months to two years before you are even allowed to file for a divorce.

In short, you may be able to prove that your spouse's snoring continues to shatter windows and putsout street lights for a radius of six miles on a clear night, but unless you can prove that your life is in danger from falling plaster you may have trouble getting your divorce.

There are, in every state, greedy lawyers whose parasitic method of survival depends upon the ruination of marriages and human life. If you are desperate enough for a divorce, you can find one of these legal creatures to aid you in collusion--which, for this purpose, means the unlawful assistance between husband and wife to illegally secure a divorce. To give a true illustration, I refer to Lee, an innocent little farm girl from Illinois. Lee and her husband had a serious argument one Sunday afternoon. In the course of the argument, the possibility of divorce was brought up and in the heat of anger both agreed. Her husband owns a manufacturing company and the following day they both met with his attorney to discuss the divorce.

Tuesday, she met her attorney which was recommended by his attorney and the four sat down to discuss it. Within a very short period of time, Lee found herself a divorced woman. In court, as the allegations began pouring from her husband's mouth, she denied them to her attorney who abruptly told her to keep quiet or she would blow the whole thing. She did and as the result her husband received custody of their children and retained most of the material items. Aside from a small lump sum settlement, she received nothing and to add insult to injury, she is required to help with child support. I recommended that Lee seek additional legal help, but at this time she is so burned out and depressed with the ordeal that she declined.

Aside from the advice to seek an honest attorney, there is

another very good lesson to be learned from this story. Do not necessarily trust your spouse when it comes to a divorce. You may have loved and lived and relied upon this person for many years, and they may be the parent of your children, but divorce can be cruel and vicious. If you are sincerely set upon obtaining a divorce, it is advisable for you to stand on your own feet, alone, starting now.

The Plaintiff

If you turn out to be the good guy, and are the one to initiate the divorce against your spouse, you are called the Plaintiff. As the Plaintiff, you will probably be required to produce at least one witness. This witness will have to substantiate the fact that you are and have been a resident of your state for the required duration of time, and may also be called on to support the essential elements of your case. Finding someone to corroborate the fact that your spouse hollers, curses and threatens you may not be too difficult. However, these could be rather flimsy grounds depending upon their severity. You would do better to produce a witness that can substantiate the fact that your spouse beats you or has committed adultery. If this is not possible, make sure that the witness at least witnesses any bruises and contusions that exist, or any broken teeth that might be lying around. Broken teeth are great! Ask any lawyer.

No Fault, Mutual Consent Divorces

There is a heavy swing toward the "No Fault" or "Mutual Consent" divorce laws, and many states have or are at present in the course of adopting these laws. It greatly simplifies divorce, and reduces court congestion considerably. It is so simple, as a matter of fact, that divorce forms can be purchased at stationery or office supply stores, filled out and executed by the divorcing parties.

The concept behind this "do it yourself divorce kit," is that neither party has to be at fault and both agree completely on the terms therein, whereas and in essentialibus thereof. It is perfectly legal and very inexpensive. However, there is one thing that should be brought to light before agreeing upon said terms.

You should realize your vulnerability at this point. Many people going through the preliminaries of divorce are in a state of emotional and mental numbness. They often agree to virtually anything to get it over with, figuring that they will find a way of coping with their decisions later. (Sounds a little like running from pain as discussed previously). It is, however, very important to base your decisions upon what you will be able to live with in the hard years to come.

Alimony and Support
What is alimony and support?   Well, one attorney defined it quite accurately as the "high cost of leaving". It is based upon the social concept of a husband's responsibility to provide for the wife and also on the contribution the wife has made in reaching their present monetary position. This contribution does not necessarily have to be financial. Decisions governing the amount of alimony and support are based upon:

A.   The marital conduct of both parties.
B.   The husband's income (present and future).
C.   The wife's income and ability to support herself.
D.   The wife's and husband's needs.
E.   The children's ages and needs.

Alimony and support are similar to taxes from a man's point of view. Unless the wife is independently wealthy, completely self-sufficient or has made no contribution to the marriage whatsoever, there is usually no way out of paying it.

Adultery and desertion by the wife still carries some weight in a few states, but it is seldom a successful deterrent to alimony.

If down the road, the husband becomes injured or ill and takes a significant decrease in income, with no conceivable hope of regaining his standard, the alimony can be reduced to fit the new circumstances. If down an opposite road the husband has a significant increase in income and his wife can prove that she can't cut it on the present alimony and that she had no knowledge of the increase when signing the divorce papers, the amount of alimony can be raised. The alimony can also be raised if the wife becomes ill or injured and can no longer help to support herself to the same extent.

How much is this high cost of leaving? A rough average for alimony is 25% to 33% of the man's income or 37% to 45% when it includes support for one child. These amounts can deviate greatly depending upon the many different circumstances. The courts generally have a domestic relations handbook available to the public which can help determine the amount.

Important Differences

Alimony is, of course, the money which is granted to the wife for her support and is usually paid in installments by the husband. Alimony is usually deductible by the husband, if he itemizes his deductions. But it is taxable income to the wife (she will have to pay taxes on it). Child support, however, is <u>NOT</u> usually deductible by the husband and the wife does <u>not</u> pay taxes on it. For this reason, many women ask for little alimony and all of the child support they can get.

The husband can, on occasion, claim the children as dependents if he can prove that he pays for over half of their total support. However, to be safe, he should have the wife agree in writing, to let him use the children as deductions instead of her.

Further, if you call it alimony, the wife upon remarrying will lose it. If you call it child support, the payments will continue until the children become of age.

Lump Sum Settlement

This type of settlement is not usually granted unless certain circumstances prevail. The decision is based upon the age of both parties, the life expectancy of each, the marital contribution from the wife, whether or not there are children involved, etc.. If there are children to consider, lump sum settlements are seldom granted.

If the couple has been married a fairly short time, there are no children, no significant contribution from the wife to the husband, and few assets have been accrued; or if the couple have been married for a long period of time and the husband is retired with no income, a lump sum settlement can be best.

Lump sum settlements are not deductible unless the husband pays in installments spread over a period exceeding ten years. Furthermore, if the wife invests her full portion unwisely and loses it, she can appeal to the courts and in some cases, get additional alimony. Another important consideration for the wife: if she settles for alimony and her husband kicks the bucket before she remarries, she can be left out on the proverbial limb due to the fact that death greatly reduces the husband's ability to provide. As a result, some women demand that alimony payments continue, even in the event of his death, payable from his estate (if he has anything left).

A lump sum settlement is the only way to go if you are the wife, without children, and plan to remarry in the near future, as alimony payments will continue only as long as you remain single.

Wrap Up

Having presented a basic look into the "legalities of divorce" in a lump sum, we are going to bring this chapter to a close with one more pleasant thought: who usually gets socked with all attorney and court costs?   The guy does, of course!

CHAPTER 4
Pass the Grief Please

(45)

Chapter 4

PASS THE GRIEF, PLEASE

You cannot prevent the birds of sorrow from flying over your head, but you can prevent them from building nests in your hair."

                                        -Ancient Chinese Proverb

<u>Lament of the Widowed and divorced</u>

The series of circumstances leading to your current state of affairs might seem to be devastating, but they are not. The word, "devastation," implies <u>total</u> destruction and even though you may feel totally destroyed, the pain which you have experienced has not only served as a valuable teaching aid, it can evolve into one of your greatest assets.

The emotional strength and character potential within each of us can be compared to the creative process of fine steel. It is subjected to devastating temperatures so excruciatingly hot it causes a complete change of state. Then it is plunged, torturously, into a cooling agent which results in its tempering, hardening and refining.

As I was going through my own tempering process, words like this had little meaning, as they were expressed by people who had never experienced my identical situation. Even though I have not experienced your own personal pain, I want to assure you that I know what grief is.

Karen, my wife, was strikingly beautiful, both physically and emotionally. No human is perfect but I believe now, as I believed then, that she was one of the best. Like every marriage, ours had some problems, but the happiness we shared significantly outweighed the unhappiness. We were actively involved in a group dedicated to the principle of making good marriages even better, and we were told by many that ours was a marriage that others patterned theirs after. I cared for my children more even than myself, but Karen was my life.

The evening of April 22, 1977, found us together on the outdoor patio of a restaurant overlooking Phoenix. The cool desert air caused her to snuggle close and I put my arm around her for warmth. As she looked into my eyes and smiled, I thought, "God, do I love you," and one of my biggest regrets is that I did not say it that evening.

My life was happy and reasonably complete. My occupation as an air conditioning contractor had plagued me with a series of heat strokes due to the grueling desert temperatures, but my business had developed to the degree where I would soon be out of the heat. We had a fine family, good health and a nice home. Karen died of a cerebral hemorrhage, caused by a broken blood vessel in her brain, on the evening of April 23, 1977.

The agony that I experienced was much worse than my own death, and I surely would have taken my life had it not been for our children. I lost faith in God and I lost my business. I started drinking heavily, and suicidal games became a part of my life. The best part of me had died and all that remained was an emotionally decayed corpse, eaten alive by the cancerous effects of grief. My only waking ambition was to sit and stare at a wall.

Eighteen months later I took what money we had and invested it in another business, but again my mental and emotional state prevented me from giving it the amount of dedication needed to create a successful business, and I soon lost it also. As a result, I was forced back into my old construction trade, working for someone else. I lost my drive, my self respect and considered myself a failure. The weight of loneliness from the loss of friends, the grueling heat, the problems and responsibilities of being a single parent, the pain of a broken relationship with a girl whom I had used in an attempt to fill the emptiness inside of me, and my critical financial state, added to my grief.

I am very familiar with grief and I wish I had known then what I know now. I may not know you personally, but as a human being, I do care and hope that my experience will help you with yours.

Dealing with Grief
Grief can be a devastating condition of mind and our minds can

destroy us if we let it.   Grief feeds on self pity and therefore, as a result of a subconscious desire for pain, we sometimes have a tendency to over-feed our grief.   This self pity feels good and somewhat comforting at first but as our grief gains strength we lose control and can be devoured by it.

Psychiatrists, psychologists and other experts in this field state that the loss of a spouse through death or divorce is the most devastating emotional experience one can have.   If you are in this position and can get a sense of comfort from this fact, it is due to your own self pity.   You are in the process of feeding your grief.   If you take comfort in another's pity and search for it, you are again, feeding your grief.   Now there are times when we all need emotional support and a reassuring pat on the back is good, but when grief-stricken, we often have a tendency to track different people down and spend hours crying over our misfortunes.   This search for reassurance can become an obsession and when no one else is present, we use our own shoulders to cry on.

Whether divorced or widowed, this is a perfectly natural characteristic, but we have to learn to resist the temptation of self pity in order to maintain better control over our grief.   You have every right to be miserable and others know this, but just realize if possible, what you are doing to yourself in using self pity.

On the other hand, don't run from your grief by refusing to discuss it or by using diversions such as drugs (unless prescribed), alcohol, sex or overwork.   You will have to face the grief head-on, and running from it just tends to string it out over a longer period of time.   As Marcel Proust said, "We are healed of a suffering only by experiencing it to the full."   Just try to live one day at a time and if this seems impossible, try living one minute at a time.

Grief can be very deceiving, especially to those of us who view it as a destructive and uncontrollable force.   As I was going through this period of my life, I became certain that all of this grief was destroying my cells and devouring my protoplasm.

Instead, my grief has proven itself to be the most constructive teacher and character builder I have ever known.   If we can see grief for the constructive and educational force that it is, we can more easily deal with it.   If we want to practice our techniques in "creative misery," however, we have merely to picture millions of little grief molecules, resembling "Pac Man," which are flooding our nervous system and cannibalizing everything in their path.

Try not to look at grief as a destructive enemy. View it instead as a valuable learning and tempering process. Let go of the past and look toward the future to the time when your pain will leave, as it really will. The future can have something bigger and better in store for you and you will never find it by hanging onto the past. One thing that keeps people hanging onto life is the knowledge that no matter how bad today is, tomorrow could be the best day of your life!

<u>Something to Hang on to</u>
One of the best ways to combat grief is to find a placebo and use it! Preoccupy yourself with something else. Pick a subject that is related to your grief, if possible, and work on it. The book that you are reading is a byproduct of my grief and so is my religion. Why religion? Because, for a while, I became obsessed with my anger at God, blaming him for my pain and for Karen's death.

Before Karen died, I had only an average understanding of God. My Super Logical Mind could not grasp the magnitude of a being who lives forever in a dimension that goes on for eternity. I could not accept the fact that the Universe had no end, because when it ended, what would be after that? Nothing? Nothing is something! How far does the nothing go? But a being that is, was, and always will be...Good God!

Sure, I admitted that there had to be something out there controlling the course of Pleiades and making everything work like a big, humongous clock, because, somehow, the theory that everything just sort of happened by accident didn't work for me.

The problem was, I did not take the time to research these questions until I absolutely had to have something to hang onto, and God remained an ominous, "grey area" in my life. Because of this potentially destructive force called grief, I have created this book, found my concept of God and have developed, yet, another philosophy of life that will get me through virtually anything. This philosophy is that the life which we have to endure on earth is very short when you compare it to eternity. Compared with forever, this life is nothing more than a waiting room, where we have to stay for a little while and now and then, we just get a hold of a bad magazine. When compared to forever, it's no big deal! Occasionally, someone like Karen enters the waiting room for a while and helps pass the time.

The Four Stages of Grief

There are four stages of grief that most of us have to live through and accept at some time in our lives. How well you do is up to you. It is impossible to say how long it will take as each person and circumstance is different. Initially grief, for the widowed, is generally a great deal more severe and prolonged than for the divorced, and if divorced, you may not even experience some of the symptoms.

<u>Stage I</u>   Numbness and disbelief are the major components in the first stage of grief for the widowed and generally result in the very absence of emotion. We should not feel guilty by experiencing this. Our lack of feeling is due to a psychological defense mechanism within us that is accomplishing what it should. Be content with the absence of emotion as it may become very prevalent in stage two.

<u>Stage II</u>   As we begin to accept the cruel reality of our fate, we will experience feelings of bewilderment and helplessness. It is of little comfort to hear that things are not as black as they may seem and that they will work out--as they truly will. Food can lose its taste and we may find ourselves waking with a start as we come out of sleep into the cruel world or reality. We tend to feel very listless, not knowing what to do. Eating, television, socializing, reading, nothing seems important.

My concern for Karen's soul, if it existed, and the possibility of life after death became paramount. I studied some of the works of Elisabeth Kubler Ross, based on the experiences of clinically dead patients which had been brought back to life. A book by David R. Wheeler titled "Journey to the Other Side," based upon the same studies also helped to assure me of life after death. This not only gave me comfort regarding Karen's spiritual well-being, it gave me something else constructive to work on.

<u>Stage III</u> We enter stage three with a reasonable amount of acceptance toward our fate, however, our feelings of bewilderment and helplessness still remain. Stage three, for the single, is when loneliness and depression become most prevalent. We may also experience a great amount of guilt even though we have no logical reason to feel guilty. It is normal to feel that there may have been something we could have done to prevent the death or divorce. We

may also feel guilty at the times wasted by not being with our spouse when we had the opportunity.

We may feed our grief by worrying more than necessary about outside circumstances like finances, added work-load, increased responsibility, etc. Depression works its grievous magic and we find ourselves wanting to sleep continuously. Our memory can lapse from time to time, leaving holes and voids in our immediate past. All hope can vanish and we may find ourselves searching for something to look forward to---tomorrow. We often feel like just giving up. This is probably the most painful stage of grief, and once you get through this, your pain will begin to level off.

<u>Stage IV</u>   As we enter this last stage of grief, our feelings of hopelessness start to subside and we begin looking for answers and methods to survive our grief. In a subconscious attempt to escape our pain, we may try to substitute the love we may have had for our spouse with anger and hate. The first positive sign of healing can manifest itself in a sense of exasperation. It is a period of mixed emotions which is caused by the healing process combatting our grief, and if suicidal tendencies exist, they are caused by our exasperation rather than grief itself. Adding to our exasperations, we can also experience a feeling of alienation from reality and our ability to make decisions can be greatly impaired. Small daily decisions like when to cross the street can become monstrous and life can become a jungle of confusion.

If these symptoms become too acute, you should definitely seek professional help. It does not mean that you are insane, and the treatment (called grief therapy) is designed simply to help you in coping with your grief, eliminating the chance for irreparable emotional damage. The most widely used cop-out (the one I used at first) is "I just can't afford it." If the above symptoms are serious, you can't afford not to.

Just hang in there and avoid excessive use of depressants such as alcohol. You are on your way out. This is the final stage and from here on the adverse emotions will begin to fade and disappear. It is not a consistent decline and you will experience peaks and valleys, but they will begin to level out and in time your grief will be nothing more than a valuable learning experience.

"Happiness is beneficial for the body but it is grief that develops the powers of the mind."

-Marcel Proust

CHAPTER 5
The New, Single You

"The New, Single You"

To me, single life means:
    Calling on friends in faded old jeans.
Having both closets all to myself
    And putting my own things on every shelf.
I hog both pillows and covers and bed,
    And breakfast on soda pop, Swiss cheese and bread.
I can talk on the phone till after midnight,
    Or read a good novel till dawn's early light.
I choose my own friends and lovers and peers,
    And look for a mate to wipe away tears.
I search for a sweetheart to hold through the night,
    And fear growing old in a sad, lonely plight.
I tell me I'm strong and need no one to share,
    But God knows my craving for someone to care.
I tell others it's great but I am not sure
    But what I just say this, to help me endure.
Why is there single life and who did create it?
    I embrace it and curse it and cling to and hate it.

Chapter 5

THE NEW SINGLE YOU

<u>Surviving the Adjustment</u>

The single world now comprises approximately forty percent of our national, adult population and yet the single is one of the most misunderstood and ignored species of our social order. Contrary to the free and fun image the public has of our single populace, the average single emerges from the indignities of divorce with tremendous financial and/or family responsibilities as well as insurmountable hang-ups. In short, the average, new single is about as secure as a deck-hand on the Titanic!

Single life can be very rewarding and fulfilling for a certain type of individual. But it can take time and a great deal of effort to adjust to it. The amount of time depends upon each individual but it generally takes the average person from one to three years. Most studies conclude that the average single remains single for less than the time needed to complete this adjustment. This means that the majority of the single world is in a perpetual state of "Suspended Emancipation!"

Why is single life so hard to adjust to? Singlization dictates an entirely new lifestyle, which is usually one hundred and eighty degrees out of phase with "un-single life". The average man is torn from the warmth and security of family and home. The increased financial burden of supporting two homes may rest on his shoulders. He also has to adapt to certain chores and duties that he is unfamiliar with. He has to learn how to cope with and adapt to solitude and loneliness. For years, he may have been surrounded with family members who constantly needed him, depended upon him and demanded his attention.   Now there is just the silence of an economy apartment.   The goals and incentives he once had are now shattered and there seems to be little reason for his existance.   He experiences a deep sense of failure and feels less a man.

The average woman experiences fear as well as a tremendous weight of responsibility.   Household and car maintenance, the complete responsibility of her children, the prospect of establishing a new career, the added financial problems of a decreased income and the fear of facing the cold, cruel world alone weighs heavily upon her. She often has to learn the dual roles of mother and father, handyman and provider.   Traditional social standards have placed her in a position, over the past years, of a dependent.   Now she is the provider.

Both of these new, single novices are going to have to learn how to cope with new moralities, new social standards, changes in responsibility, sexual deprivation, loneliness, depression, rejection, disappointment, new forms of entertainment, new methods of utilizing time, a new type of friends, new fears, the need for new capabilities, and in short, new methods of survival.

Add to this a sense of failure and the inferiorities that usually accompany divorce and you have quite a problem!   It's not as hopeless as it might appear but it's no emotional picnic either.

Single life is similar to a bed of spikes.   It is not painful, depressing or uncomfortable...once you get used to it.   It's just the getting used to it that can cause the problems.

In an effort to escape all of the emotional discomforts of adjustment, many singles jump right back into marriage, not out of love but out of desperation and need (which can feel just like love), and in doing so, they accomplish nothing and benefit little from their wrenching experience.

Many people say that there is something missing in their lives. The part that's missing can generally be found within one's self, but most of us have a tendency to try and fill this void with someone else. When they fail to live up to our expectations or demands, we can become very hurt and blame them for our pain.   Learning to accept responsibility for our own decisions is the first step to adjusting!

It's good to be able to need others.   The problem is that we can, all too easily, over-depend on others or fate, and not enough on ourselves.   Why do we have a need for others?   I personally believe one reason is that humans, like whales and certain other creatures of this earth, are monogamous.   We have a deep rooted instinct to be paired.   Whether this is true or not, studies conducted by Penthouse magazine show that the greatest majority of men would prefer to have a _sexually exclusive relationship_ with the right woman, than to be single with many sexual partners.   (Surprising, Huh?)

Still in all, I believe the element that makes this desire so critical is the fact that our society is obsessed with pairing, marriage and sex.   How to get the ideal mate or find the ideal sex partner by wearing Labordini support jox, splashing on Liquid Pig-Parts Cologne, eating Passion Toasties or using a flower scented douche?

Friends and family often join the national opinion that _everybody_ should be married (especially yourbody) and this programming serves to add to the emotional stress of a single.   This tells the emotionally devastated new singles that something is wrong with them and creates a tremendous desire to be paired like "normal" people.   Other problems, like work and financial stress, insurance and credit problems, employment biases, loneliness, cold showers and undernourishment add up to take their toll, too.

New singles generally feel desperate.   "Here I am, at my age, (18 to 102), a failure and having to start all over again."   They get the "times awasting crazies" and fear that if they don't find their place in this new single world by day after tomorrow, it will be too late.   The bill collectors are screaming, all their hair is about to fall out, their faces are developing wrinkles and their financial capabilities are incompatible with their needs.   If they don't find someone soon, no one will want what's left!   They often feel that their problems are insurmountable.

"Here I am, all alone with no one to trust or to depend on, not even myself."   They often feel that the world is unfair and is to blame for their predicament.   They may spend a year in the confirmed belief that they cannot last for one more day.   They tend to run out in a panic, shooting off in every direction and spreading themselves so thin that they accomplish nothing.   Most divorcees enter the single world with hostilities, inferiorities and more hang ups than Ma Bell.   They view their past as a desolate failure rather than a valuable learning experience and many get trapped within the confines of their own emotions.

Now that we "old pros" have had a smug look at the new single, it's our turn.   It's time that we demonstrate, first hand, what being together is all about.   In order to acquaint the novice single with some of the new insecurities and neuroses that he or she will have to adopt, I'm going to lay raw, the truth on what singles are all about.

Contrary to social beliefs, singles are not only human, many are almost normal. Singles do share one consistency, however, and this is their general lack of consistency. In short, singles are usually one way or the other, both at the same time.

Singles buy nice cars but save matchbooks with two or more matches in them. They buy good clothes and generally wear gym shorts, old jeans and T-shirts with advertising on them.

Singles are usually very clean, but they wash with tiny pieces of saved soap. When the pieces get too small to use, they squash and squeeze them together, into a larger lump. After bathing with saved soap, they splash on very expensive cologne (generally something with a foreign sounding name).

Singles memorize all of the best wines by name and buy generic wine for personal consumption (it's usually kept in a Pinot Noir bottle). Some singles do buy very good wine though, as all singles like to spoil themselves. As a rule these are the ones whose entire nutritional existence depends on good wine, free meals and generic crackers.

Singles usually choose very nice apartments but furnish them with throw pillows and bean bag furniture. Lamps, renderings and decorator items are all first-class but their end tables are often wooden crates, with uneven lettering, advertising anything from Grape-o wine to gun powder. Scattered around you will find accents like digital clocks, chromed lamps and posters. Singles generally keep their pillows in the front room and their etchings in the bedroom. (Would you like to see my etchings?)

Stereo systems (which are a must) are generally the best that money can buy but the stereo cabinet may consist of boards, artistically balanced on cinder blocks. Singles generally choose nice apartments because it's often just them and their apartment against the world. For this reason most single's apartments have a distinct, individual character about them. This character can resemble anything from Twentieth Century Old to Early Dracula.

The three decorator themes, most used by singles are (1) Very earthy, (2) Very sophisticated, and (3) Very earthy and very sophisticated. Most singles use plants to compliment an earthy theme. Plants are also neat to talk to. They just set there and listen and never find fault or give bad advice. If you don't love them and take care of them, they die, but never complain about it. Some singles don't like plants though. They think the plants talk about them whenever they leave the room!

Singles' homes generally have four main storage units that they live out of: the oven, the dishwasher, the dryer and the car. In visiting another single, it's a good idea to check the garbage disposal before running water in their sink. In a last ditch effort to pick the place up before you arrived, they may have stuffed their dirty socks into it.

Mirrors are also a favorite decorator item and can be found just about anywhere. As a matter of fact, overhead mirrors, falling from ceilings onto beds have probably killed more singles even than bad eating habits. Aside from being dangerous, the only drawbacks to overhead mirrors are when you come home after an unproductive evening and find yourself looking up at yourself, staring down on yourself lying there all alone. Or like when your mother drops by to visit and accuses you of becoming conceited.

Most singles hate to cook. If it doesn't come in a box, can or bottle, God probably wouldn't want you to eat it anyway. He wouldn't have made canned ham, crackers and cream soda if you were meant to slave over a stove! There is one exception however, and this is eggs. If eggs ever become illegal, the U.S. single population will almost surely expire. Raw eggs, cooked eggs, eggs with canned ham, eggs with canned salmon, eggs with mushrooms, eggs with anchovies, eggs with cream soda. Some people believe that all of these liquid chickens create certain bodily fluids within the average single and this chemistry is what draws singles to other singles. This is called Emotionalistic Eggnatism or simply E.E. in the research laboratories.

Wine is currently the national drink for singles, however, cream soda comes in for a close second. Perrier also occupies a space in most single's refrigerators. No one seems to really know what it's for, but it does carry a certain social prestige. It's more than likely the name because singles all love foreign sounding names. It gives one an edge in being able to pronounce it and makes one sound worldly and sophisticated.

Some single girls have developed a new feministic hobby which seems to be sweeping the country. This new hobby is called "Barfing." It's relatively inexpensive as the only things you need are food and a finger, and it allows its participants to eat all they want and still stay trim.   This is an effective way to control weight. But you can develop a barfing syndrome called Bulimarexia or you can merely get sick every time you eat something.   This can not only be very embarrassing on dates, it can cause a physiological disorder resulting in swollen salivary glands, cramps, potassium depletion, fatigue, convulsive seizures and God knows what else!   It can also cause psychological problems, as most who do this are ashamed of it.

Singles are usually very active and seldom have time for hobbies.   They do often have interests, however, many of which are in the field of sports.   This is because singles, in an effort to look good, are very preoccupied with   physical fitness. The two favorites are, of course, jogging and bicycling.   This type of exercise allows you to perfect the technique of heavy breathing while, at the same time, provides the possibility of meeting someone else with whom you have something in common.

Jogging and bicycling have become so popular that through the course of evolution we are developing a complete, new strain of human being.   One characteristic is the notorious Black Lung, the result of exercising and heavy breathing through smog alert conditions.   Other characteristics are, of course, flat feet, tiny bodies and enormous legs.   It is rumored even that some "baby singles" have actually been born with tiny sweat bands around their foreheads.   Doctors in Los Angeles cite a case where a single mother's severe heartburn was caused by her unborn son's Adidas sweatshirt.

Other singles' interests include sailing, skiing, diving, tennis, racketball, dancing, partying and other singles.   TV occupies the space as the number one form of home entertainment in the unsingle world, while the telephone has become the entertainment center for the average single dwelling.   Most singles have little, tiny televisions and big, humongous telephone bills.   Zone and long distance calls contribute slightly to this high cost of conversing.   However, the extras are the real culprit.   Many singles have phones that will do just about anything but flush the toilet, and I'm sure Ma Bell is working on that.   A two line phone (call waiting) is a must for any single.   The attitude behind this is that you may be talking to a number five when a real Ten calls you.   If the line is busy, the Ten may never call back.   Answering machines are also in vogue.

Some single guys collect expensive wine bottles that they usually find in the garbage cans behind ritzy restaurants.   Of course some singles own these ritzy restaurants which greatly enhances their collective efforts. At any rate, it's fun to write dates and girls' names on them like "Bridgette, Dec. 16, 1983" or "Tammie, March 5, 1984" and set them on display around the apartment. Sticking candles in them and letting them burn down also adds a certain sense of sensuality.

Singles do have a few hangups here and there and sex is one of them. They often feel guilty when they do and invariably feel regret when they don't.

Most singles love sex even more than good food, but many are undernourished in both categories. As a matter of fact, if it were not for physicals, many singles would probably have no sex life at all! One reason for this is due to the fact that with the fast changing social standards of today, no one is really sure who is supposed to play the part of the sexual aggressor. Some women are trying to take the traditional role of an animalistic pervert away from the men, and many are fairly good at it! Both sexes do need practice in their new roles. For an example, women are going to have to learn how to be more gentle in their tactics and persuade a man in such a way as not to make him feel used or cheap. On the other hand, guys are going to have to learn the importance of virtue. Don't be too easy and always say no when you mean maybe! The single guys' #1 Law of Social Reform states: "Say no, then negotiate."

Most singles, at some time in their life, splurge recklessly on the extravagance of satin sheets. This sensual form of potential danger has injured countless numbers of singles as the result of slipping out of bed. One single in Kansas not long ago accidentally hung himself with the same rope that he used to tie his pillow onto the bed with. As far as sex is concerned, satin sheets are a waste of money, as anyone who starts off on them will invariably end up on the floor anyway and the neat thing about a floor is that it's fairly difficult to fall off your carpet!

Satin sheets can help a few singles, however. If you have become bored with regular sex, satin sheets can provide a delightful challenge.

Singles are generally just a little neurotic. One reason for this is because they usually have time to sit and think. They worry whether or not the little light went out in the fridge when they closed the door. They wonder that the inside of a basketball really looks like. They worry about falling space junk and running out of toilet paper if a nuclear war occurs.   They worry about the fact that Mr. or Ms. Right has not called and as they sit there waiting, they make up hundreds of hypothetical and infidelic reasons.   When the phone does ring, they are usually too mad to talk.   They worry about drinking too little or leaving the party too early and worry about the bags under their eyes the next morning.   "Will they go away by themselves or will they require surgery?"

Singles often buy the smallest, sportiest convertible they can find, then live in a constant fear of tall dogs.

A single may spend weeks trying to figure out a way to break off a relationship without hurting the other person.   Finally, when they do, and the other person isn't hurt, they spend the next several weeks worrying over the fact that the other person wasn't hurt!

We singles do most of our worrying when we're down, but we do a lot of worrying when we're happy, too.   This is because when happy, the only way we can go is down.

Singles worry and fret in their attempt to find someone else to love. When they do find someone, they worry and fret about falling in love.

Singles usually worry about others liking them.   They want others to like them until they do, then they worry about others becoming too dependent on them.

Most singles really, in truth, do have it together, though. Because of this, you should never straighten a crooked picture on their wall or close a cupboard door.   It was probably like that for a carefully thought out reason.

Singles are generally hypochondriacs.   They constantly worry about getting sick, all alone, with no one to care for them.   Nobody really knows how many singles endure the lonely torment of the "Dissolute Droops!"   Or how many eventually expire all alone with only the pale reflection from their overhead mirror to keep them company in their last hours.   When singles do something they really do it right and illness is no different.   When singles suffer, we suffer from: "stripped throats", "twenty-four day" flu and "exploding" appendixes.   If you ever want to get out of a date, just tell the other single that you have stomach cramps, sore throat and a high fever but that you would love to see them anyway!

Singles, in their quest for better health, are less likely to smoke. They drink a lot, get little rest, worry continually, dress inadequately, take downers to sleep, uppers to wake, grass to heighten and diets to lighten.   Yet, they will stand there in a silk shirt or blouse, shivering from exposure, nervousness and malnutrition and say "have you ever seen what nicotine can do to a rat's back?"

Most singles really feel persecuted.   They're sure that they were the only one not invited to Clyde's party Saturday night.   The fact that they don't know Clyde has little bearing on the case.   They are also sure that everyone at Monica's party fell in love except them, that they were the only one at the single's bar that didn't leave with someone else, or that they are the only one in town with no plans for next Saturday night!

Most singles hate to eat out alone.   There is something very defeating about walking up to the reservationist and saying, "Lichowietz, a party of one."   Furthermore, singles know that when those same defeating words come booming out of the paging system, everyone in there will be craning their necks to see who this poor lonely person is.

Another problem that dining singles endure is the undeniable fact that all single seats are located in the darkest little corner, right between the restrooms and the kitchen.   Restaurant owners assure us that they don't hate singles, it's just that sitting there all alone we tend to depress the "normal" people.   What do they think normal people do to us?   Perhaps they haven't heard that almost half of our national population is single.   At the rate it's going, they may be seating the un-singles in dark corners before too long!

Dining singles generally learn quickly what to order.   The best method is to ask the waiter what he recommends and then order the opposite.   If he recommends Veal Scallopine, you automatically know that it's the oldest thing on the menu and that it has been saved specifically for some unsuspecting sole single.

Singles love fads. One of the newest fads is complete independence.   We singles go out and convince one another that we have surpassed the immature need for anyone else and that we love our complete independence.   Then we each go home and wonder why we are lonely, while everyone else is doing so well!

Tattoos are also really in vogue now and some single gals are getting tattoos in places that I refuse to discuss here.   A personal interview with the manager and sole proprietor of Cervical Graphics, Inc., states that feminine tattooing has increased by several hundred percent over the past years.   In going one step further, I found a survey taken to determine what turned men off and on.   The survey concluded that 80% of the men interviewed were turned off by women with tattoos.   Why?   I believe that it has something to do with some secret little subconscious fantasy that all single guys have hidden somewhere in the back of the hypothalamus, above the brain stem. Even though the girl in their arms is wearing a see-through blouse, has approached them on the possibility of sex and swears like a drunken drill sergeant, this little voice in the back of the single guy's mind is saying, "Maybe I am really the first.   Maybe she just had an accident as a small girl.   Maybe this is still virgin territory!"   When you run across a tattoo on her tootoo, you realize beyond any shadow of a doubt that this territory has not only been explored extensively, it has been charted and graphed!

Now single guys may like to fantasize but that doesn't mean that we are gullible by any means.   We realize that the chances of having a natural birthmark that says "Go Baby" and signed "With Love, the Green Bay Packers" is about a hundred to one.   Another more obvious reason for this lack of like regarding feminine graffiti should be obvious.   In all respect, girls, how would you feel about a guy who insisted wearing a flower behind his ear?

What else do these surveys indicate?   Of the men interviewed:

<pre>
        80% were turned off by heavy makeup
        70% were turned off by excessive body hair
        05% were turned off by pregnant women
        75% were turned on by perfume
and 75% were turned on by lacy lingerie
</pre>

Singles can really get <u>caught up</u> in the act of physical salutations.   For an example, single guys generally like to kiss. There is the Hello Kiss (generally on the lips), the Goodbye Kiss (generally on the right temple), and the That's Alright Kiss (generally on the forehead).

A problem often encountered is the fact that some girls don't like to be kissed that much!   Instead of telling the guy, however, they simply turn their head quickly, which often results in the guy getting his moustache caught in her earring!

This type of physical attachment will invariably occur at formal parties where everyone is trying to make a good impression and where no scissors are readily accessible.   Added to this difficulty is the obstinate reluctance singles have to ask for help.   If a couple insists on staying on the dance floor with the guy breathing into the girl's ear all night, you can safely assume that this is what happened. If there is some doubt in your mind, simply wait for the tempo to pick up, as it's the fast dances that invariably give them away.

It's also a good idea when approaching the kissee to check their mouth for foreign objects like toothpicks, cigarettes or potato chip dip. Otherwise you can withdraw punctured, burned or foaming at the mouth!

Singles like to hug and embrace too, which can also be very embarrassing. The guy can get his watch caught in her hair. She can get her brooch caught on his belt buckle or she can get her eyelash caught in his gold chain.

Single guys generally have fairly nice cars. They usually keep these cars very clean and looking their best. This is because the single guy's car is similar to a game bird's mating feathers. They clean them and preen them and keep them in shape because they strut around wearing them a good percent of the time and the better yours looks, the more chance you have of attracting the hens. This automotive hygiene is also due in large part to the fact that the average single guy has heard or read somewhere that women are basically tidy.

Single gals seldom volunteer the use of their cars to go on a date and their main excuse is the lack of automotive hygiene. They almost always say the same thing, "Forgive the way my car looks, I didn't have time to clean it yesterday. Can we take yours? It's so pretty and clean!" Actually, bad automotive hygiene is nothing but an applied example of feminine genius. By always taking the guy's car, they save gas.

CHAPTER 6
Seven Stages of Singlization

Chapter 6

THE SEVEN STAGES OF SINGLIZATION

These Seven Stages of Singlization are not necessarily accurate for everyone. But they provide a very true picture of the basic patterns that most singles tend to take. Most singles are about as consistent as Mexican hash so there may be deviations in the peculiarities of each stage or you may find yourself bouncing in and out of some particular stage at times. You may whiz through some stages (particularly the first two) so quickly that they seem to be nothing more than a momentary thought. There are also many variables which can affect our adjustments individually, such as menopause, age, religion, pride, insurmountable hang-ups and committal type relationships. These Seven Stages of Singlization are not examples for you to try and live up to, but are designed to provide an insight into your present position and to make clear many of the pitfalls that may be encountered. During the first stage, there are significant differences between the divorced and widowed single, so we will cover both examples separately.

Stage One (The Widowed Single). The widowed single usually enters this stage in a state of numbness with little feeling of pain or loss, only disbelief. This phase can last for days or even weeks. They then enter the realm of reality and pain. The smallest problems can seem insurmountable and everything can appear hopeless. Severe depression can consume them. They can experience the loss of taste, the loss of motivation and the loss of a will to live. They often feel an unfounded sense of guilt for no reason. This Stage can last from several months to years. As a matter of fact, widowed people have been known to get caught in this stage and stay there forever.   In order to do this, however, you have to have a strong drive for self-induced torture and must really enjoy playing the part of the victim.   This might seem like a cruel statement, but the truth is often cruel.

The widowed single may not have the same type of bitterness and emotional scarring that divorced singles have but the devastating pain they feel is a by-product of love so they often feel that they may never open themselves up to pain through love again.   It can be just too agonizing.

Generally the first positive sign of healing manifests itself in the form of exasperation, anger and rage.   This is GREAT!   Let it out.   Cry, scream, throw things and then get ready to enter Stage Two of your Singlization.

<u>Stage One (The Divorced Single).</u>   The divorced single usually enters Stage One of their new single life with feelings of pain, hostilities and inferiorities, but also Determination.   They may have doubts as to whether or not they did the right thing but these doubts are usually masked by their determination to make it work.   They are often driven by the obsession to prove their Ex wrong, and this is not bad.   This tends to kindle their fuels for survival, as later on, they may realize the true meaning of an emotional energy crunch.   The divorced single often experiences hostility toward their Ex and sometimes the world in general.   These hostilities are normal and acceptable to a degree but when they evolve into hate, you are asking for problems.   Hate can be devastating.   An interesting fact about this cancerous emotion is that you soon become a slave to the person you hate.   If you are fortunate enough to have parted wedlock as friends, you will progress in your new world much faster.

Divorced singles are not usually content to merely store up inferiorities from marital put-downs by their Ex.   Singles, being singles, often do it up really right by creating even another emotional put down in the conviction that they have failed in marriage. Society has placed so much importance on marriage that it has become the number one qualification for social acceptance. As a result, the divorced single tends to feel that he or she has failed miserably in comparison to others.   With more and more divorces occurring, this will be less and less a factor, but this self-induced stigma still prevails.

At this point, the divorced as well as the widowed single has begun to develop emotional scarring, and many refuse to even consider the possibility of a relationship. "Boy, not me, never again. I'm going to reap the fruits of single life forever!" It may be advisable, though, to keep some sugar handy because the fruits of single life can be very bitter at times and the sugar will help considerably if you have to eat your words. It is OK to feel this way, though. Any emotion or attitude is OK right now if it is honest.

The feelings set forth within these two categories can be experienced by either divorced or widowed singles and are not specifically limited to one or the other, however, one thing that all new singles have in common at this stage is their apprehension and uncertainty of what lies ahead and what will be expected of them as singles.

Stage Two. This is the stage of experiencing. It contains the same hostilities, inferiorities and determinations as found in stage one but we now begin to search for truths as well as for our place in this new lifestyle. We begin to feel the desolation of loneliness and consider the possibilities of dating. Generally at this stage, the new single is very inhibited and cautious but many plunge right in. Some date for the companionship and fun of it and others mistakenly embark in search of their legendary Mr. or Ms. Right.

As our new adventurers progress deeper and deeper into the wierd, enchanting mysteries of single life, their expectations begin to crumble. Things like social disease, bad dating experiences, the pain of rejection, fits of loneliness, and financial problems can transform subconscious fears into morbid realities. They find inconsistencies in other singles that they were unaware of and begin to feel isolated, as if suspended between the married world and the single world. They try desperately to fit in but refuse to change their attitudes, and no one else seems to conform to their way of life.

They experience jealousy at seeing other couples together. They usually consider their friends fortunate when they enter into a relationship and wonder why they, themselves, can't find someone. Everyone and everything else in the world seems to be paired and they begin to wonder "what's wrong with me?" They become increasingly impatient and tend to try on relationships out of desperation and need, instead of love.

The inability to fit in, the painful experiences in dating and crumbled expectations will often blend together to make this new life a casserole of confusion.   In order to regroup their emotions and thoughts, many, during the course of the next two stages, will enter periods of social hibernation.   They find a hole, climb in and regress from society.   Friends and family can't stand this, but these are the times that are most effective in healing and personal growth, so Do It!   Just don't allow yourself to get into a permanent rut of social regression.   If it lasts longer than three or four months, force yourself back out and try some different approaches.

<u>Stage Three</u>.   This stage is generally ruled by complete desperation.   It is a time when we are most prone to sacrifice principles, be what we feel others want us to be or do anything necessary to find our place in this frustrating new world.   We often find ourselves taking part in popular fads, discussions and activities that really seem absurd to us.

Our tendencies for relationships or marriage "on the rebound" are at their highest level.   This stage can be the weakest and most vulnerable time of our life.   At this place, we have a tendency to enter all of the classic traps (described later) and we often want to believe whatever anyone tells us.

Many of us start spending money just as if we really had it and later wake up to find ourselves in a state of financial anemia.   We often build our self esteem on superficial principles and lose self-respect by hiding our true image under some popular disguise.

Emotional scarring can build like bugs on bread and you can become trapped in this third stage if you are not careful.   When this emotional scarring crusts over, it eliminates one's ability to feel--and without emotion, you will remain locked in the solitary confinement of yourself.   If I ever open a single's bar (which is highly improbable), I will definitely call it "Stage Three".

The longer you remain in this partytime stage with its emotional denials, the more your callousing will build and the harder it will be to get out.   Only when you realize that the superficial structure of this stage is not stable enough to build your life on can you progress to the next stage.

<u>Stage Four</u>.   This is a time of total submission.   The time that you finally hit rock bottom.   You have tried virtually every means and nothing seems to work.   Your self pride is weak, your emotional callouses have built to the point that you may never trust or love

again, and you resign yourself to the fact that you may just have to grow old and lonely, all by yourself. You may never have anyone but yourself to rely on and you can feel completely defeated. This is the most emotionally devastating and yet the most emotionally awakening stage in the mystery of singlization.

You have to spend many long hours just getting to know yourself. Eventually you discover that you are pretty good company and you even start liking yourself (your real self). You sense a new awakening within you and search for answers in an attempt to broaden this feeling. You develop a new sense of hope, and desperation begins to be replaced with a calm assurance.

This awakening can only become a reality through the desperation of having to turn away from the <u>use</u> of others and looking to yourself for fulfillment. This fourth stage is the first really constructive plateau and from here on, you build.

How long does it take to reach this plateau? Each person is different and it depends on where they are emotionally and mentally. It also depends on the circumstances such as how many relationships they have entered into and the duration of each. (Emotional callouses and binding relationships slow the process considerably). An average rule of thumb, however, is from one to three years. My duration of time was a little over three years. Widowed singles usually do take longer to find their way through the first two stages, and divorced singles generally have a little more trouble with Stage Three.

Stage Five. Armed with your new self-awareness, you enter the stage of bettering yourself. You may turn to single's sharing groups, religion, exercise, hobbies, a new occupation, travel, meditation, education or any other means of self-construction. You have an insatiable desire to gain more of this fantastic feeling of self-worth by improving yourself mentally, physically, spiritually and/or emotionally. You find that dating and being with friends takes on a new meaning. You lose the desperate need to have someone else to depend upon. You learn to like yourself and project your own image to others instead of the false image of what you thought they wanted. You take pride in the realization that others like you for yourself and you concentrate on fulfilling your own expectations rather than another's expectations.

Your emotional callouses begin to wear down and even though

you can start to feel again, you are still very leery of relationships and particularly marriage. For some, this is a time of celibacy and they tend to support platonic relationships more. You learn the secrets of self-honesty. You find the inability to see problems and their solutions clearly was due to your lack of self-trust resulting from your tendency to fool yourself into believing whatever you wanted to believe. The world, and life in general, takes on a new simplicity and you start looking at life from a new perspective.

Stage Six. This is the stage of transformation. You look for honest answers instead of answers that support your desires. You rebuild your old principles and programming to meet your new awareness and life takes on a new meaning. You are reasonably complete now except for a partner with which you can share your new joys. The pain of your previous life still haunts you and you refrain from becoming too involved with anyone emotionally. This time, however, it's your choice.

You fear that in entering a relationship you could lose your new awareness. You question the ability of someone else to see you as you see yourself and fight the possibility of returning to a previous stage through the criticisms and lack of understanding of a new partner.

Your self-contentment can serve to trap you in this stage. It is not a bad place to be but again, this is your decision. It is important, however, to understand what can exist in the seventh stage.

Stage Seven. Should you get this far, the seventh stage is a plateau of self-realization. It is a place for your total commitment in love, if you so choose. You analyze the progress you have made since your previous marriage. You realize that you are not the same person and that your new wisdom will prevent you from making the same old mistakes. You know that you will not depend upon someone else to provide you with your own happiness. You will rely on others only to fulfill the attitude of happiness within yourself.

You understand the importance of communication, consideration, affection and sharing that will contribute greatly to the success of a relationship or marriage. You realize that marriage, like single life, will have pitfalls and that it does not provide the Utopian type of contentment that society often projects. Its main contribution is the ability to share life and a common goal with someone else of great importance. That's all, but then that is quite a bit. The decision is yours.

7
CHAPTER
Starting Over

Chapter 7

STARTING OVER

The first step in starting over is to sit down and calmly evaluate yourself. You're similar to a computerized robot in as much as your emotions and behavior are the result of your past programming. If you're unhappy, it can be due to inaccurate programming, because accurate programming usually creates actions which benefit us. With correct programming, you might have chosen a different mate, learned how to hold a marriage together, or how to accept circumstances that you have no control over.

Our programming starts the second we leave the womb. We find that by crying, we get what we want and we also learn to rely on others to take care of our needs. Our tendency to return to this postcervical utopia stays with us throughout our lives. Many of us have found that crying about our problems no longer helps; but we do it just in case someone might hear us and come to our rescue. The result is a society of humanistic robots with emotionally wet pants who spend a great deal of time running around crying. Improper programming can cause you to think that the successful robot has learned how to change its own pants. In truth, the successful robot is the one that has learned how to control its kidneys (or in a robot's case, its selenoid valve).

There are many examples of improper programming. To illustrate this, let's review just a few of the most common tapes.

Tape 1: Passive Programming

As a child we were taught that we should be seen and not heard, to obey and not argue. No one loves you if you stand up for yourself. That's called sassing back. As a result, many of us enter the carnivorous jaws of society thinking that if we are passive, we will be loved and provided for. Many still do not understand that passiveness breeds disrespect and projects vulnerability. As a result, they can't seem to figure out why they are always being hurt and taken advantage of.

Tape 2: Treat Programming

When we were good kids, many of us got treats. This showed us that we were loved, and programmed some of us to believe that we could buy another's love. Love can mean a new doll or a ball, an afternoon at the movies or even a cookie. This can program us to put a material worth on love, which, for obvious reasons, rarely works.

Tape 3: Appearance Programming

Parents' incessant drive to keep their kids clean, and society's infatuation with physical beauty, has programmed many of us to put too much importance on external appearance. As a result we have a tendency to forget about the inner beauty and concentrate too much on the physical beauty (our own, especially). If we do not come up to the high standards of appearance that we want, we feel inferior and this inferiority is reflected to others.

If we are exceptionally attractive, we often let our looks become a burden to us. These are the people who never go swimming at swimming parties because of their hair or makeup and who never lay in the hay on hayrides. No matter how hard they try they can't seem to let down and be themselves. Why? Because they feel their attractiveness is all they have to offer. This lack of self-assurance often projects a snobbish image when, in fact, there are few people who are genuine snobs. Most are just very insecure because of improper programming.

Tape 4: Favors Programming

As children, we were often rewarded or loved only when we did Mom and Dad a favor or completed our chores. This programmed us to believe that the secret to making people like us is to do for them. The result is that we sacrifice for others; and when our efforts go unnoticed, we feel that we have been cheated and taken for granted. This is relative to Tape 2, only here we try to buy another's love with our labors instead of cold, hard cash.

Tape 5: Escape Programming

Many of us learned as children that living in a dream world and ignoring the unpleasantness around us was the only way to go. As kids this philosophy is not so bad. Adult life, however, requires us to differentiate between truth and fiction. It demands a sharp, concise sense of reality. These escapists are usually the people who say "I thought everything was great in our marriage and then suddenly, a divorce!" The truth is that they were programmed to ignore the danger signs, another example of fooling one's self.

Tape 6: Helpless Programming

As a child, many of us found that in order to get out of responsibility all we had to do was act helpless. If we were supposed to mow the lawn, we just had to run over the cat one time and we were never asked to mow again. If we were supposed to dust the mantel, we could knock a ming vase off accidentally and presto, no more dusting. You can bet the next time we said we didn't know how to do something, our parents listened!

Men, to a large extent, have corrected this programming in order to traditionally provide for their family; but many women still use this programming. Some tend to rely on a cute, helpless act with a sprinkle of sex appeal to survive in the single world. When someone refuses to buy this act and socks it to them (as in the case of Hanny Helpless who paid $35 to have her windshield debugged), they complain that everyone is out to take advantage of the poor helpless single gal.

The position that, as a woman, you know nothing about that type of thing, and therefore it is not your fault, is just more science fiction. You will have to reprogram yourself to be better advised in areas of possible vulnerability. The truth is, gals, the world is cruel and will gobble up anyone who is helpless and weak, female or otherwise. Projecting a helpless image is just asking for trouble, even though a sprinkle of sex appeal here and there never hurts.

Tape 7a: Humility Programming

Many of us have been programmed to believe that self-praise is the same thing as conceit, and coming from ourselves to ourselves, it is very superficial in its benefit. It's a known fact that we all need praise and positive strokes but due to our programming, we tend to rely strictly upon others for it and look to ourselves mainly for criticism. This, of course, can easily establish a negative self-image. Not only that, it can cause sort of an inferiority syndrome. It has already been established that others can't like us unless we like ourselves; and if we rely on others to like us first, how can we ever get started?

At a single's discussion group I attended not long ago, the topic for discussion was "what is my best quality?" The topic had trouble getting off the ground. No one really wanted to say anything good about themselves for fear that others would look at it as conceit. Many wanted to change the topic to "what is a friend's best quality," but the team leader stood firm. There was quite a bit of hedging such as: "I like my independence;" "I try to take care of my body;" "My sensuality is very important to me;" and finally a guy said, "I like my skin, I think I really have neat skin!" Everybody laughed and his skin turned red and from that moment on you couldn't get a word in edgewise.

Most of the qualities brought up were personality rather than physical attributes, but suddenly everyone had an obsession to pat themselves on the back. After the discussion was reluctantly adjourned, everyone was exuberant. During the social hour that followed, I noted that the personalities in the group had changed tremendously. People were erect and self-assured. Timid voices had become bold and practically no one was withdrawn. Everyone had experienced a fleeting evening of self-confidence and self-esteem.

The one person we all need praise from the most is ourselves. If the term "self-praise" does not compute, try "self-confirmation." Just confirm the fact that you are OK. Later you will realize in all truth that you are a one-of-a-kind, super-fantastic person. There is no one else in the world exactly like you and as a result, the world would not be the same without you.

Tape 7b: Humility Programming

The biggest debit resulting from humility programming of course is loss of self-esteem and its byproduct, self-confidence. Some people act self-confident but are not. Would you really like to be able to tell if someone really is self-confident? The easiest way is to give them a compliment and watch for their reaction. You can tell them that you like their shirt. If they reply, "Oh, it's just an old shirt I've had for years," they are rejecting your compliment, advising you of their lack of self-confidence and telling you that you have bad taste. How many people have you insulted this way?

Some people will argue that this has nothing to do with lack of self-esteem or confidence and that it is the result of being shy. I will counter with another question. What is the difference between shyness and the lack of self-confidence?

Psychoanalysts say that shyness is a conscious awareness of subconscious conflicts raging deep within the psyche.

Physiologists believe that it is inherited.

Sociologists, psychologists and behaviorists feel that it is due to social programming.

They all seem to agree however that (a) the lack of self-confidence is the result of low self-esteem, (b) that shyness and low self-esteem have a significant correlation, (c) that when shyness is prominent, self-esteem is low, and (d) when self-esteem is high, shyness becomes virtually nonexistent.

Tape 8a: Manipulation Programming

We have all been programmed to get our way through manipulation. Many mistakenly use destructive manipulation such as the rationing of favors and sex, adverse mind games and guilt. Others use fear through intimidating threats like breaking off a relationship, dating others, physical abuse, etc. These methods worked on you when you were a child, but they won't work now. Why? Because no one likes to fall victim to destructive manipulation; and as adults, we have a choice as whether or not to accept it. Most will not.

People who are victims of destructive manipulation might not even realize it. They just know that they are unhappy with the relationship for some reason and choose to get out as the result. The propagators may not even realize that they are using destructive manipulation. The only thing they know is that relationships just don't seem to work for them, and they wonder why.

If we are happy with a relationship we will tend to stay in it, and there is nothing quite like constructive manipulation for getting our way and making friends and lovers happy at the same time. Some examples of constructive manipulation are: Praise, Affection, Support, Sharing, Consideration and positive strokes in almost any form. As pointed out previously, others will be far more dependent upon you for positive strokes than for negative strokes. Stroking can cause static electricity in people, the same as with dogs and cats, and positively charged people are more anxious to please you than are negatively charged people.

Constructive manipulation should not be confused with the total giving and surrender of one's self. If a person is too easy to possess, particularly at the first stage of a relationship, it seems to take the challenge out of it and the relationship can end up on the rocks. You can use love, praise, support and the other tools of constructive manipulation without giving yourself; mind, body and soul. Just use these tools honestly and you will create a masterpiece. Really start liking people. Make each person you're with, at each particular point in time, the most important person in your life!

Tape 8b: Manipulation Programming

There are many different modes of manipulation; however, one of the most common is through debate. Often during the course of a debate you realize the other person is correct; but your Pride Protection device in your "I am not at fault circuit" clicks in and it allows you to cloud the input so that you can continue the debate under the guise that you are still right. The technical term for this mode is "fooling yourself." You fool yourself into thinking you are right, just because you don't want to be wrong or because it fulfills a desire.

Now the big problem arises when you enter this type of debate with yourself. To illustrate this, let's create a hypothetical debate between you and yourself.

One day in a supermarket you run smack dab, nose to bellybutton, into the someone of your life. Your heart reels and your mind skips a beat. Your metabolism instantly changes state and you erupt into a heterosexual hidrosis of hormonal secretions. Over a subsequent cup of coffee you find that your new, perfect person is Jewish, seventeen years old; does not smoke, drink or take part in sports, and is homosexual. You, in fact, are Catholic, thirty eight, and the only thing you like better than smoking, drinking, and sports is a good heterosexual fling. You say to yourself, "Self, this is love!" Yourself says, "Listen, this can't possibly work out!" But you have never been known to listen to yourself and you also know that yourself is very weak. So you say, "Hey! I know there's a couple of small problems to work out, but this is the real thing!"

So, with the grace of a high-diving hippopotamus, you plunge right in. Yourself was trying to be honest with you, but you were not being honest with yourself. As the result of fooling yourself, you manage to get you and yourself into another one of those hopeless and painful situations that you're so good at, and you will probably cry and complain to yourself through the whole wrenching trip. When are we ever going to learn to stop fooling ourselves?

Tape 9: Pattern Programming

People tend to lock themselves into certain patterns. For instance, a person may have been married to an alcoholic for a long period of time, programming themself to survive with this particular type of problem. As a result, they subconsciously feel very comfortable with it even though few would realize it. Therefore they are drawn to the same type of relationship which can provide them with the same type of problems. It's quite similar to a habit in as much as we have become used to the peculiarities associated with our past and tend to subconsciously search out relationships which are similar. Some of us are programmed to seek out relationships with those who will completely dominate and rule us--or abuse us. Sometimes we form programming patterns which allow us to enter into what we believe are "safe" relationships. Love affairs with married people or relationships with those so different from us that things could never work out. When they don't work out, we often stand there in our own bewilderment and wonder why.

These are anything but safe relationships and will invariably result in a wrenching, tearing emotional experience.

Corrective Programming

There are so many examples of incorrect programming within the lives of each of us, it would take another book just to list them all. The important thing is to consider the possibility that your old programming and resulting attitudes may need some reformation. Start by looking for some new answers and when you feel overwhelmingly right about something that doesn't seem to be working for you, look at it with an open, honest mind.

If the bad programming on our tapes is too deep, we can erase it ourselves; but this is not always easy to do. Quite often we have to hire a professional deprogrammer called a psychologist. The problem is, some of us were programmed to believe that psychologists are basically bad so we refuse to get reprogrammed.   This attitude is also the result of incorrect programming, as psychologists are not basically bad. They are just basically expensive. If you can reprogram yourself and save money, this is great, but remember that there is help out there if you need it.

Reprogramming ourselves will become easier as time goes by. We can start right now by thinking positive; talking about positive subjects; looking for virtues rather than faults, and trading our negative attitudes for positive attitudes. (This is what the psychologist would probably tell you anyway.)   It takes time to learn how to do this, so don't get discouraged.

The emotionally magnetic alternations on our tapes have been impressed deeply into our minds over a long period of time, but they <u>can be</u> changed.   One way is verbalization.   Let's say that one of our programs most worthy of changing is Acceptance Programming. We may really be tired of trying to fit everyone else's expectations and trying to be accepted and loved by everyone we meet.   To change these grooves, we can start by saying aloud, "I'm through trying to please everyone else!"   Now just stating this will not change our programming or cover over our previous alternations.   We will have to verbally repeat it aloud over and over. (It's recommended that you don't do this in public.)   It's also a good idea to write it down as often as you can and put it in a place where you will see it.   Prayer, self-hypnosis, meditation and sleep-reading are also methods that are successful in reprogramming one's self.

Selecting and wording your new program can be very tricky. For example, if you decide that you are through trying to please <u>anyone</u> else, you may find yourself unemployed and/or very lonely, as total independence may not be what you are after.   Out of anger or pain, you might choose to program yourself to never love again, and for obvious reasons that would be a mistake.   It is very important to come to honest terms with yourself before you start changing your life.   You may have to live it for a long time.

Corrective programming requires you to have a basic working concept of one of the psychological components found in every computerized robot of the humanoid variety. You have to understand the operational sequence of your Main Pride Protection Device, located in your "I am not at fault circuit."   This device was initially designed to protect our pride, subsequently energizing our self-esteem mode.   But excessive, incorrect programming can overload this circuit which limits our ability for self-understanding because it fails to allow us to make an honest appraisal of ourselves. In short, we can't see which program to correct because our Main Pride Protection Device will not allow us to see our faults. When this happens, we cannot be reprogrammed.

In the highly technical field of computerized robots, this is commonly referred to as "The Nurd Neurosis." To illustrate this, we will refer to the last of our tapes on incorrect programming.

Tape 10: Nurd Neurosis Programming

Practically everyone who has ever drawn a breath is a victim of this programming. As kids, we were often punished for being wrong, and in school, we were given incentives for being right. If you were right, you passed; if wrong, you flunked. As we grew older, we found in the world of employment that people were hired or fired as a result of their ability to be right.

In game shows, the right contestant leaves with the goodies and the wrong contestant gets ulcers. Society has inaccurately programmed us to believe that if we are right we will be considered intelligent, successful, desirable, competent and admirable; but if we are wrong, we are nothing more than a hopeless, half-witted Nurd that doesn't have both oars in the water. It's no wonder that most of us refuse to ever be wrong. I mean, who wants to be a nurd?

Studies in criminal behavior conclude that the average con artist actually cares for his victims and never considers himself wrong for taking their money. He justifies his actions by believing that he has given his victims a gift of happiness by letting them believe in a fantasy or dream that they wanted to believe in. Al Capone, one of the coldest blooded murderers and gangsters this country has ever known, was quoted as saying, "I have dedicated the best years of my life to giving people the lighter pleasures, helping them to have a good time, and all I get is abuse, the existence of a hunted man." Can you believe that? Big Al's programming to never be wrong was definitely getting in the way of his self-honesty. He was lying to himself and, as a result, he could never make the accurate self-appraisal needed to correct his programming even if he wanted to.

Everyone is at fault some of the time, and no one is perfect. If you are looking for a no-fault, perfect person in yourself or in others, you will be a constant product of disappointment. If someone openly and willingly admits to you that they were wrong about something, you don't condemn them. As a matter of fact, you tend to become very righteous and feel a deep respect for their honesty. But then this is probably because you are more understanding and forgiving than the average person, right?   If you were to admit that you were wrong to the average person, they would more than likely jump up, point an accusing finger at you and scream, "NURD! NURD!"   If you believe this, you really are a Nurd!   When you are wrong, try admitting it and see what happens.   You may be pleasantly surprised. On the other hand, don't go from one extreme to the other and develop a "love-me-cause-I'm-always-wrong attitude."   People may not think of you as a Nurd but they may consider you a moron.

<u>Emotional Reflections</u>
     We have all been programmed, from the time of mother's milk, to abide by the scrutiny of others and to care what others think of us. When we find ourselves single and alone, it's almost like having no one to even validate our existence.   This tends to add to our sense of loneliness and insecurity.   As a single, however, you will have a great opportunity to get to know yourself.   Being alone more, you will be forced into the position of becoming your own best friend.   The emotions and dependencies that you may have funneled toward your spouse will now revert back to you and as a result, you will begin to confide, respect and like yourself more and more.
     A common theory shared by many psychologists and experts in the field of human emotion is that:

> Self-worth can be obtained from <u>only</u> one source.   It is said to be created in each of us <u>only</u> by what we see, reflected from the eyes of others.   It is <u>only</u> when others respect us that we can have respect for ourselves.   It is <u>only</u> when others love us that we can love ourselves.   It is <u>only</u> when others approve of us that we can come to terms with our own egos.

I disagree!   This concept is very accurate when applied to the adult members of today's average family, but not necessarily so with the average single.   When you have someone to bounce reflections of your self-worth off of, you use them.   They are like an emotional mirror that you can look into to see what and how you are. Sometimes these mirrors are warped and give back a distorted or inaccurate reflection, so we divorce it and go shopping for another mirror. The fact remains, however, that we all form a very great dependency on others to serve as our emotional mirrors.

When we divorce our mirror, or it becomes broken through death, we are lost and search desperately for another one. Because of the possible inaccuracy of our old mirror, we are not always sure what our true image is and we want desperately to find out. "What is my purpose? I have no identity!"

Well, cheer up. I spoke earlier of the self-contentment and self-esteem that was possible in single life by being exposed to loneliness and relying on yourself more? You guessed it! This gives you the opportunity to use yourself as an emotional mirror. You will find that a person's self can be the most accurate emotional mirror one can have. If you are honest with yourself, it will project a clear, accurate image every time. This ability is possible only when we turn away from others and look to ourselves for support.

It is much easier to use others for our mirrors and as long as they are around, we will tend to do so. But without the presence of others, we are forced into this transition. One thing that I want to make clear is that this emotional mirror philosophy is not meant to make you so self-sufficient that you will need no one else. It should simply teach you how to become more self-sufficient in the appropriate areas. Mutual need is a beautiful thing and it is necessary to help us fulfill our joys and emotions.

This chapter deals to a great extent with becoming self-confident and developing the self-respect that may have been weakened as the result of previous programming. This self-confidence, however, should not be confused with total independence.

The development of emotional calluses often result in total independence. This is very confusing to those in this category, as totally independent people tend to fool themselves into believing that they need no one else. The fact is that we do all need others to depend upon. It has been said: "No man is an island unto himself." It's good to have a dependency upon others so long as it is not a total dependency and it can be controlled. Many singles believe that if you depend on others at all, you will inevitably be disappointed. This may be true to a certain extent, so the trick is to hit a happy medium. You have to develop enough independence to sustain yourself through the times of disappointment, resulting from the failure of others. But don't try to achieve happiness through total independence as you are very unlikely to succeed.

The hardest part of making this emotional mirror transition is learning how to be honest with yourself. If someone is not totally honest with us, we learn not to trust their advice; and it's exactly the same with ourselves. If you are not completely honest with yourself, you learn not to trust your own judgments and this results in indecisiveness and inhibits your ability to make correct decisions or see solutions to your problems clearly.

CHAPTER 8
Classic Traps

Chapter 8

CLASSIC TRAPS

Generally, new singles are very vulnerable, confused and desperate. Most new singles can't stand the thought of thinking. This wastes valuable time. Their decision-making capabilities are about as solid as a Kleenex full of Jell-O but they refuse to lay back and regroup their senses. They often make instant decisions on selling homes, plotting life-long careers at college, traveling around the world, buying expensive luxuries, getting skinned alive by dermatologists, investing their limited funds, selecting their new friends (anyone will do), or finding a new spouse. Singlization has a way of eating holes in one's security blanket. So to keep their insecurities from showing through, or because of an acute state of fear, many refuse to wait and consider the alternatives. The sum total is often loss and more heartache.

In a blind panic, they throw caution to the wind and plunge into the futile attempt of gaining the experience needed to establish their new lifestyle by next weekend. As a result, many end up, bogged down in one of the "Classic Traps," some of which are listed below.

<u>Unrestrained Sex</u>

Many singles, usually in one of the first three stages of singlization, feel that they need an overabundance of sex. Many look at sex like a squirrel looks at nuts. They feel that, while it is available, they should get as much as possible and store it up for hard times. The motives for wanting sex are what we are concerned with right now and some of these motives are:

1. To prove that they are desirable.
2. To fulfill a physical desire or need.
3. To fulfill an emotional need.
4. Because they feel that it is expected of them.
5. Because they don't want to be considered frigid, impotent or homosexual.
6. To satisfy a vendetta against the opposite sex.

Sexual freedom, for the first two reasons, can be fulfilling for those who are emotionally tuned for it. But, when you sacrifice your own principles, the result can be very destructive. The proverbial guilt, experienced the day after the night before, is not the only principle we have to consider. One of the main characteristics which separate humans from lower class animals is our ability to feel compassion and love for one another. Many people suppress this, but it still exists, buried deep within our psyche. When our sexual cravings result in the emotional injury of others, we can also experience a degree of emotional injury, and even the <u>subconscious</u> reality of our guilt can chip away at our self-image. Regardless of where we are emotionally, it is very difficult for the average person to share sex without some degree of commitment and/or dependency. Contrary to the popular belief that this is entirely the other person's problem, it is also yours.

Most new singles are starved to death emotionally and like the fat person, who overeats in an attempt to satisfy emotional hunger, new singles often over indulge in sex. They try to solve their emotional problem through a physical means. The type of sex found in item 3 is, of course, the best kind. This is the kind of sex that'll make your toes curl under! The problem is that this type is possible only through love and love is not that easy to find. New singles often have a tendency to try and fall in love with anyone in hopes of finding this euphoric sex aid, and then become wrenched out of shape when their expectations are not fulfilled. Remember you probably won't make love to everyone you fall in love with and you should not try to fall in love with everyone you do.

Sex, for the reasons listed in items 4, 5 and 6 can be very unfulfilling and destructive and only through an honest self-appraisal can we determine our emotional state and motives.

Frenzied Social Activities

There is nothing quite like a frenzy of social activities to break us down physically, financially, and when the activities are finally over and we are alone, emotionally. We can run only so far in an attempt to escape our feelings, and when we do stop, our feelings catch up to us. When this happens, we usually find that we have made them much worse than they really are. This is a typical example of the price we have to pay whenever we run from anything.

Trying Never To Be Alone

This is closely related to Frenzied Social Activities, except for the fact that we can be as lonely in the center of a large party as we can in solitude. Being alone does not have to mean loneliness, unless we become obsessed with the fear of it. There is no one in this world that you have more in common with than yourself. Try being your own companion and don't fear the prospect of being alone. By fearing and trying to escape something, it evolves into a bigger and even more fearful monster. When you do finally turn and face it, and after your fear of it subsides, you will be amazed at its insignificance.

Overwork

Being a productive form of escapism, we often consider overwork as a perfectly acceptable way of running away from ourselves; but this can also result in an obsessed fear of our feelings. Many of us overwork, not only for the monetary gains but to also render ourselves so exhausted that we will sleep during our idle periods. This trap can result in a physical breakdown, or because weariness can cause depression, it can result in a very depressed state of mind. At any rate, as with any form of escape, it can weaken and terrorize us.

Depression Through Depressants

Escapism through too much television, alcohol and drugs is like fighting a fire with gasoline. Alcohol and many drugs are severe depressants and so is television to a large extent. By relying on depressants as an escape, we only become more depressed. This causes us to indulge even more in these depressive elements and before you know it, we have become addicted to depression.

Overeating

Overeating is like a lot of other Classic Traps. We are trying to satisfy an emotional craving by using a physical means. Overeating will no more satisfy our emotional craving than music will satisfy our hunger. So, as a result, we just continue to indulge and bulge!

Social Regression and Withdrawal

Like all forms of escapism, this trap can lock us into a rut through our fear of what lies out there waiting for us. A certain amount of social withdrawal is good, but when our obsession for withdrawal becomes overpowering, we may need psychological help to overcome it. It's important to keep check on it and to be able to distinguish between our desire for solitude and our desire for social escape because of fear.

Sadistic Tendencies for Self-Destruction

These tendencies include, but are not limited to, suicide. They can also include alcohol, drugs, accidents or an over-abundance of any destructive element. We often take the attitude that we will get back at the world or show others how much we are suffering through self-inflicted damage. Uncivilized man, for centuries, has been involved in the practice of self-inflicted torture in an attempt to physically express his emotional pain. We may be civilized, but in many cases, we are driven by the same deep rooted, emotional tendencies that our original ancestors had. Self-inflicted damage can in no way help us with our problems, and no intelligent person could logically believe otherwise.

In an attempt to be a logical, intelligent and civilized person, we may deny that these tendencies exist. They do exist, though, buried deep within us and it's important to understand the futile motives behind our occasionally destructive nature in order to control them. The next time you're down and find yourself crouched in the corner eating worms or abusing yourself in other ways, ask yourself – why? Take a good, honest appraisal of your motives. You are probably not drinking that tenth martini just to get drunk!

Denying Ourselves

One of the "classicalist" traps that we singles are noted for is getting involved with groups or individuals that we have absolutely nothing in common with, except maybe desperation and the desire to belong. In this trap, we often deny ourselves completely, and become whatever others want us to be. We are not usually happy in our counterfeit parts, but we feel that we belong so we play our part to the bitter end, hoping for a standing ovation of some type. People are strange. Many give up a marriage to be their own person but when they become single, they try desperately to be like everyone else.

Our desire to be socially accepted can cause us to fall directly into the carnivorous jaws of a Classic Trap called single snobbery. In past years, the media has painted a picture of the ideal American single, and most of us, at some time during our "singlization," try very hard to fit into this picture. The "sophisticated picture" of the ideal American single is one who is well- versed in the theater, dancing, contemporary music, trivia, classic films, travel, French cuisine, literary works and virtually any other subject that might arise. This sophisticated example of "Supersingle" is insurmountable in the areas of wit and intellectual sword play; a virtuoso in the art of single sophism, and is the unwavering specimen of self-assurance, etiquette and charm.

There are many groups and organizations which capitalize on the insecure single. They promise to take this insecure example of social rejection and transform him or her into a polished product of social acceptance. Social research schools will teach you to be exactly what others want. You can become an expert on favorite subjects and the games that some singles play. Whether you acquire your education from a polishing school or on the single battlefield, you can learn how to always be "En Garde" against human error, insecure in the things you say and in constant competition with those around you. You can also learn how to select your peers, lovers and potential mates, based upon superficial principles. You will not allow others to see you for yourself and their judgments will be based upon how well you can act. But most important, you will learn how to present a false image that is difficult to maintain and will haunt you with the belief that the real you is not good enough.

This single stereotyping is not limited to the sophisticate. The "red-neck society" has its own form of single snobbery. Red neck acceptance is based a great deal on fighting, swearing, drinking, independence and sex, although you are more likely to be accepted for yourself.

I have found few singles that really enjoy the social jousting that is so prevalent on the single scene. Whether you are a member of the "blood, guts and beer social club" or a connoisseur of French cuisine, the best person to impress is you!

The Rebound

The obsession to escape pain and loneliness can create the most ominous trap of all. This trap, discussed often throughout the book, is called marrying on the rebound. The desperation felt by new singles has caused more wrong marriages than irate fathers, and it's nothing more than a shortcut to failure. The most vulnerable victim for this tenacious trap is probably the custodial parent whose companionate and sexual needs are overshadowed only by exhaustion and sheer frustration. You may be convinced that, next time, the only motive you will have for marriage will be love but I can assure you that when we become desperate enough, we can fall in love with anyone.

Wrap-up

In analyzing these Classic Traps, it may be worthwhile to note a couple of things. First, each trap is the result of trying to escape pain instead of facing it. Second, the ensnaring qualities of each is self-perpetuating. In other words, it's similar to flypaper; the more we struggle, the more ensnarled we become. The more ensnarled we become, the more we struggle, and so on. This creates a syndrome of "Perpetual Emotion." To illustrate, let's take another look at the fear of being alone. This fear causes a tendency in us to try and escape by staying busy and in the company of others all the time. In trying to escape this pain, we build it into a bigger monster than it really is which causes an even greater fear of it, which causes an even greater drive to escape it and so on. It is self-perpetuating.

The greatest problem that we have in fighting these "perpetual emotions" is that, being invisible, we can not see them and understand them. It's like getting into a boxing match with The Shadow! If we give them a physical form, however, they become more tangible or visible to us, and that brings us to a somewhat tangible world of emotional monsters known as Sleeping Dragons.

CHAPTER 9
Sleeping Dragons

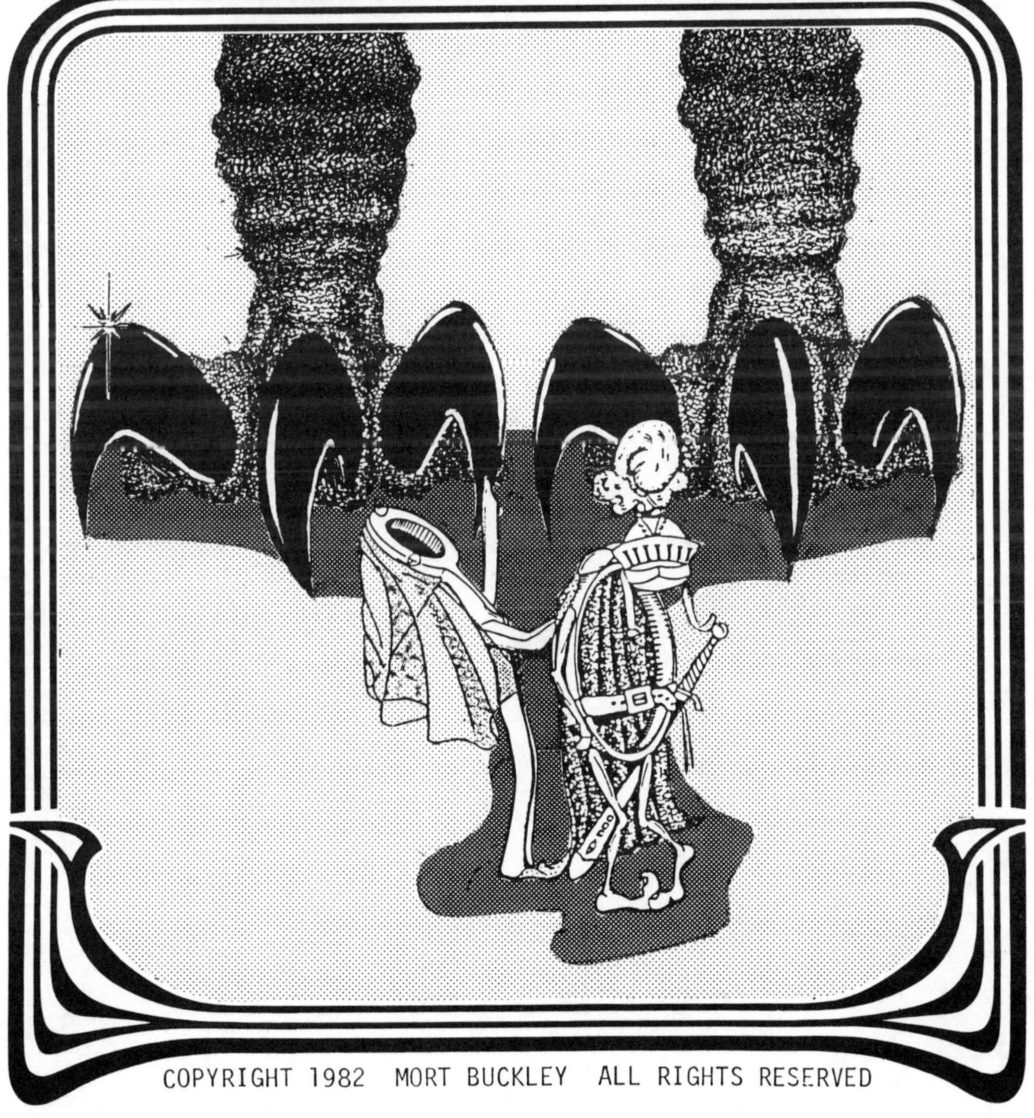

Chapter 9

SLEEPING DRAGONS

It's easy to tell others how to slay their dragon, which has just got up on the wrong side of the bed, but when we come face to shinbone with one of our own, it's another story.

Dragons are tough!

Not only that, our own dragons are invisible to us. Others can see them, but we can't. These big fellas like to sleep in our subconscious mind and because we can't see them, we sometimes like to pretend that they are not even there. The problem is that divorce and singlization have a way of waking dragons up and you don't just ignore an irate dragon, especially when he's inside of you!

Our dragons are so fearsome to us that we often spend all of our time running from them instead of trying to face them--which, as pointed out previously, makes them bigger and even more fearsome. Living within the vast dimensions of our minds, these dragons know our every thought, which does give them an edge. Being entities of a physical universe, we tend to use a physical means in combating these emotional monsters which usually just results in getting us bogged down in one of the Classic Traps discussed previously.

We are products of a physical dimension and as such we often have trouble seeing or understanding emotional elements from an intangible dimension. Also, when people become singlized they are bombarded by a ton of different emotions all at once, which can be very confusing. By separating these emotions and transforming them into a tangible form, we can better understand them. Thus, the Dragons awake!

There are many different types of dragons within the mind of each of us. For the purpose of this chapter however, we are going to limit our course in Dragonology to five basic species. The dragons of: Insecurity, Desperation, Anger, Loneliness, and Depression.

DRAGONS

<u>Class</u>: <u>Invisibilia</u>, <u>Order</u>: <u>Emotionivora</u>, <u>Family</u>: <u>Dragonidae</u>,
<u>Genus</u>: <u>Draconis</u>, <u>Species</u>: <u>Miscellaneous</u>

THE DRAGON OF INSECURITY (<u>Draconis</u> <u>Insecuratorious</u>)

The Dragon of Insecurity is one of the first dragons on the scene. He is a very, very shrewd guy with no weapons at all except for his arsenal of tactics. Some of these tactical weapons are: Feelings of rejection, self-pity, false security in fate, low self-esteem and defeatism, all of which lead up to. . . Insecurity!

Dull brown in color and resembling a snake, he paralyzes or hypnotizes us into total submission. Like a twenty-five ton parasite, he latches onto his prey and drains it of will and strength. This, of course, softens us up for the other dragons. Like all serpents, he is very slow and subtle in his approach but his attack is swift. One of his favorite strategies is to convince us that things are hopeless. He tells his victims that the whole world is against them and is responsible for their misfortune. He smothers them with self-pity, then like the serpent in the garden, he says "rely on fate and it will see you through." He knows that instead of taking the responsibility for our own lives, it's much easier to do nothing, then when nothing happens, we can blame fate and say, "Well, the world did it to me again."

He feeds on our insecurities and convinces us that we are unattractive, stupid and unworthy. He assures us that, because someone can't keep a date or has other plans, it's because of rejection. When we allow him to destroy our self-respect or self-worth, we are close to defeat. When we stop caring for ourselves, we stop caring about ourselves and at this point, we can let anything happen to us. This is when we generally start trying to be someone that we are not.

In many instances, we try to transform ourselves into one of the thousands of fictitious personalities that we see daily on tv or in the movies. Someone who is forever strong, never wrong, totally desirable, in complete control of every situation and always in complete control of themselves. I doubt that there is a human in this world who can live up to the average, superhuman image that society has programmed us to strive for.

At any rate, old Insecuratorious loves for us to lose our identity. He is also the dragon most responsible for our wrong decisions as the result of self-deceit. He hates praise or strokes from anyone, particularly ourselves, and his worst enemy is self-esteem. The best weapons to use against him are periods of self-fulfillment and personal honesty.

THE DRAGON OF DESPERATION (Draconis Desperatorious)

The Dragon of Desperation is a little guy (only about the size of an average six-story building) but he is very wiry and fast. It's his job to keep us in a preoccupied panic and in a continual state of confusion. This way we can't concentrate on defense tactics that could help us with the bigger dragons.

He utilizes tactics like panic, fear and impatience and works in conjunction with the Dragon of Insecurities. Old Desperatorious will always show up soon after Insecuratorious has started softening us up. This is the dragon, most responsible for driving us into one of the "Classic Traps." He realizes our human tendency to run from pain and uses his magic to make our fears of pain appear much larger and worse than they really are. As the result of this increased panic, we inevitably run blindly right into one of the Classic Traps.

Time is his greatest asset and security is his worse enemy. For this reason we usually have to slay his big buddy (Insecuratorious) before we can deal with this little guy. As a rule, when the Dragon of Insecurities has bitten the dust, Desperation returns to his cave and goes back to sleep. It's sort of like killing two dragons with one stone.

THE DRAGON OF HATE (Draconis Hateorious)

The Dragon of Hate is a big, red, fire-breathing Emotionivora whose ill-tempered personality has won him few friends, even in Dragondom. Actually, he needs no friends as he works entirely by himself. "Big Red," as he is called in dragons' social circles, does not fool around. He is very fast and his attack is swift although he has little stamina and gives up quickly if he meets resistance. One of the main secrets to his success is that anger, which is the preliminary stage to hate, feels so good to humans.   He quickly convinces us that the target of our hate is the victim when, in truth, the hater becomes the victim.   Divorced singles and jilted lovers are his favorite prey. He makes us forget that the hostilities we have are often just the product of pain resulting from the love that we have for one another. Sometimes we hate in an unsuccessful attempt to stop loving.   In short, we may be hating someone who loves us so much that the pain is making them act weird.   This fine line between love and hate can make anyone act weird, even us.

His magic venom infiltrates our minds like a cancer, destroying healthy cells and replacing them with decay.   Old Draconis Hateorious will transform his host into a bitter, living corpse if he can.   The bitterness resulting from hate can actually ruin our very lives if we let it.   One of the best defenses against Big Red is to be a little selfish with our criticisms.   Don't waste your valuable energy in an attempt to perfect others because you cannot do it!   Our search for faults in others is generally just a product of our own insecurities.   Realize that we often look for faults in others, in order to make us look better through our own eyes.   With this revelation tucked away in one of your psychological pockets somewhere, use it. As it is said, "Speak well of your enemies because you are the one who created them."

Instead of hate, create a compassionate type of pity for the slimy, good-for-nothing low life that this subhuman really is.   Take comfort in that fact that you are so much better.   The conformation that "Old Low Life" has a few good qualities will give a certain credibility to your assumption.   Honestly look for something good in this impersonation of a person that you hate.   It may be hard to find something, but look anyway.   Then if you have it in you, openly verbalize these qualities (the more the better) to someone else or at least to yourself.   There is nothing like it for putting out Big Red's fire!

THE DRAGON OF LONELINESS (Draconis Loneatorious)

Possibly the toughest dragon of them all is loneliness.   We load our semi-automatic dragonslayer with ammunition like frenzied social and work activities and the constant company of others.   The thing we have to realize, however, is that this fella has a hide so thick that it is impregnable, and not only that, he feeds on this type of ammunition, using it against us.

Frenzied social and work activities and constantly being in the company of others only serves to increase our fear and pangs of loneliness when we are finally alone. The pain of loneliness combines with the type of letdown we always feel after a big social fling and can cause severe depression. The best method of slaying this dragon is to starve him to death. Accept the loneliness you feel. Experience it, learn from it and let it introduce you to yourself. Insecurity makes us feel an urgent need for others, while desperation blows our fear of loneliness so far out of proportion that we become terrified of facing it. When we do, however, we find that being alone does not necessarily constitute loneliness and that solitude can indeed replenish the soul. Solitude does not have to be an enemy. It can be one of the greatest aids in finding one's self.

This, like many other antidotes in this book, is not easy. But it seems to be the only one that works. Now, by experiencing loneliness, it is not suggested that you become a hermit and refrain from dating or being in the company of others. Just don't let it become an obsession which governs your very existence. Remember, solitude does not necessarily dictate loneliness. You can be just as lonely when in the presence of bad company as you can when alone!

THE DRAGON OF DEPRESSION (Draconis Depressionatorious)

The Dragon of Depression is, by far, the largest and most dangerous dragon we can encounter. He has finished off more people than any other dragon known. He is referred to simply as "Irving" by his dragon buddies, but don't let his name fool you. Old Irving is huge, flat black and rapacious in nature. That is to say, he follows other dragons around and feeds off their victims. Some of these victims have allowed themselves to become too weak to fight back and he completely devours any remains like a big, black vulture. His method of attack is by suffocation and once he has you down, it's hard to get away from him. It's like trying to move fifty tons of dead weight that's sitting on your head! He's so fearsome that many people commit suicide rather than face him, not knowing that belonging to the vulture family, he is really just a big, overweight chicken.

Depressionatorious, or "Irving", is the only dragon that uses any type of physical means to subdue his prey. This physical means is illness. When we give up to the point of letting Irving pin us, our physical defenses collapse and we often get sick. If there is anything in this world worse than getting sick, it's being sick with a fifty ton vulture sitting on your head!   Believe me, it's no laughing matter!

Irving may be big and fearsome but he is also very timid and we have to literally lay down and give up before he can defeat us and eat us.   He hates things like cheerful apartments, clean surroundings, personal hygiene, warm baths, good food (other than human), self-pride, activity and friends.

Another one of Irving's vulnerabilities is in the predictable patterns of his attacks.   Even when we are successfully back on our feet, old Irving will continue his assaults, but with a predictable pattern.   Our emotions fluctuate in cycles, similar to a bio-rhythm chart, with peaks and valleys. We are emotionally high, then low, then high, then low.   There is always a low following every high and as a result, you can expect Irving to invite you for dinner shortly after you come off of one of your highs.   Plan for this and be ready for him.

<u>DRAGON ANTIDOTES</u>
There are numerous crusaders that can and will assist you in your fight against the forces of these emotional monsters.   Some of these are:

<u>Self-improvement</u>.   This is without a doubt the best crusader in the world.   In fact, it seems to be essential.   Almost every single I have talked with has instinctively gone on a crash program for self-improvement at some time prior to their personal fulfillment.   This prescription can take form in the area of physical exercise and/or educational improvement.   It not only serves to keep you active, it will also increase your feeling of self-worth.

<u>Physical Exercise</u>.   Exercise is fantastic, particularly when it is used to the extent of bettering your physical appearance.   Try jogging, swimming, skating, tennis, racketball or bicycling. If you can afford it, enroll in a good health spa or a class that teaches martial arts or dancing.   Singles often tend to go overboard on everything so, as a word of caution, take it easy, particularly if you are not used to physical exercise.

<u>Educational Improvement</u>.   Bettering yourself mentally and socially is also a fantastic antidote.   This can include academic

courses through schools and colleges as well as fine arts, trade schools, etc. You not only keep your mind active and experience an increased sense of self-worth, you can better yourself in the area of employment. You will also be surprised at the number of singles you will meet who are also using this as a method of combating their own dragons.

Keeping a Diary. Keeping a diary or a daily log on your emotional state may seem a little foolish and self-defeating at first thought, but it is surprising what you can learn about yourself. The keeping of diaries, for emotional health, is an age-old remedy and is still used as a valuable tool by modern psychologists today. By reflecting back through it, you not only can detect improvement (which is always good for the morale), you can analyze many of the problems which cause your grief. For instance, you may find that depression peaks out at 6:00 p.m. daily. By analyzing it, you may find that this is the time of day that you and your Ex usually sat down to eat dinner. By readjusting your dinner schedule, it's possible to effectively reduce your anxiety for the rest of the evening. Your diary need not be exhaustive in its content; however, the amount recorded is up to you.

Hobbies and Interests. These are great antidotes for Dragon Fever. Most of us have had a desire to fulfill certain interests or creative desires but have never indulged ourselves with the time needed to do it. So, how about now? This is the time to be good to yourself by concentrating on things that will bring you self-contentment. Be a little self-indulgent for a change. Your interests can range from writing piano concertos to collecting animals to put in your ark. There are so many interesting things in this world that no one has a right to be bored and depressed, unless they want to. Get into art, creating, writing, collecting, music, gardening, etc., etc., etc. Also, there are probably many organizations within your area that are filled with people who share your same interests. Go to your local library and look through a book titled "The Encyclopedia of Associations" which lists thousands of organizations within each area of the nation.

Helping Others. In some philosophies, this is regarded as the main secret to happiness and self-contentment. Whether true or not, the fact remains that it does often bring a feeling of happiness and self-worth to the benefactor. There is a tremendous need in the various organizations which are dedicated to helping the mentally retarded, the physically handicapped, the aged and the poor. If you are already depressed, however, working with the oppressed can be very tricky, so rely on your own instincts.

Communication. This can be a very valuable tool to use against loneliness. Emergency "Hot Lines" are often set up, between singles, to be used in the event of a sudden attack of "The Dragons" and is usually very effective and helpful to all parties involved. It's good to talk these feelings out (if not overdone) and the benefits of moral support are obvious. Some, however, have a tendency to create an over-dependence on their phone mates, or to rely on this type of communication as their only aid. This can result in greater emotional anxieties and added pressures if a member of your "support team" cannot be reached or is not particularly receptive. Something else to remember is when you continually dump on a particular person, they too can become depressed. Continual dumping and the resulting depression can wear a friendship thin, so don't abuse this privilege.

Environment. It is usually a good idea, emotionally, to start over with a new residence, since living in the same surroundings can serve as a constant reminder of your past. You may choose a house, which can be a good investment, or an apartment, which will relieve you of major upkeep and repairs. This, of course, depends largely on your financial condition as well as the area in which you live. In choosing your new domain you should pick something comfortable and cheerful; an environment that will support you for better or worse, in sickness and in health. It will sometimes just be you and your apartment against the world, so pick one you can really be friends with.

Fighting the Grungies. When we become depressed we often add to it by allowing ourselves to fall into a state of "Grunginess"! We don't comb our hair, we refuse to shave and we allow our home to evolve into a cannibalistic monster that acts like it's out to get us. Remember that one of the best ways to fight old Irving is by cleaning up our act and keeping it clean. Sometimes the Grungies feel good and will support us, but never when we are depressed.

10
CHAPTER
Recipe For Personal ~ Pie

Chapter 10

RECIPE FOR PERSONAL PIE

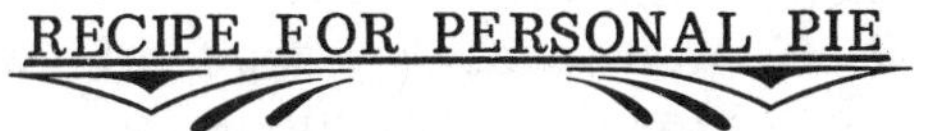

THE MIRROR

If you get what you want
In your struggle for self,
And the world makes you king
for a day,
Just go to the mirror and look
at yourself,
And see what that man has to say.

For it isn't your father,
or mother, or wife,
Who upon you their judgment will pass,
The fellow whose verdict counts most
in your life,
Is the one staring back from the glass...

He's the fellow to please...
Never mind all the rest!
For he's with you right up to the end.
And you've passed your most difficult,
dangerous test,
If the man in the glass is your friend.

You may fool the world down the pathway
of years,
And get pats on your back as you pass,
But your final reward will be heartache
and tears, if you've cheated the man in the glass.

                    -- Author unknown

The Latitude of Attitude

When I first became singlized, I was so bitter that I could care less what the world thought of me.

When I started dating again, I became obsessed with what the world really did think of me.

Recently, however, I've come to the realization that the world has never really thought of me at all!

This realization was probably one of the most profound realizations I've ever realized. It happened one day when I was late for work. As I pulled up to a stop sign at a busy street, I quickly looked to the left to see a long line of cars coming about a block away. A quick glance to the right assured me that if I hurried, I could make it, but this Nurd on a bicycle was in my way! By the time he had peddled his tush past my point of trajectory they were upon me and I was hopelessly blocked in front by a hundred cars or more. "Well," I said aloud, "the world did it to me again!" As I sat there steeping in my own stew, waiting for a break in traffic, it suddenly came to me. The world wasn't really against me. Circumstances had provided the means for me to feel sorry for me and I had done the rest. It wasn't the nurd's fault or the world's, it was mine! At that point in time I began to realize that I alone was responsible for all the unhappiness that I had elected to heap upon me. I had told myself that I could never be happy until I had financial security, so...I couldn't. I had convinced myself that I could never be happy as a single and that I could never find someone to replace Karen in my life, so...I couldn't. I had subconsciously placed myself in a completely hopeless situation.

I have found that happiness is an attitude and it is controlled mainly by our own decision to be happy. The world can't control your happiness any more than other people can. They can influence your happiness (or unhappiness), but _only when you give them that power_! The nurd on the bicycle didn't have the power to make me unhappy until I gave it to him. Why did I do that? Because I had decided to be unhappy and was just looking for an excuse. It's miraculous, the amount of power that we often give to others. When I took this power away from nurds on bikes, and accepted the responsibility for my own attitude, a whole new world began opening up to me. By telling myself that I couldn't do something, I couldn't. By telling myself that I was unhappy, I _was._

Many of us have a full-time hobby of convincing ourselves that everything is wrong and nothing is right.   We run around complaining about this and that, stewing over the way others have let us down, worrying about world problems and telling ourselves that everything would be alright, if only.... This just creates the climate for unhappiness and makes it easier for us to find it.   Now I realize that when you're up to your neck in emotional monsters, it's hard to remember that your main objective is to be happy.   The fact remains, however, that you are the only one capable of controlling your own attitude and there could be no happiness without a little unhappiness to base it on.

I have also found that <u>unhappiness usually starts with the desire to be happier.</u>   Think about it.   By telling ourselves that we would like to be happier, we're selling ourselves on the idea that we are discontent with the present, and what is happiness if it isn't a present state of contentment?   Many people confuse happiness with joy, and spend their entire life in a partytime search for an unending source of the stuff.   But joy, being an exhilarated state of happiness, is a rare and fleeting commodity. Enjoy joy to the fullest degree when you have it and be content to await its return when you don't.

A New Concept in Goals

Being happy and content does not mean that we should not set goals.   It simply means that we should be content with our lives at present and content with the goals we have set.   Don't allow your goals to become an obsession that governs your state of mind and don't sell yourself on the idea that unreached goals will constitute personal failure.   If you do, they will.   For this reason I disagree with the theory that you should set your goals as high as possible and then put a time limit on them.   Perhaps this is one reason why so many fast rising business people can't find happiness or contentment.   One of my biggest mistakes was the tendency I had to set myself up for failure.   I was notorious for setting my goals too high and expecting too much from the goals that I did achieve.

I make this statement even in view of all the wailing and gnashing of executive teeth out there!   I can hear a million computerized minds saying "Ridiculous!   The higher you set your goals, the better.   Buckley just doesn't have what it takes to reach his goals!"   Well, if that were true, you wouldn't be reading this book right now!   Millions of <u>unread</u> manuscripts are trash-canned each year and the chances of an unknown author getting a book published are about one in zilch.

I sincerely believe that I can accomplish anything I want, if I want it badly enough and that's the catch! We often set our goals higher than our desire to achieve them. When they crash and burn, we feel a sense of failure. Why do we fail? It's not because we are incompetent or inferior, it's because we didn't want to achieve our goal badly enough. We set the goal higher than our desire to achieve it. There's nothing like this for creating inferiority complexes, but singles really do it up right. We all run around with the confirmed belief that ours is probably the biggest and best inferiority complex in the entire world! This creates the climate for unhappiness and from there, all we need is an excuse.

Through these goals we often set ourselves up for disappointment or failure. For instance, we may go to a single's bar for no other reason than to score (sexually). As the evening progresses the desire becomes an obsession, going far beyond the reasons of physical gratification. It becomes paramount, almost to the degree of life and death, to prove to ourselves that we are OK and desirable. If we fail, we consider it an omen, testifying to the fact that we are some kind of a reject which is neither desirable nor worthy. The truth is, for some unconscious reason, we may not have wanted it enough. Some of us set ourselves up the same way by expecting too much from certain people or dates. When our expectations don't materialize, we become very disappointed or take it personally.

On the other hand, singles are also great at predicting their own failures in advance. We may go to the same single's bar (as an example) for the same reason but with the preconceived prediction that we will bomb out and PRESTO, we do! Singles have been known to predict in advance that a certain date is going to be a real bummer and whadaya know, it is. It's almost like we set our goals to fail, and we do! In short, goal setting is very important but should be handled with a heaping helping of Emotional Moderation. Set your goals in this case to have fun, and go with the prediction and attitude that you will...and you will. Don't give outside forces the power to disappoint you, and they can't!

Emotional Callusing
Confirmed singles work really hard at being single and like most hard working people, they develop calluses. The only difference is

that instead of physical calluses, singles tend to develop an over-abundance of emotional callusing which is the bi-product of emotional pain.

All humans have some degree of emotional callusing. It starts at the time some big jerk in a green uniform pulls us reluctantly from the womb and starts slapping us around. Some degree of emotional callusing is good. In fact, it is necessary for us to be able to cope with life. Singles, however, in their lust to get all of a good thing they can, often overdo it! Whenever we are jilted, rejected, used, cheated, conned or shunned, we have a tendency to develop another protective layer of this emotional protoplasm. These calluses help to prevent pain by lessening our ability to feel. If we can't feel so well, we don't hurt so bad. Sounds great, right? "Hey George, bring me another heaping helping of those EMOTIONAL CALLUSES, I want to feel no pain!" There are a few drawbacks!

Heavily callused hands are similar to wearing gloves. They feel no pain--or the pleasure of touch--and the same holds true for our emotions. A callused heart does not feel the pain of love, or its pleasures. Like gloves on a hand, many singles erect walls of emotional callusing around their feelings as an insulator against pain and they stop feeling altogether.

Most singles believe wholeheartedly in this philosophy, but they believe that it's mainly the other singles that refuse to let their walls down and feel. As a result, we all run around in our protective little barriers, peeking over the tops now and then to see if anyone else has made the first move. This example of "perpetual emotion" is the biggest factor in the spread of a social neurosis that I call "The Sex War Syndrome." The affects and causes of The Sex War Syndrome will be covered more extensively later, but for now it's important to analyze it outside the realm of human sexuality.

Because of the unique problems associated with single life, most of us experience a great deal of emotional pain from time to time, as the result of empowering others with the ability to influence or even control our own personal attitudes. It was stated earlier that a few emotional calluses here and there are a good thing to have, but the "here and there" is the tricky part.

The single's tendency to overdo everything good, often makes us regress from friends, family, sweethearts and strangers alike. We usually learn the benefits of being self-sufficient at an early stage of the game and this new power to control our very own attitude, all by ourselves, can be very consuming.   As a result, we often put on the skids to all vulnerability; even to those that we already love.   The problem is, <u>Love</u> <u>is</u> <u>Vulnerable!</u>   I have heard countless singles emphatically state:

"I will never allow myself to depend on anyone again."
or:

"I will never allow myself to be vulnerable again."
What they are really saying is:

"I will never allow myself to feel again!"
This is a prime example of emotional callusing in an advancing stage.

Love always produces pain as well as pleasure.   We cannot experience the fantastic pleasure of love without experiencing a certain amount of pain with it.   The contemporary single with an over powering obsession to escape <u>all</u> pain develops a tendency to run from love even though he or she craves it with a purple passion.   Pain has a way of pushing old buttons within our subconscious minds, reminding us of old experiences, so at the first itch of pain most of us pull up our wall of calluses and refuse to chance it.

This is very frustrating to the single whose main goal in life seems to be that of committing emotional suicide by falling into a vulnerable type of love with everyone that shows a passing interest in them.   How do we know who to trust?   I trust those who have earned my trust, by determining when the pleasures of love significantly outweigh the pains of it.   Trust and love should not be confused at this point.   I try to trust everyone with a companionate type of love but trust only a few with the power to influence my personal attitude.   (There are many types of love which will be covered later.)

Our Emotional Deodorant

We have all heard the old maxim "We are what we eat!"   Well, God help us, because if this is true, the average single is nothing but a skin covered garbage disposal.   Another tantalizing tidbit of truth is that we are also everything that we do.   Our psyche is like a camera. It records for a lifetime everything we do, say, feel or think.   The really rotten things are dumped into our subconscious garbage cans and hidden from sight, but they're still there peeking out at us with beady little bloodshot eyeballs, and this putrid pile of unpleasantness actually becomes a part of our emotional self.   Just as the anchovy omelet and hot fudge sundae I had the other night became part of me, physically, the degrading little lie that I told about someone out of anger a while back became a part of me, emotionally. As a result, somewhere deep within the subterranean canyons of my psyche, there is another beady-eyed little creep, leaning out of his garbage can screaming "YOU'RE A LIAR!"

Now we all have sort of a psychological sanitation crew in there, too, and it's their job to keep our emotional garbage in check. The problem is that during certain stages of our life we start dumping more garbage in there than our crew can handle. This, in turn, causes a decomposition that no one can stand, even ourselves. Have you ever known someone whose personality stinks? Well, their emotional body odor may well be due to an over-filled garbage can.

Every self-respecting human on the face of this earth has developed a personal code of ethics and regardless how stringent or lenient this code is, we should try our best to live up to it. If we don't, personal pride is impossible to achieve. The articles that we incorporate into our personal code are up to each one of us individually. I have found that the more articles one has the stronger one's character and personal pride becomes. There is no better emotional deodorant on the market than to establish your own code and practice it.

Our Greatest Lie-ability

For many of us our greatest liability is our ability to lie. The truth is often dull or filled with those beady-eyed little creeps that we don't want others to see or the truth may not fit our desires, so we modify it slightly and it becomes a lie.

We are all liars?   I have lied to myself as well as others in the past and will undoubtedly do it in the future. This is because I am pure human. Being a human being, I will never attain perfection and would be lying to myself again if I thought I could. Now many of us (myself included) have used this theory of imperfection as a cop-out under the guise that since perfection is impossible, we may as well stop trying and really live it up!

As pointed out previously, the big problem occurs when we are dishonest with ourselves. We would not trust someone else that continually lied to us and similarly we stop trusting ourselves. Our personal lies usually result in wrong judgments and decisions which, in turn, create failure in our lives. When our lives become filled with failure, it destroys the faith that we should have in ourselves and this clouds our ability to see the solutions to our problems clearly. Over a long period of time we even become uncertain as to when we are telling ourselves the truth or lying. As a result, we often begin to rely on others to tell us what to do. These others, which are not always experts on the subject of us, can give bad advice and all of a sudden we have no one to depend on. Our world becomes a lonely, confused dimension of despair and we tell ourselves that it's not our fault. It was the fault of our Ex-friend who gave us the bad advice, or the world in general is to blame.

Honesty is an art that has to be learned and practiced. Most of us at this point will say "but I am honest," and you may be. Honesty, however, is a relative term. How honest are you? Are you honest enough? Let's take another quick look at one of the heaviest burdens we have in achieving personal honesty, the honest realization that we are wrong when we are, and the resulting ability to accept the blame. Everyone suffers to some degree from the Nurd Neurosis and never wants to be wrong or at fault so, as a result, we all have that tendency to fight for being right. Sure, we will admit that we're wrong if someone proves it beyond any shadow of a doubt and we have no other way out, but even then we tend to show that we were only half wrong, or that our error was due to a misunderstanding. It is still <u>Not Our Fault</u>! We are not only trying to fool the other person, we are trying to fool ourselves.

We have all heard the maxim "We can't be honest with others if we are not honest with ourselves." Well, this is very true, however, the reverse applies also. We can't be honest with ourselves if we are not honest with others. Honesty imparts a feeling of honor and integrity which becomes addicting once we find its worth. Honesty is a philosophy, a way of life, and it has to be practiced in whole; not in part.

Dishonesty is very self-defeating. It imparts a subconscious message that we disapprove of ourselves and have to lie in order to cover up our inferiorities. We often lie in order to cover up the garbage that we don't want others to see. As a result, it just lays there steeping in its own fumes. As an example, when we're late for an appointment or date, we often resort to a preposterous lie instead of admitting that we are human and as such we screw up now and then.

Some singles are so unsatisfied with themselves that they portray a fake image and try to be someone they are not. We often lie to ourselves in order to cover up what we should see but don't want to, or in order to believe something that we should not.

Lying is one of the greatest destructive manipulators in the world and we often resort to lying in order to get our way. This tells us that we don't have what it takes to get our way by using conventional methods.

Then there are singles who fool themselves into believing the very worst of an Ex-mate or lover. They run around spreading degrading lies to the point of believing it themselves and allow their obsession for hate to deteriorate their own self-respect.

These are just a few examples of how "Truth Decay" can damage our "Moral Hygiene." The secrets to acquiring personal honesty are not that easy to find. It took years of lying to get many of us as confused as we are, and unconfusation is not going to happen overnight. You can run out into the street and scream to the world "SOMETIMES I PICK MY NOSE," and you probably won't see any improvement at all. The only way to achieve it is to practice it. In time the benefits of personal honesty will become more and more apparent, instilling a desire to live it to the fullest degree.

Honesty is many things to many different people but to me honesty is being myself and respecting myself enough to show others who and what I really am. I don't expect them to like me; but if they do, that's great. This is a phenomenal statement for a Pisces to make and the transition was not easy.

Now at the same time, it's a good idea again to hit a happy medium. Like anything else, honesty can be overdone! There's nothing like a little honest criticism to obliterate friendships, rile strangers and annihilate relationships. There are some people indeed who will not accept criticism at all, in any form. Honesty, however, is the best policy and when used proportionately with diplomacy, you can even keep friends.

CHAPTER 11
Dating Again

Chapter 11

DATING AGAIN

The Itch

Dating again can be similar to experiencing an incredibly horrible itch, in a very private place, while trying to carry four cups of steaming hot coffee to your waiting guests. You have to maintain control because every eye is upon you and yet the itch is so bad it's causing you to walk funny. The itch is like the desire for sexual companionship and the four cups of steaming hot coffee are your inhibitions and fears. The waiting guests represent all of the other people who are involved--the relatives who would not want you to scratch that itch; your friends who cite your sexuality as a wedge to force you to; the opposite sex waiting to see if you will. And practically everyone is watching to see how well you do it!

Many new singles at this point decide to hold off on dating until their fears subside and their confidence builds. The main inhibition shared by most, however, is simply the fear of rejection. Each is afraid that he or she will not be accepted by the other. Oddly enough this is the most common fear shared by the majority of the single race and if you wait until you get over it, you may never date again. The only way of gaining confidence is through experience so you may as well get started. How do you start? The easiest way is probably through friends that are single or friends that know someone else who is. The hardest way would probably be the bar scene, but with this you usually know right up front what's expected of you. There are many ways to meet other singles and this will be covered later in the book, but for now let's concentrate on what to do and what to expect.

(121)

The Magic Formula

The best advice is to <u>do little, expect nothing and be yourself.</u> The simplicity of this formula may be very disappointing but I can assure you that it has taken many singles years of heartbreaking experimentation to come to this simple realization. Before we dissect and analyze our formula, I would like to share the difficulties of a few of my first dating-again experiences with you. The stories may be a little over dramatized, but they are a very accurate account, and they are true.

My first date, subsequent to the loss of my wife, was set up by Pete, a good single buddy who seemed to understand my inhibitions and fears. He suggested that we double date the first time so that I could get to know the girl. I had noticed her in his office on a prior occasion and remembered that she was extremely cute. I knew nothing else about her except that she had a four-year-old daughter and was divorced.

I spent one whole week preparing for the date with a $20 haircut, a new pair of slacks and a new midnight passion blue shirt. The big night finally came. I nervously applied toilet paper, stype stick and Savage Animal Musk cologne to my smooth shaven and profusely bleeding face. I rolled on my Sex Scent antiperspirant deodorant, donned my new clothes and put on my best pair of shoes (the ones that I was married in, thirteen years prior).

As my date and I sat in the tiny rear seat area of Pete's sporty new car, I tried to remember some of the witty and profoundly intellectual conversations and routines that I had been creating for the past week, but I drew a total blank! I started wondering what was expected of me. Should I hold her hand or maybe put my arm around her? Since my hands were dripping with sweat, I decided that the best route was to put my arm around her. The only problem was in deciding how to go about it. I reached back to my thirty-five years of experience for help. I remembered at sixteen I would stretch and casually lay my arm on the seat and then let my hand nonchalantly fall onto her shoulder. As I calculated the limited size of my surroundings, I determined that there was just not enough room to stretch. Not only that, there was only a three- inch clearance between the top of her head and the ceiling of the car and even if I could navigate that three-inch gap, there was another problem. Due to the limited room, I found myself sitting on the hand that was attached to the arm which would have to go around her.

Pete, my veteran single buddy, kept looking in the rearview mirror to see how I was doing and there I was, sitting on my hand!   In a fit of desperation I pulled my hand from beneath me and from between us, swung my arm (which had gone to sleep) in a long arc overhead and hit the ceiling with a loud, resounding BONG!   My elbow ricocheted off the ceiling and onto the top of her head, messing up her hair and then onto the back of the seat.   After apologizing several times, I settled back to one of the cruelest realizations of my entire life.   At that horrible second, I realized that the flame retardant in my new midnight passion blue shirt had created a chemical reaction with my Sex Scent antiperspirant deodorant and was producing a terrible odor, so strong that it was burning our eyes.

I looked at her in horror for some kind of reaction.   She was just sitting there with her jaws locked and eyes staring straight ahead.   I felt that if I withdrew my arm and accidentally hit her in the head again she could lose control.   I wanted to tell her that it was not me, it was just my deodorant but somehow that didn't seem like the thing to say.   In a last ditch effort to regain some of my composure, I asked how old she was.   Without breaking her stare, she replied "Nineteen!"   This bit of information served only to boost my chemical reaction.   The rest of the evening got progressively worse and I remember being elated at the fact that she at least waved goodbye to me as we parted company.   I learned a lot about chemical reactions that night but learned three other things about dating as a result of this and many other encounters, which has helped a great deal.   **You guessed it!   Do little, expect nothing and be yourself.**

In reflecting back over this first date, I realize that I may have tried a bit too hard, I did expect too much and I definitely was not myself.   I blew $20 on a haircut that did not help at all.   I bought a new shirt and refused to wash it because I was afraid it would lose all of its shine.   I experimented with dangerous chemicals that almost asphyxiated a car full of innocent people.   I had psyched myself up about the date to the extent that I almost killed myself shaving, and the resulting nervous perspiration was definitely my main downfall. Instead of being myself, I almost broke my arm trying to do what I thought was expected of me, and I had spent days creating routines and conversations that I was sure would make me look witty and intellectual.   Instead I looked like a thirty-five year old moron with bad hygienic habits.   If the truth were known, she was probably just as apprehensive and insecure as I was, even before I exposed my armpit. If I had confided the truth and then laughed it off, it may have helped the situation as nothing could have hurt it, but I was too preoccupied with my false image to have even considered this.

Instead I sat there like a skunk on a log hoping that perhaps all of her nasal membranes had been seared from a freak ammonia accident or that maybe I would wake up and find that it was just a bad dream. Further, I was trying to impress her with someone else's image and not my own. If she had fallen for a false image, I would have had a very hard time living up to it on future dates and, as a result, any type of relationship was doomed from the very start anyway.

I realize that being yourself is easier said than done, but by practicing this philosophy, in time you will find that it pays off and that people will be more receptive and easier to be with.

On another date not long thereafter I took out an attractive girl of twenty-five. After a trying evening of indigestable food and single's bars, she suggested that we go back to her place, stating that her Ex had the kids for the weekend. I lit the fire in the fireplace and settled back with her and a glass of good wine. I was in complete control as our conversation drifted from current affairs to human sexuality. I remember feeling very proud of the way I managed to swing the conversation, however, I have since wondered just how much I had to do with it. The warmth of her body snuggled close to mine filled me with an erotic mixture of hot desire and apprehension. With my heart pounding, I looked down into the deep warmth of her beautiful brown eyes. As I opened my mouth to speak, she gazed into my eyes and said "Ya wanna screw?"

It was like being hit broadside with a firehose. She had snatched the control right out of my hands. My programming, based on input two decades in the past, read out "this does not compute; connection terminated." Dumbfounded and confused, my reply still amazes me. I said "Dogs screw, I don't!" With that I put on my coat and walked out of her place into the brisk winter air to take another cold shower - which I might add does not help, contrary to popular belief.

The moral to this story is, of course, expect nothing. People are just not like they used to be. This failure was due to the fact that the date had not lived up to my expectations. I had based my strategies upon expectations that were not fulfilled. I had everything carefully planned in such a way as to insure my complete control, but some women think nothing of taking the control right out of the man's hands and are very liberal about it.   When my plan hit a snag, I didn't know what to do and acted out of sheer desperation. The realization of what I must have done to her has haunted me ever since.

One of the areas that I have had a great deal of trouble in is with blind dates.   The most unique date of my life was set up by Paul, an Ex friend who was married to a Korean girl named Lee. Paul called one morning and explained that Lee's unmarried sister was visiting and asked that I join them for dinner at an exclusive club that evening.   He assured me that she was beautiful, described her as the type of girl that could pass as an international model, and indeed she was.

I rang the doorbell at precisely seven p.m. as per instructions. Lee was in a bathrobe trying frantically to get showered and dressed and explained that Paul had left to pick up the rest of the group whoever they were, and said that her sister would join me in the living room shortly.   I nervously sat down on the divan and reasoned with myself that this would be an opportunity for us to talk and get acquainted.   Under normal circumstances this would be true except for the fact that after she did join me, I discovered that she couldn't speak a word of English.   "Hi," I said, "my name is Mort."   She giggled.   "Uh, what's your name?"   She giggled again.   "Uh, do you speak English?" I asked, pointing to my mouth.   She nodded quickly with a big smile and rubbed her stomach.   "How could your stupid-assed brother-in-law do this to me?" I asked with a large grin.   She returned the grin and shrugged which did alarm me!

When Paul returned (after a period which seemed to be days) he admitted that he had forgotten to tell me about this slight problem, but assured me that Lee could translate for us.   He then quickly changed the subject by introducing me to Lee's other sisters (none of whom could speak English) and their husbands who were to accompany us.   We decided to take two cars, and the drive to the club was uneventful except that I felt that I was the center of their conversation and couldn't figure out what was so funny.

The three brothers-in-law were all wearing a type of European suit without collars and the club's dress code specifically stated "collars only."   After creating a big scene, Paul decided to take the three of them back to his place for a change of shirts.   This left me alone with five Korean girls, only one of whom could speak English.

The club is built on several levels with stairs going everywhere. To my amazement the girls, when traversing the maze of steps, would clasp their hands holding them close into their stomachs, stoop over slightly and ascent or descend sideways, one step at a time. Aside from the fact that everyone was staring at us, we didn't reach the second level until a half hour later. We found a very good table (quiet and perfect for talking), got the directions to the ladies lounge (which was back down on the lower level) and ordered drinks.

I ordered a scotch and soda and Lee ordered a round of Grasshoppers for the girls. After an hour or so, Lee called Paul to see what was keeping them. It seems that in the course of introducing the guys to a new hallucinogenic, American custom, he had managed to get everyone, including himself, stoned. Lee took my car, returned to the house to pick the guys up and left me alone with four Korean girls, whose English vocabulary consisted of one word, Grasshopper! After a few drinks, we evidently started speaking in tongues because I faintly remember having one of the most interesting conversations and evenings of my life. Lee returned about one a.m. without Paul or money which left me with a $65 liquor tab, but it was worth it.

The moral to this true story is evident. Don't worry about customs or the way you have to act and don't worry about what to say. Just do little, expect nothing and be yourself.

How Long Should We Wait?

The answer to this question is not less than thirty seconds, nor longer than you want to wait. Many of us have so conditioned ourselves to be a faithful and true spouse, that the thought of dating again can cause strong guilt feelings. Only through the experience of dating will you overcome this, if it applies to you. Dating again can and probably will create a series of new emotional crises in your life so it's a good idea to start dating just <u>before</u> you feel that you are ready for it, but <u>after</u> you feel you can handle it.

Reasons for Dating Again

The best reason to start dating again is for companionship, either physical or emotional, depending on where you are. There are quite a few considerations to this, however, so please read on. The worst reasons for dating again are because:

1.   You want to find your new, perfect person.
2.   You feel that it is expected of you.
3.   To prove something to you or to your Ex.

     If you decide to date again for any of these reasons, you are just setting yourself up for disappointment. Why? Because you are expecting results from dating that cannot be realized.

Mr. or Ms. Right

     Another good tip in dating again is to forget about Mr. or Ms. Right.   Adam and Eve were the last two people created specifically for one another and we all know what happened in that relationship! It is advisable, therefore, to forget all preconceived requirements of your ideal mate (except, of course, for the sex) and sort through the ones on hand.   Those who establish certain characteristics for their perfect mate usually spend half a lifetime in their futile search and end up with someone who is 180 degrees out of phase from their original concept anyway.

The Rebound

     The biggest problem that many new singles encounter in dating again is a psychological phenomenon called "Being on the Rebound." During the course of their previous marriage they may not have even been aware of any emotional relationship with their spouse, however, following the divorce, they usually experience a sense of emptiness and loss.   This is caused by the abrupt absence of an emotional condition that they had become accustomed to.   As a result, they experience an emotional withdrawal similar to the physical withdrawals associated with the abrupt absence of nicotine, alcohol or other drugs.
     Because of these unpleasant side effects, the new single generally has a tendency to try and fill this emptiness with anyone they feel attracted to.   They often fall in love with the relationship and what it can do for them, instead of the person.   As a result, many are ready for a commitment after only one or two dates and some, even before that.   The experienced single has learned that quick commitments usually result in an emotionally wrenching experience and therefore is generally more cautious.   The Rebounder often interprets this caution as rejection when the relationship is not advancing at the pace they want it to, and in an attempt to spark the

other's enthusiasm, they blow the whole thing. This Rebound tendency becomes most prevalent during the second stage of singlization but it is not limited to new singles. Anyone who is the recent victim of a broken relationship can find themselves on the rebound. This usually takes place at the same exact time that they stop saying "I will never, ever fall in love again."

The big danger develops when two singles, on the rebound, meet each other. This can be similar to introducing two pieces of flypaper, as they can immediately become hopelessly stuck on each other. This instant bond can even result in the ultimate commitment of marriage out of the desire to fill their emotional void rather than out of the love that they _should_ feel for one another. This, of course, will almost always end up in disaster. Love is a form of emotional dependency and so is the infatuation that can be experienced from being on the rebound. They both feel the same and they both fill the emotional void within. The main difference is that love lasts, and infatuation does not. It _can_ evolve into love in time, but the important thing to remember is the number one rule of commitment. This is not to even consider marriage until you have known the other person for at least nine to twelve months. When we find someone that interests us, we are generally on our best behavior for the first few months and it takes time to expose the little green monsters that all of us hide under our thin candy coatings.

<u>Emotional Misunderstandings</u>

Often, particularly new singles, suffer from a perpetual feeling of rejection. This is due, in part, to the emotional calluses that _other singles_ seem to have, as well as the joy they seem to experience from not having to please or answer to anyone else. In their obsession for friendship or a relationship, new singles sometimes create certain expectations and designs on acquaintances or dates. There has probably never been a new single with more of a tendency to do this than myself. I would meet a girl, calculate her assets, determine that she was for me and plan our whole future within the space of our first date. I would call the very next day to see what she would like to do and would be utterly shattered if she had other plans. I would feel deep rejection, my pride would be obliterated and I would lose the will to live for another week or two.

Actually, it wasn't rejection at all. In fact, I learned later that some of the girls wondered why I never called again. Some of them may have been interested and may have also felt the sting of rejection.   In the majority of these cases my failure was due, simply, to a big emotional misunderstanding.

Some singles, especially seasoned singles, are a lot more cautious.   Some singles may not want a relationship with anyone. Some singles may want to become friends first (a painfully slow process).   It's nothing personal as a rule, it's just that some singles are selfish and want to make their own decisions and establish their own plans.   I shudder to think of the relationships and friendships that I sabotaged as the result of emotional misunderstandings.

The best advice here is to expect nothing and just enjoy your date for what it is at the present.   Don't make plans and designs and let your friendships and relationships develop naturally, at their own pace.   Girls: Don't sit home, waiting for the phone to ring; and Guys: Don't start your blueprints on the future until you have something to draw them on.

Public Enemy #1

When I started attending single's discussion groups, retreats, seminars and workshops, I did so just to get the feel of certain single attitudes and feelings that I could not pick up on in other places. Like some of my acquaintances, I stereotyped these people as all of "the Bleeding Heart Majority."   I have since found, however, that this single division is comprised of models, business owners, blue collar workers, the rich, the poor, the intellectual and the not-too-intellectual.   The one thing that they DO NOT have in common is class or type!   They do have a very common goal, and this is the desire to relate to and be accepted by other people for themselves. Their common fear is rejection--the single's Public Enemy Number One!

Now I'm great on a one-to-one basis, talking about a subject that I have some control over, and where the devastating effects of rejection are isolated, but in these groups, you can always find me in the darkest corner, sitting behind the tallest single. If it's the type of group where everyone has to give their first name, the trauma of the evening is awaiting my turn to say "I'm Mort."   I'm afraid I'll screw up!   As the names get closer, my hands get sweatier.   My mouth gets dry and my throat becomes parched.   I usually cough, just to reassure myself that my larynx is still there and I silently practice my name over and over to make sure I won't forget it at that last, crucial second! "My name is uuuuuuuhh..." Do I raise my hand and take an active part in the discussion? You gotta be kidding!

Taking a chance and baring my soul to one person is hard enough but to a group....My God!

I do get some comfort though in knowing that the average single is _almost_ as afraid of rejection as I am. This became painfully apparent last night at a single's seminar. As I sat on the floor with a hundred or so other singles, and many more being turned away, I had another one of those profound realizations. I realized that almost everyone had three things in common:

#1 We all had a driving need for the others.

#2 We were all afraid of being rejected by the others.

#3 We all misinterpreted the other's needs and motives, and this misunderstanding was what kept us all apart, in our own little emotional cubicles.

After a hard day's work, we all rushed to get ready, driven miles to get there, sat on a hard floor with no seats or backs to rest on, no smoking, no scratching, and we all had to listen to each other's stomachs gurgle for two solid hours with only one fifteen-minute break. Why were we all willing to do this? The answer is NEED!

Now many singles, in an effort to ignore this profane word "Need" will maintain that they just went there to score. I won't buy that. There are many easier ways to achieve sexual gratification or to even find a sexual partner. The problem is that in more conventional single's hunting grounds, you can become very intimate with someone else's body but not with their feelings. We were all there to find a more intimate relationship with a fellow human. We were all looking for a person or persons to relate to on less animalistic and more humanistic terms.

Why did most of us endure this experience and leave without finding what we came after? The answers are: Gross misunderstanding and the fear of rejection. We were afraid that the other person would reject us and they were afraid that we would reject them! As a result, most of us went home with the attitude that if the others didn't like us, we wouldn't like them either, and another layer of emotional callusing was added to our protective barriers.

This gross misunderstanding of other's needs and motives can cause us all kinds of problems. Single life has a tendency to create all types of complexes within us. In an attempt to hold back somewhat, for fear of rejection, a guy may approach a woman with an indifferent attitude. The woman senses this "distancing" and may, in return act somewhat aloof and indifferent herself. Both may feel that the other has rejected the other.

With the preoccupation of sex on the single scene, many singles accept or reject others strictly on physical appearances with no consideration at all about what kind of a friend this person would be. Many men feel that ALL women are out simply for an expense-paid fling and many women feel that ALL men are out for free sex, which also causes "distancing" and ultimately, rejection. The fear of love's pain can cause the same results. In short, when someone rejects you, it's generally because of their personal hangups and it has little to do with you personally.

In order to be a successful single, you have to take some chances. As a matter of fact, you have to experience a great deal of rejection. Psychologists tell us that on an average, less than one percent of the people we meet will actually accept us, and the ultimate, bare-faced rejection rate is fixed at an unsettling twenty-five percent. But remember that when someone rejects you, it's probably not because of you, it's because of them and their problem.

The DoLittle Majority

The single world is comprised of a vast ocean of people from different races, cultures, ages and ethics, but one of the most troubled groups is what I call "The DoLittle Majority." The majority of this majority consists of women in their middle to later years, who are looking for men in their middle to later years, who are dating women in their middle to earlier years. So why do younger women often like older men? Is it because of those round, little bellies, their thinning hair or those sexy wrinkles? Well, this varicose virility may have something to do with it but, essentially, younger women like the security, stability and emotional gratification that older men can provide.

Now, this creates a big problem for the seasoned women. If their counterparts are dating younger women, who's left for them? How can a member of the seasoned majority compete with real teeth, firm profiles and tight skin? That's the problem! The majority of this majority think in terms of competing on a physical basis and face it gals, you may be fighting with somewhat of a handicap!

There are essentially only two basic elements which form man's desire for women. These are: the physical element and the emotional element. The physical element is the easiest one to detect in a woman. You can tell if you like a woman physically within the space of a quick glance and men naturally have a compulsion to go after the easier element first.

A great many women who are running over with this hormonal protoplasm know very little about the really profound stuff, Emotional Gratification, the same youthful elixir which hides the wrinkles on older men.

As people mature their physical forte is replaced with wisdom, the food of the gods. Wisdom may be a little more subtle but it's not a bad exchange. So use the tools that you have!

I encountered a mature, heavyset lady at the supermarket checkout stand the other day by the name of Rose. Her disposition, attitude and bubbling nature made me love her instantly. There was something that told me, at that particular point in time, I was the most important person in her life. Rose, I think you are terrific and you almost make me wish that I were twenty years older!

Contrary to popular belief, the best route to a man's heart isn't necessarily through his stomach. Try going through his psyche! Let men become dependent on you for the emotional food you give them. Let them know how great they are and how much you think of each one personally. Make him the most important person in your life, at that particular point in time and you can do no wrong. I'm not suggesting for a second that you smother them with false compliments and counterfeit praises. People can usually tell a phony. Honestly look for the good in men and let them know it.

Now let's discuss the BIGGY---incentive! I'm convinced that many of the "DoLittles" that complain the loudest, do the least to correct their situation. It's a big, scary world out there and it is filled with pain.

There are fears of manipulation, abuse, perversion, failure and heaven knows what else! It's easy to see why a girl would give up easily, sit back and put the blame squarely on the shoulders of the men who are dating younger women. Fear is also a terrific incentive to stay overweight or unattractive. Many women fear that their sagging cells will turn men off but they refuse to do anything about it and if there is anything better than sagging cells for turning the opposite sex off, it's a bad self-image!   If you don't think well of yourself, you can't expect others to.   If you are serious about this thing, and have a bad self-image, tune yourself up!   If you have trouble submitting yourself to the grueling subversities of exercise and diet, keep reminding yourself of what's at stake.   Life is made up of priorities.   Make your choice and live with it but don't give up and tell yourself that you have no control over your own fate.

Don't mourn over the cells that the years have taken away from you, use the skills that the years have given you.   Just hang in there, honey!   You've come a long way.

Sex and the Dating-Again Experience

It would be very easy at this point to give you my own conclusions concerning the moralities and personal attitudes of sex and the dating-again experience.   My conclusions work well for me, but they may not work for you.   So, staying true to my original plan, I will grit my teeth and simply advise you of some of the concepts that you might use to base your own conclusions on.   We are going to just touch lightly on some of these concepts because the subject of "sex and the single" will be discussed in detail, later.

The biggest asset that one can possess is self-respect.   You have to respect and like yourself before you can expect others to.   Self-confidence is very closely related to self-respect and is often reduced to nothingness through the course of divorce.   Those emerging from the clutches of divorce, quite generally, have managed to add a vast quantity of self-defeating doubts to their growing collection of insecurities, especially in the area of sexual prowess.   Very few divorces are the exclusive product of sexual incompatibilities, but this self-induced stigma seems to flourish, particularly in the minds of some divorced singles.

In an effort to recapture self-confidence and defeat these insecurities, some singles take on the impossible task of making every member of the opposite sex fall in love with them.   In their minds this is accomplished by getting the opposite sex into the sack and proving their sexual excellence.   There is a subconscious belief that this type of trophy hunting will not only boost one's sexual self-image, it subconsciously helps to vindicate one's vendetta against the opposite sex as well.   It's true that as the result of a successful score, we can realize a certain amount of pride from the fact that someone else finds us desirable, but if this someone else has to pay the price of pain for our jacked-up ego, it can be very costly to us also. This someone has given us a special gift, and we may have, in turn, rubbed their nose in it..(so to speak!) This becomes very easy when we put up walls against feeling and move into our own shell of emotional calluses. You can do this, if you want, but I can assure you that it can get very lonely in there all by yourself, and emotional calluses are not that easy to get rid of once they form. At this stage you may decide to inform your next trophy that there is absolutely no commitment and this can vindicate you from all responsibility, but does it? Just be honest in your appraisal as these emotional calluses usually form on a subconscious level and The First Law of the Single Psyche states: "All subconscious emotions are just conscious enough to get in our way."

This is one philosophy that few seasoned singles agree with. Most have the attitude that we cannot be responsible for everyone else's happiness or hurt, and I agree completely...to an extent! The only disagreement I have is to the extreme degree that many singles live this philosophy. If we can't hit a happy medium in our compassion for others, it can be very self-destructive, resulting in chronic, emotional scarring. The effects of this emotional scarring can create a psychological neurosis that I call "The Sex War Syndrome," which is discussed later.

Because the prospect of sharing sex is so inviting, most of us tend to fool ourselves into believing that we can have sex free without paying anything for it. This, however, is seldom possible. In some cases, we do get a bargain but in many other cases, the price of promiscuity is awesome. Now, at this particular point, I can feel the vibes of thousands of singles whose entire emotional existance depends upon "free sex." These vibes are saying "I have free sex all the time and have never...er, almost never paid any price!"

Well, this may be true for some individuals, but in considering the delicate emotional state of the new single and their dating-again experience, I am going to cover some of the prices for "Bargain Basement Sex" and will get into the price structure for veteran sex later in "The Sex-War Syndrome."

First of all, the act of sharing sex has a very strong tendency to form commitments between its two consenting enthusiasts. This feeling of obligation has probably caused more wrong marriages than the proverbial shotgun, and has created an equal amount of painful relationships. Our conventional compulsion to not hurt a friend and to retain honor often joins with our desire for sex and the chemical reaction produces a psychological super glue that often binds us to a hopeless situation.

Secondly, many new singles use sex as a manipulator under the theory that sex will provide an incentive for commitment and will end up in a meaningful relationship. They do not yet realize that any relationship worth having cannot be purchased, and as a result they often buy into a painful experience. Also, in many cases, the manipulator becomes the manipulatee because the tendency for commitment works against the non-committal nature of many singles and blows the chances of a relationship before it even starts.

So, in a nutshell, some of these bargain basement prices for sex include:

1. Loss of self-respect through the sacrifice of principles (usually temporary).
2. Damaged pride resulting from a final rejection or the realization of being used sexually.
3. Low self-worth as the result of hurting another.
4. The pain of a lost relationship which may have never existed.
5. The formation of emotional calluses resulting in the effects of the sex-war syndrome.

I have not painted this depressing picture of sex in an attempt to force anyone into celibacy. If you are single, it's a safe bet that because of the unique problems associated with single life, you will probably share sex with someone or someones. I simply want to make you aware of what to expect and supply some information that can assist in determining why, when and who. Moral, personal and religious issues regarding sex are up to each one of us individually. The main attitude of the sexcessful single, however, seems to be at the point of being very selective in choosing sex mates and they generally have to feel something, both physically and emotionally for the other person. Surprisingly enough, this even holds true for many men despite their sex-crazed reputations.

At this point, I am not going into detail concerning "the sex-war syndrome" but I think it is appropriate to explain its origin. To do this we will take a look at the contemporary Adam and Eve that started this whole mess. The names have been changed to protect the guilty.

Buckley's Theory of Evolution

My theory of evolution is unique inasmuch as there is no missing link. Scientists believe that the Yetti (Abominable Snowman) may be the missing link in Darwin's theory but few, if any, have ever actually met one. I say this even in spite of some of the bad dating experiences that I've been told about. We have all heard of the Yetti, but without actually encountering one, it remains a myth; something to talk about but not to fear.

Similarly, there are two species of human-like monsters inhabiting the single world that you will undoubtedly encounter and I assure you that they are really real! The unsuspecting nature of the new single, makes for fair game so if you are not prone to be cautious after dark, it might be advisable to read on!

We are all aware of the evil that lurks in the dead of night, whose vampire-like lusts drive it in search of young virgins (or not so virgins) to ravage, use and leave heartbroken with maimed virtue that soon becomes just one more notch on a mirrored bedpost. Who is this masked stranger, you ask? I know him by name only. It's..."THE INCREDIBLE HUNK!"

This Casanova type creature (usually male) devours the innocent, emotionally rapes the unsuspecting, and plunders the sexual loot of any young maid or made he can. In order to better understand the nature of this vile villain, let us take a short trip back through time to when he was known simply as Joe Snurps, mild-mannered shoe salesman in the metropolis of Blite, Arizona. In tune with most shoe salesman, Joe had a roaming eye that went beyond looking at feet, and as a result, Joe's boss was never satisfied with his ability as a salesman. Joe's wife, whose only hobby was writing Joe's diary six months in advance, was bored sexually and had the proverbial 24-hour headache, seven days a week. Joe never talked about it but down deep he was sure that it had something to do with his sexual prowess.

Joe was a real nice guy but had only a few friends. One sold Ferrari's, one was a stockbroker, one was into selling municipal bonds and one who used to be a broker for hospital rooms was retired at age twenty-two. Joe always had trouble keeping up with his friends and his wife never let him forget it.

Finally, out of desperation to find a new him, Joe got a divorce and started all over again. He went out and bought a handful of gold-filled chains, a silk shirt and a used Corvette. After a few painful and expensive encounters with the opposite sex, Joe's emotional calluses started forming. With each painful experience he got tougher and tougher emotionally. Finally one day Joe meets Sally Snibbles, a little widow on the rebound. Sally figured that Joe was just about the greatest thing since Peppermint Schnapps, (of course she would have felt that way about any guy with gold chains).

Sally Snibbles was really good to old Joe but he never could let himself become vulnerable enough to care for her. He did need her for the companionship and to help recharge his feelings of self-worth. He promised her the world but gave her a broken heart and a dirty set of sheets. This made Joe feel kinda bad in a way, but his guilt was overshadowed by a wonderful new sense of being desired. He shook Sally loose from his leg and walked out the door in search of other desperate women to con and get even with. At this point Joe has been callused to feeling and addicted to being desired. He is out to get even with the world and women in general.

Now it's time to reveal another, equally evil creature whose shapely shape lurks in the shadows of single's bars and stalks and strikes its unsuspecting prey in inconspicuous places. This parasitic leach, with its cancerous conscience, knows no boundaries and attacks the strong and the weak alike. No, my friends, we are not discussing Herpies 2, we are talking about something much worse; we are talking about WONDER WOMB!!

This voluptuous villain does not rape, ravage and plunder the virtues of her victims because, as we all know, the traditional role of being used and abused sexually belongs to those of the female gender. So, in staying true to the Geneva convention of sexist roles, she rapes, ravages and plunders her victims financially. Like the Incredible Hunk, Wonder Womb focuses her attack on the most vulnerable area of her victim's anatomy, his pocket!

The magic little tool she uses (synonymous with her name) has extracted more money from men than the best agent the I.R.S. has ever employed. Her bedpost is not notched but it sags under the heavy strain of gold chains viciously ripped from the throats of those who have loved her. How could anyone be so cruel and vicious? Well, let's take a closer look. Let me introduce you to Wonder Womb, alias Sally Snibbles.

This theory of evolution illustrates simply that we all have a tendency to be the product of our environment (and it is covered more extensively under the chapter titled "The Sex-War Syndrome.")

It's good to realize that not all singles are night creatures.

Many singles have a better handle on life than unsingles do and some are just impersonations of night creatures, however a word to the wise should be sufficient. (If you are not wise, there is a chance that you soon will be.) How can you tell if you meet one, you ask? Simply look for the signs: unquenchable desire for adoration; infidelity, lies, selfishness, overspending of your money, etc. What do you do if you meet one? Girls, get out fast! Guys, count your change, you could have married her!

CHAPTER 12
Custodial Parentinitis

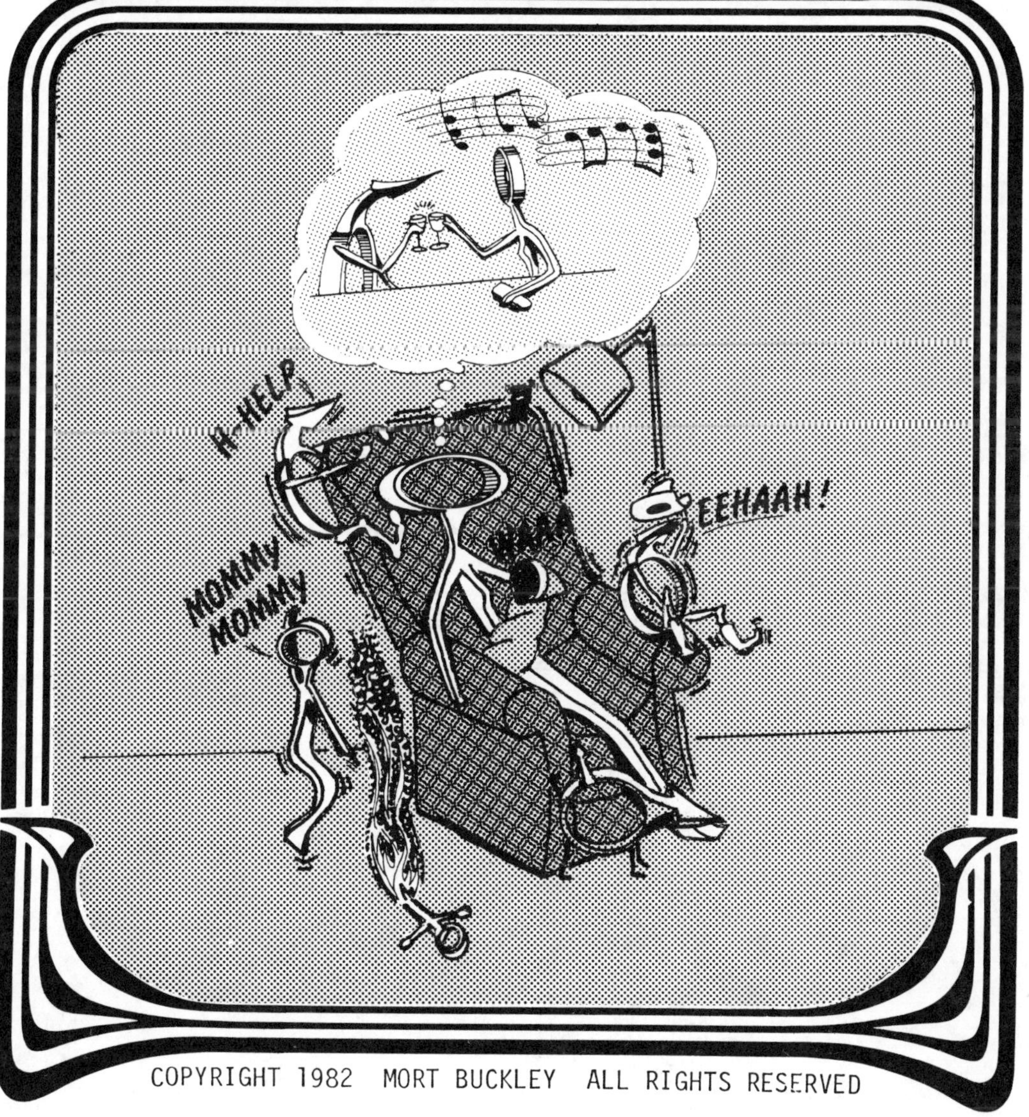

Chapter 12

CUSTODIAL PARENTINITIS

The single society seems to split itself into two separate divisions at this point: the Free Single and the Notsofree Single. The Notsofree Single is rumored to have contracted an illness called "Custodial Parentinitis," and most free singles avoid them like the plague. You can tell if someone has "Custodial Parentinitis" by certain symptoms such as financial anemia, black circles under the eyes and a tendency to fall asleep while making love. The abbreviated name for this genus is simply the "Custodial Parent."

Out of the many types of people in this country, my heart goes out to the responsible portion of these Custodial Parents. Their lives can be a monotonous kaleidoscope of daily routine, constantly trying to fill the positions of both mother and father. For some, there is no one to even relieve them occasionally on a weekend and the complete responsibility of raising the children correctly and providing for them rests on one set of shoulders. There is no one else to help make the decisions that will mold their children's lives, and the knowledge of this responsibility can be one of the heaviest burdens in single parenting.

They often take no time for friends or self-indulgences except during the short period between their children's bedtime and their own. Their day starts with the mother's traditional role of getting the kids up, fed, dressed and off to school or the nursery. They then take the traditional role of the father by going to work to earn a living for their family. The work day is often interrupted with school and home emergencies as well as chores which have to be taken care of during the lunch hour.

After work and on weekends, there are meals to prepare, the

house to clean, laundry to do, grocery shopping, bill paying, household repairs, gardening, car maintenance, doctor and dentist appointments, on and on. One normally small inconvenience like a sick child on a work day can become a tremendous obstacle. There is often no one else to confide in and everything rests solely upon them. Custodial Parents die in many ways but you will never hear of one resting to death.

This can create a fantastic human being in those who don't weaken. They can find self-pride and contentment that few others will ever experience, and they seem to attain the secret admiration and respect of everyone, including themselves. These hardships can also build a strong family unity as well as a responsible and capable character in the children. Some singles (particularly the weekend parent) envy the custodial parent for not having to live alone and for their free access to the children. This, however, is not as neat as they might think. Custodial Parents seldom have the time to adjust to their new single lifestyle and few ever have the freedom needed to get in touch with themselves. They are basically leading a single's life with few of its benefits.

Many Custodial Parents are so preoccupied with their hardships that they fail to realize the opportunities of raising their children as they want, in an unchallenged atmosphere, and the really close parent/child relationship that's possible through mutual need. Each single parent has an opportunity that few marrieds have in which to form a fantastic relationship with their own children. This is possible because with the correct attitude, they can easily form a greater dependency upon the children.

Kids from broken homes have a tendency to be very insecure as it is. One parent is gone, what happens if the other goes? They were once secure with the unity of both parents but fate has taught them that security can be a very temporary commodity. They need the feeling of being depended upon and the parent needs the feeling of having someone to depend upon. What a fantastic illustration of supply and demand!

Children do have some trouble adjusting to the new lifestyles of a single parent home. Their ability to adjust is determined greatly by the __parent's__ ability to adjust. Kids are far more elastic and adaptable than adults are. Therefore, the kids are usually a lot further down the road to recovery than the parents think. The problem is that the kids often choose to keep it a secret! The act of insecurity is almost a foolproof method for obtaining attention and getting their way. Their need for attention at this time is at an all time high, and the parent's output may be at an all time low. Consequently, kids will fight for this priceless commodity in any way they can.

If attention can't be obtained through pity or guilt, they often resort to gaining it in a disruptive or even violent manner. This negative behavior pattern can manifest itself in the form of broken windows, sudden illnesses, family fights and feeding the canary to your pet piranha. Subconsciously the kids are reciting the old maxim "Love me or hate me, but don't ignore me." If you can put their energy to work in a constructive manner, and distribute your attention by way of "Prime Time," you can help to alleviate this problem somewhat and your canary will be forever grateful!

<u>Attitude</u>

The correct attitude in custodial parenting is quite a bit like sanity. It is naturally very important but often impossible to maintain. The first step in controlling your attitude is, of course, to understand it. To do this, let's take a look at some of these seemingly insurmountable problems that most custodial parents have.

<u>The Time Problem</u>

This is without a doubt one of the biggest problems that custodial parents encounter. To illustrate, let's take a look at an average weekday itinerary of the average, weekday, custodial parent.

1.   Wake up (if you have had time to go to sleep).
2.   Find your brown turtleneck sweater (the first place to look is on the dog because the kids worry about him getting cold).
3.   Remove the newspaper from the roof (you need it to wrap lunches in and the kids complain when you wrap their sandwiches in toilet paper).
4.   Put plenty of deodorant on and get dressed (no time for a shower).
5.   Get the kids up, feed them, pack lunches, get them to school and drive to work (don't rush, you still have ten minutes).

<u>NOTE</u>: If Junior's strep throat isn't better, you will probably have to locate another babysitter FAST, as the old one has probably caught

it by now!

6. Call the high school principal and the child psychologist from work and cancel all afternoon appointments. They will have to manage without your help today.
7. Figure out some way to get your oldest daughter from school to the orthodontist without leaving work or asking anyone else for favors.
8. If you have time, you might try to figure out some way to pay the orthodontist.
9. During lunch, send a check for your delinquent utility bill to the water company, your delinquent water bill to the utility company and deposit the post-dated check at the bank. (This fouls up everybody's computer and buys you time to make your checks good.)
10. Make an appointment to have the car transmission replaced Saturday (if it lasts that long).

NOTE! Try to find a garage within ten blocks of a grocery store so you can go grocery shopping while they work on the car.

NOTE! Get a price quote on a new engine, too.

11. Call the plumber (your neighbors are tired of you using their facilities).
12. Call the finance company to see if your loan went through for the twenty gallons of gas you will need for next week.
13. After work, go to the two hour PTA meeting so that you can listen to your youngest daughter's thirty-second group recital.
14. Check Junior's impetigo and give everyone their ringworm medicine.
15. Replace another of your neighbor's broken windows and get your autographed football back.
16. Check and see if your parents are still living at the same place and explain why you haven't had time to call.

Miscellaneous things: Do laundry; get prescriptions filled; balance checkbook; pay bills; help the kids with homework; fix dinner; wash dishes; empty trash; pick up house; make out tomorrow's itinerary; get some sleep if you have time.

Just about the time you feel that everything is under control (which is seldom), another emergency arises. It all just testifies to the fact that you don't have time to do everything. This heavy burden of responsibility is self-imposed but nonetheless, can be a very depressing element in the life of the average custodial parent. Every responsibility that we do not have time to meet can cause guilt if we let it. When there are more responsibilities than we can handle, guilt and frustrations can run rampant. The solution is simply to let some responsibilities go and recognize the fact that there is no longer such a thing as a "Super Parent." It's rumored that Super Parent died of a stroke, two and a half years ago, anyway.

In deciding which of these super important responsibilities to let go let's first consider your personal time. Some degree of social life and recreation is a number one must. A good, healthy attitude requires some degree of nourishment, particularly if you are adjusting to a new lifestyle. In my book, this is a number one priority because without it, your attitude will decompose under the guise that you are sacrificing for your family. In truth, however, your family will be the victim because of your resulting bad attitude.

Many single parents refuse to answer their own needs because of guilt, or the belief that they would be putting their own desires before the children. As a result, they turn themselves into a sadistic, parental robot. They deny their own emotional needs and resent it all the way. This often creates an attitude which makes the children even more insecure. Many single parents use this ploy in an attempt to prove to themselves that they are fit parents in spite of their divorce; or they simply let their children manipulate them through guilt.

It is true that the kids probably don't want you to socialize at this point. They are very insecure at this stage and tend to clutch and hang on for dear life. They have lost one parent and do not want to chance losing the other; even for an evening. One important thing to bear in mind though is that kids, being kids, tend to base their decisions more on emotion than logic, and the family has to depend upon the parent's experience to make the correct and logical decisions.

With your time for the family reduced as it is, it can be difficult to ignore the painful screams for attention as you walk out the door, but do it anyway. One hour of constructive time with the kids, as the result of your break, can be far better than a full evening of destructive time resulting from a negative attitude. On the other hand, socializing can easily be overdone, so try to hit a happy medium.

Another one of the most important rules to follow is to set aside <u>at least</u> thirty minutes each day for yourself. If you can, take an hour or more, but use this time to do something for you. Something that you would like to do but do not <u>have</u> to do. You may be surprised to find that your life will not crumble nor will the world stop turning because of this extravagant abuse of time. The greatest portion of this book has been written in thirty minute segments and even if I never sell a copy, its value to me is incalculable.

Major efforts in the area of repairs, gardening, dusting, cleaning, ironing, folding, filing, waxing and polishing are often considered as unimportant luxuries in the lives of custodial parents. It's true that surroundings greatly influence personal attitudes but you may have to let some things go and this is a good place to start.

The kids can be a great help and at the same time benefit from the experience, but even with organized child labor, you may find yourself buried alive in the murk and mire of custodial parent responsibilities.

You may be able to significantly reduce this responsibleness by uncomplicating your life somewhat. Most of us have hundreds of items that we never use and which serve to just clutter our lives. These priceless bits of clutter take shape in the form of old toys, clothes, mooseheads, utensils, household items and countless other treasures that we either fall over or which peer out from under dust covered coats with beady, little eyeballs to haunt us. The less you have, the less you have to take care of. If you choose, you can have a grand liquidation sale and use the money to buy a timesaving appliance such as a dishwasher or microwave. One word of caution: Junk was described by someone as "something that you never need until after you get rid of it," so use discretion.

Another consideration is in sharing a home or an apartment with another single parent or someone who likes kids. This reduces the financial burden, work load and insecurities, while at the same time allows you to share the responsibilities of babysitting. This is a very intricate decision, as this arrangement is similar to marriage without its physical benefits. As a result, there are few of these arrangements that work out successfully. I have found some instances, however, where this type of arrangement has provided a very happy and supportive solution to some of the problems of custodial parenting. How long has it been since you told someone, "It's really great to feel needed?" That long, huh? I agree, I'm tired of being needed too! It's a widely known fact that the average human being has a tremendous need to feel needed but the average custodial parent definitely has more than his or her share of this feeling. There are thousands upon thousands of people out there who feel useless and want desperately just to feel needed and here we are just dying to feel not so needed. So why not spread it around a little? Stop hogging all of this fantastic feeling and share it with others. There are church groups, Big Brothers and Big Sisters organizations, senior citizens groups, bored neighbors, friends and family members just panting for the chance to help someone.

A great majority of the single population, however, seems to have developed a tremendous sense of independence and refuses to accept anything that might be considered charity. The one thing that we should realize though is that people are motivated only by their own personal desires. When a person offers to help someone else, they do it not for the other person, but for themselves, and they get their own reward out of it.

Try accepting help graciously and reward your benefactors with a simple, heartfelt...Thanks. Most people understand the plight of the custodial parent and therefore expect no gratuity, either financial or otherwise. Just be gracious and let them know how appreciative you are. If you feel that someone is offering their assistance in the hope of having the favor returned in an objectional way, let them know right up front where you stand but try not to jump to unprecedented conclusions.

Another good way to utilize time is to plan it. Get yourself an appointment book and plan each minute of the day. At this point you may be thinking to yourself, "I just don't have time to do that!" You might be surprised, however, at the amount of time that you save. Plan not only the daily business routines and household chores but your personal and family time as well. Stick to your time table as closely as possible with few, if any, deviations. Within a short while you will learn how much time to allow for each function and when you finish something sooner than planned, make it a point to spend it on yourself. Relax and Veg Out for a while. Pick out a nice piece of wall and stare at it.

Now let's consider our time with the kids. Ideally you should spend as much time with the kids as possible; constructive or otherwise. With the problems associated in single parenting, however, most of us are simply unable to spread ourselves thin enough to cover everyone's needs. Our parental time can be minimized to an extent though, if the remainder is of prime quality. One way to achieve this is by utilizing our time more effectively. You can start by throwing out the tv tables, unplugging the television and using your dinner period as a time for talking and taking an interest in one another. Discuss the day's events, problems and plans, and always try to save a positive experience to wind it up with. You may have difficulty establishing this habit as there will be times when a special tv program is on or times when other circumstances will interfere. Just do your best and take pride in the fact that you are trying. A problem can also materialize in the fact that the kids may not be receptive to an inanimate television set at first, but in time they will more than likely start looking forward to this evening encounter.

There are many other periods of time to utilize, like while driving, doing minimal chores around the house, getting dressed, etc. If you share the household chores with the kids, and can maintain the correct attitude while doing it, you might be amazed at the amount of prime time you can realize from such a constructive effort.

By distributing responsibility evenly throughout the family, many single parents feel that they are being mean, selfish or shirking their own duties. In truth, they would be teaching responsibility as well as satisfying their children's needs to be needed. It's very important for children to feel that they are a necessary part of the family unit. Because of previous impatience, chastizing and denials by parents, the kids may be hesitant to accept the responsibilities at first, but the basic humanistic instinct to be productive and necessary still exists somewhere within their cute little psyches. The problem is that they are as good at losing their psyches as they are at misplacing their shoes, so you may have to work on this a bit!

<u>Utilizing Prime Time</u>

Kids need to feel needed as much as adults do. In traditional two parent homes where the adults rely on each other, the children are usually cheated of this feeling. Furthermore, they are often raised without the practical experience of self-sufficiency and independence. They are a cared for but unnecessary element of the family unit. Single parents have an opportunity that few married parents have, to develop self-confidence in their children and to create a strong family bond by making them feel like a needed and productive component of the family.

By accepting responsibility and feeling necessary, the kids will sense that they do have some control over their own destiny and as a result of this independence, they will release the death grip they have on their parents somewhat and feel more secure.

Another thing that you might be surprised at is the amount of help they can actually be.   Children as young as four years old can be remarkably adept at dusting, keeping toys picked up, taking care of their own rooms, emptying waste baskets, etc..

The development of these household skills may require a certain amount of patience on your part, as Junior will inevitably empty the trash into the toilet, thus plugging the works up and Sis might dust the inside of the fireplace with her Great Grandmother's wedding gown. If, however, you can maintain some degree of sanity while overseeing the chores for a while, things will correct themselves as the kids learn. Just remember to always be very specific with your instructions.

One of the biggest hangups that you might encounter is the undisputed fact that it would be much easier to just do it yourself. But by doing this you will only be temporarily satisfying the needs at hand and the kids will not learn a thing.

So how do we go about convincing them that they will benefit by working their poor little fingers to the bone? The answer is relatively simple in theory, but much more difficult in application.

How to Organize Child Labor

(1) Explain the necessity for their help and make them feel that you are depending upon them to do their part. Don't look at them as you would a non-productive plant or pet which only <u>needs</u> and <u>never</u> contributes.

(2) Take an interest in them and their problems. Reward them with praise for their efforts, more than their results.

(3) Show them that you DO trust them, even if you don't. Give them specific responsibilities and allow them to resolve their own difficulties without your help.

(4) Make them feel important by discussing family decisions, and feel free to share some of your innermost feelings with them. Ask them for their opinions, realizing the inexperience of their

answers; and take an interest in their complaints.

(5)   Allow yourself to depend upon them for emotional support and love, and make them aware of your dependency.   Again, just bear in mind that because of their youth, they are not always a dependable source of support or advice.   Don't rely on them as you would another adult and don't expect too much of them in this area.   It's easy for the single parents in their need to rely too heavily on their kids for support and to be gravely disappointed when the kids are not able to provide it.   A child of any age, however, can supply a tremendous amount of love and support particularly when we need it the most.   Use a great deal of physical contact and touch whenever possible, but try not to embarrass them in front of their friends.

(6)   Try not to <u>force</u> them into accepting responsibilities. Provide an incentive for them to want to, by overlooking the mistakes resulting from an honest attempt, and by offering praise, gratitude and corrective instructions. Try substituting a display of disappointment instead of anger when they waiver in their duties and make them aware that you are <u>disappointed</u> when they let you down. If this doesn't work, go back to anger!

Kids have an uncanny ability of taking over the role of parent and turning you into the child. This becomes painfully apparent when they do start accepting responsibility as this can make them feel just like big people.   It's extremely important to realize this and maintain your position as "King of the Hill."   Don't make the mistake of eliminating discipline (whatever type you choose) or accepting their views as gospel because of a new tendency to view them more as an adult.   You have to maintain their respect if you expect to function as a good parent.

Another problem in organizing child labor can very easily arise if the children are over-burdened with chores. The best way to establish the amount of their work load is to provide them with the incentive to help, then gauge their capabilities by the results of their efforts.   I have found that by establishing certain chores each child is responsible for, you can more easily keep track of the quality as well as quantity of work.

<u>The Depressants of Adolescence</u>

The resulting trauma and shock that can result from the very mention of work, especially in the area of adolescence, can be a very perplexing problem. Kids who are forced to work against their better judgment have been known to develop chronic cases of Sweeper's Elbow, Dishrag Fixation (diagnosed by long periods at the sink, fondling the dishrag), Vacuuming Vertigo (dizziness), assorted varieties of Dusting Disabilities and, of course, the notorious Workious Decubitus (decubitus relates to the lying down posture).

Kids in the process of coming down with a severe case of adolescence usually display many different symptoms, but one of the worst seems to manifest itself in the form of "Adolescent Alogia" (the failure of speech) or its opposite counter-symptom, "Verbal Diarrhea." Occasionally adolescents have been known to produce these contradictory symptoms both at the same time which can result in a severe disorder known as "Parental Breakdown." Keeping communications open between parent and child during this stage is similar to picking yourself up by your own shoestrings, however, it is of paramount importance to try.

No matter how desperately absurd your adolescent's attitude is, you should make an attempt to understand it. Realize that in their opinion, it's foolish to waste energy doing superfluous things like work when they should be conserving their strength and concentrating on banging up the family car, misplacing their valuables, staying out past curfew and competing with friends to see who can make the lowest grades in school.

One of the most profound questions asked by parents today is, "Why didn't I have all these problems during my own adolescence, when I had all the answers?"

No matter how infinitesimal our adolescent's problems may seem to us, they can be monstrous to our children. An ignored "Hello" for a teenager can be equivalent to a call from the I.R.S. to us. The adolescent is right at the point of being grabbed up by the heels and dropkicked through the great goalposts of life. The transition from the warmth and security of childhood to the cold realities of adulthood would make anyone act weird. Add to this the gnawing, new emotions of puberty, the new weight of responsibility and the sudden need to learn how to cope on their own, you have an oversexed, apathetic ball of nervous energy, bent on transforming the world to fit its own needs.

So far the best method I have found is to feed this nervous energy by keeping them active. School, sports, group activities, academic challenge, Scouts, household chores, music, art, family activities (including their friends), etc.

How do you develop their interest in these areas? Simply by taking an interest yourself and providing tons of encouragement. You don't necessarily have to take part in everything yourself, just create the way (transportation), the incentive (through encouragement), and push a little. Kids are smart and they realize that an occasional prod in this direction does not constitute enthusiasm or interest on your part. Get in there and PUSH! Show enthusiasm in the directions you want them to go. If they act disinterested or turned off, keep pushing. You may even have to force them initially but make up your mind and stick to it. Kids need the security of a solid decision. When parents show weakness, uncertainty or disinterest, kids lose confidence and often decide to make their own decisions.

Assure your kids that you trust them, but don't do it for a second. Dishonest you say? Sure it is and they have the very same tendency. For instance, I know that you have heard the universal cry of the teenager: "But why can't I? Everybody else does!" Well, I've talked to "everybody elses'" parents and have found that practically nobody does! To add to the perplexing problems of modern day parenthood is the fact that today's parent has fallen victim to the scourge of ever-changing social standards. We were kids during that time when everything we did was the kid's fault, and now, we're parents at a time when everything the kids do is the parent's fault.

Friends and peers are, of course, one of the most important factors which form our kid's molds. It is, therefore, very necessary to encourage your potential delinquent to associate with friends which have the correct character. How do you determine the choice and influence the selection? You might consider the possibility of getting your kids into a church or religious organization with a wide variety of teenage functions. Whether you are religious or not, there is nothing like this type of organization for instilling the values and morals that most of us want in our kids and a slightly over-righteous teenager beats a delinquent every time.

Financial Anemia

When it comes to finances, many custodial parents become suicidal. As a matter of fact, statistics show that two out of three single parents would probably commit suicide at some time toward the end of their life if bullets and sleeping pills were not so expensive, and with the price of gas now, no one can afford to asphyxiate themselves. As a result, most single parents just accept the fact that they are trapped within the confines of their poverty and learn to live with it. There are some hints that can help you to cope, such as:

* Leave your electric garage door open so when they turn off the electricity, you can still get your car out.
* Never lock your doors at night. If a thief breaks in, he may lose something of value.
* Convince your kids that it would be fun to camp out in the backyard and rent the house to someone else.
* Call the Salvation Army regularly for pickups, but never give away your discards. Try and trade them for something worthwhile that they may have on their truck.
* Sign your kids up for the free lunch welfare program at school and give them a doggy bag to bring home each day.
* Shut your car engine off in the middle of an intersection and have courteous motorists push you from gas station to gas station until you reach your destination.

Aside from these helpful hints there are some tried and true suggestions which can help combat the side effects of financial anemia. The most effective attitude I have found for me is to convince myself that we don't **NEED** this and that. I have sold myself on the philosophy that we essentially need only air, food and water and everything else is just luxury. Sure, I would like the kids to be able to wear clothes to school and I would like to drive a car with an engine that ran, but we don't really _need_ these things. Another helpful fact is in the realization that most other single parents are in the same boat. Aside from learning to manage, taking shortcuts and trying to better one's self through advancement, there is little else one can do except to accept it. You can either make the best of a situation or the worst of it. One thing for sure, though, complaining and worrying does make it worse.

<u>Sex and the Custodial Parent</u> (<u>Are</u> <u>you</u> <u>kidding</u>?)
When the guy on the screen kisses the woman and passionately whispers "your place or mine?" you can bet that neither are full-time custodial parents. The only reason I would have for bringing a date home would be to watch the late show with the kids. Having a

physical relationship in my place would be similar to trying to hold up the Los Angeles police department. What do you do in a case like this? Find a way, as you inevitably will. "Necessity is the mother of invention" and desperation helps a great deal too.

One of the hardest decisions that single parents have to make is how honest they should be with the kids regarding their personal life. I hesitate to advise on this, however, I will share the philosophies that single parents generally have and interject what I have found to be some of the pitfalls.

Philosophy #1: In this theory it is believed that parents have to provide a perfect example for their children to follow. The notion is that kids can't understand human weakness or the difference between an adult with experience in handling certain affairs, and themselves, as children. The fear is that if it's good enough for Mom or Dad, the kids will feel that it's good enough for them. Aside from our unexplainable obsession to keep the kids virgin as long as possible, there are other well-founded reasons to fear adolescent promiscuity and if they consider the parent promiscuous, they will have more of a tendency to follow. Additionally, they fear that if the children were to find out about a physical relationship, the kids would lose respect for them and single-parenting without child-respect would be impossible to say the least.

As a result, most of these parents are locked into the reality of living a lie. Further, they expect and demand that their children develop certain strengths and convictions that they, themselves apparently cannot. If and when the children do weaken, they feel ashamed that they did not live up to the shining example and expectations of their parents. Lies and cover-ups usually result and this is when kids run into trouble with no one to turn to. If you choose this philosophy, prepare yourself for a disappointment and try to understand that your child, being a chip off the old block, is also only human if he or she comes to you in trouble some day. Also be very careful and hope that you never get caught.

Philosophy #2: "The kids have their sex life and I have mine. They leave me alone and I leave them alone." This attitude is shared by a great many single parents, but not the majority. I have determined that this attitude is found mainly in singles who choose to seat themselves so deeply in their own frustrations that they cannot take on any other problems, namely their kid's. Because of the pressures and unique problems they face, many single parents become obsessed with obtaining emotional relief through physical means and little else matters. This, of course, is a problem of attitude and unfortunately they are looking in the wrong place for emotional relief. But regardless of their personal views, their apparent indifference for the children is sensed and they consequently lose all influence in guiding their children's lives. Even though kids may fight this influence, they all have a subconscious tendency to rely on the experienced parent for advice and support if the parent seems to care! The most trouble-prone kids are the ones that have to learn strictly through the painful trial and error process and who grow up believing that no one really cares anyway.

<u>Philosophy #3</u>: This is probably the philosophy most widely used among the younger to middle-aged single parents and is located somewhere between Philosophies 1 and 2. Here the parent attempts the somewhat difficult, but honest approach. They explain to the children that sexual intimacy is a beautiful gift that one person can give to another through love. That, if sex is abused and used outside the realm of love, it can be very painful, dangerous and self-defeating. They explain the dangers of heartbreak, social disease, pregnancy, sexual perversions and so forth. They explain that, with the right person, they, the parent, will more than likely share sex. Here the pitfalls are possible resentment and jealousy on the part of the children, the loss of respect and the dreaded philosophy that what's good for you is good for them. The only way around the pitfalls in Philosophy #3 is to use the correct type of approach. If you have previously raised your children in the confirmed belief that all extramarital sex is bad and if you decide to modify this belief slightly, don't do it all at once. Break it to them carefully and gradually. Talk to them about sex and your modified views for a while before clearing your conscience.

<u>Philosophy #4</u>: Avoid the issue and maybe it will never come up! This philosophy is science fiction in its purest form and you had better have your strategies planned before it does come up! There are few things worse than a parent who stutters when confronted by their kids about sex.

<u>Philosophy #5</u>: Abstain from extramarital sex completely and try to raise the children likewise. If, after a couple of years of single life, you are still that strong in your convictions, you may as well throw this book away and write your own. Before you do, however, keep in mind two things:

1. For your children's sake, remember that all people may not be as strong as you.
2. Your determination not to marry out of desperation will have to equal your convictions on celibacy. At any rate, Good Luck! (seriously).

The philosophy, or combinations thereof, that you choose is up to you. Your considerations, however, should be based on the age of your children, as well as the morals, philosophies, rules and convictions that make your family the unique unit that it is.

The "Negative Reaction Syndrome"

This is one of the biggest problems facing the average single parent home. The Negative Reaction Syndrome consists of negative reactions within the family unit, caused by negative reactions which result in...more negative reactions.

The average single parent, confronted with financial problems, limited time, insecurities, loneliness and heavy responsibility, is about to fall out of his or her tree as it is. Their overtaxed nervous systems have already developed a leaky condenser in the vertical circuit and their internal overloads are at the point of Melt Down. The complete parental machine continues to operate in a state of near malfunction.

As you pour over and over the bills in an attempt to balance your deficits by using the basic math you learned in high school, Junior walks in with a simple grade school question like "What does the integer of a negative 22 minus the absolute value of a negative 4 equal?" ZINGO! That was the straw that did it! Your pressure relief valve opens and in a burst of unsubtleness, you loudly convey the message that you couldn't care less what condition his absolute value is in and to remove his integer from your presence immediately. This tells Junior that he can't confide in you. He walks out and kicks the dog which bites the cat which claws his sister who throws sand in Junior's mouth and you scream, "WHAT'S WRONG WITH THIS FAMILY!"

In an attempt to get to the bottom of this problem, you ask Junior why he kicked the dog. "'Cause Sis wasn't around," he cries. Puzzled, you ask Sis why she threw sand in brother's mouth. "'Cause it was open," she sobs. Realizing that you can't argue with logic like that, you go back to your budget and Junior hits Sis in the stomach. Don't bother asking him why he hit Sis in the stomach as he will say,

"'Cuz she turned around too fast!"

So how do we fight a Negative Reaction Syndrome? With a Positive Reaction Syndrome, how else? It was your decision on how Junior's interruption would affect you in the first place. If you choose to let it affect you negatively, does that make you a bad parent? The answer is No, it just proves that you are human and anyone that worries about being a good parent will do their best to control their attitude once they have learned how.

On one hand, none of us are perfect and we should accept this fact. On the other hand, we should not use this Perfectless Person theory as an excuse to fall short. Somewhere in the middle we should do as well as we can and take pride in the fact that we are.

13
CHAPTER
Single Parenting Can Be Fun?

 SINGLE PARENTING CAN BE FUN?

Supervision

Supervision is no problem when it comes to single parent kids. It's the lack of it that causes the problems.   What do you do? Find a capable babysitter?   Impossible!   Patience Plaze of Mildness, Montana was the last capable babysitter known to mankind and she had a stroke three years ago.   INcapable babysitters are a dime a dozen.   You can always find a sweet, incapable babysitter anxious to be there at home, waiting to greet your kids as they return from school.   Finding one willing to stay after that is the hard part.

Where have all the good babysitters gone?   Statistics show that due to occupational hazards, 18% have joined a convent, 12% have jointed the Peace Corps, 3% have joined the Foreign Legion, 21% have joined the Armed Forces, 31% are in mental institutions and 15% have never been found.

If the kids are old enough to accept responsibilities (twenty-two and up) you can leave them alone.   If not, a nursery school or juvenile detention home is recommended.   If you do decide to leave your kids to fend for themselves, you will definitely be doing a lot of "Parenting by Phone!"   In time you will become so adept to this verbal form of nonverbal communication, that you will actually be able to tell whether or not there is trouble just by the way the phone rings.   You will also learn how to understand the message before their sentence is even finished.   For instance, if they call cheerfully just to say "Hi," tell them the answer is NO!   If the youngest child is elected to call you (the one that can't talk yet), you know that the others have done something so horrible that no one wants to tell you about it!   When they start a sentence with "You know" as in "you know our neighbor's window?" or "you know the old lamp on the mantel?" you know it's broken. "Uuuuu," is also a dead giveaway. It means that they haven't figured out how to break the news to you yet!

Kids also have a way of telling you something over the phone without actually telling you. For instance, if they call to say, "I just wanted to tell you that we had a blown fuse but don't worry because the fireman replaced it for us," don't say okay and pass it off. Otherwise when you get home from work to find that two-thirds of your house somehow, mysteriously, turned into ashes, they will say "but I told you on the phone!"

The two most important abilities that a single parent should retain are:

1.   The ability to keep a sense of humor.

2.   The ability to count your existing or surviving blessings. For instance, when the kids call to tell you that during the course of their baseball game Junior batted the ball out through the living room window for a spectacular home run, just be glad that there wasn't a skirmish over home plate because that was more than likely the TV set!

The Parental Child

There are many facets to single parenting that can reduce a well-adjusted child, wise parent into a ball of blubbering rubbish. But the one I find most effective is the problem of role swapping.

A lady friend and I were sitting on the porch enjoying each other's company one evening, when all of a sudden the door flew open and my daughter stomped out under the guise that she was looking for her barrettes. The enjoying suddenly stopped and as a matter of fact, I quickly withdrew my arm from around my girl friend. I immediately became the child, caught in the act and my daughter had become the parent who had decided, in a not so subtle way, to call a halt to this disgusting display before it got out of hand.

This example is but a small pea in the great goulash of confusion that I have experienced as a single parent.

My daughter has even been known to wait up for me to return from a date. She would meet me at the door with a third degree like, "You're home kinda late, aren't you? Where have you been? What were you doing?"   Guilty or not, my eleven year old daughter could break down my self-confidence and back me into a defensive corner like no prosecuting attorney on earth could.   My first reaction was to come up with a preposterous story like I had a flat tire, ran out of gas and then fell asleep at the movies.   In time, however, we learned the importance of honesty and mutual support and as a result, we are a <u>great</u> <u>deal</u> <u>more</u> honest with one another.

As with any relationship--friendly, parental, romantic or otherwise--there are certain feelings and secrets that I choose to keep to myself and, as discomforting as it is, I realize that the same applies to my children.   The overall communication and support between us, however, has reached new and exciting proportions and I would not return to the loneliness and uncertainty of what we had before for anything.

Parental Romance

The amount of time that single parents can give to their children is often limited.   Weekend parents are usually unable to see their children as much as they should, and custodial parents are often too busy putting out fires and taking on the responsibilities of both parents.   Single parents do need time for themselves, though, and they often choose to spend this time with other adults, usually of the opposite sex.   This quite often creates jealousy and makes the child feel neglected.   Many children attempt to take the place of the absent parent by assuming the role of the man or lady of the house. A new stranger in the form of their parent's friend can represent a challenge and having one's place in the family challenged this way can be a very traumatic experience, further adding to their insecurities.

Under the guise of self-preservation, kids will often try to manipulate their parents through guilt, or drive the intruder off in some way.   How does a sixty-five pound weakling without a second grade education drive a full grown, worldwise intruder off?   How about picking their nose and wiping it on the intruder's leg?   The milk-in-the-lap, gum-in-the-hair or basketball-in-the back tricks can also be effective.   The teenage son of a good friend told one of her dates that the man's intentions regarding his mother had better be honorable.   A young son of another friend asked a male caller if he was the guy his mother had been dreaming of.   A teenage son of a girl that I had been dating informed his mother that she had been spending too much time with me (he had the time right down to the last minute) and accused her of neglecting her own family. The daughter of another friend loves to advise her mother that a man is on the phone by screaming "Hey mom, it's another one of your boyfriends, I think it's old Noodle Nose!" The same lady quietly slipped into her house late one evening in hopes of sharing an intimate glass of wine with old Noodle Nose and found her underwear as well as other personal paraphernalia strewn all over the place. To add to the shock, a short time later the dog came running out of the daughter's bedroom wearing the mother's negligee.

One of my daughter's favorite ploys was, "I hope you don't cook 'cause I do all the cooking around here." The object of who would do the cooking was irrelevant in this case as the inevitable struggle for dominance was the implied message.

With adequate dating material at an ever depreciating level, it's of paramount importance to find a quick solution to this perplexation without resorting to the use of ropes and gags. To help, I have listed some suggestions that seem to work for me as well as many other single parents.

1. Sit down and discuss <u>certain</u> aspects and problems with your kids, regarding your dating experiences. Make them a part of it. Ask for their opinions even though you don't necessarily take stock in their answers. Diplomatically relate a few bad points as well as many good qualities that you see in a particular friend. (Make sure that it's nothing that you wouldn't say to your friend's face). Don't allow yourself to get into a debate where you end up arguing in favor of your friend as they will immediately assume that it's you and the intruder against them.

2. Try to convince the kids that this intruder is not actually a rival, but is depending upon them for support, friendship and desires their acceptance.

3. Don't push them into accepting your friend too quickly. Allow them to develop trust and acceptance at their own pace.

4. The one thing that you should demand is the show of respect that is due an adult. Let them know that this respect is due, not because of your relationship, but because of your friend's stature, as an adult. If an adult cannot attain respect, the show is over!

5. Include the kids in some of your dating plans such as picnics, parks, drives and family related activities. If your child wants to bring a friend, try to oblige.

The question of whom to bring home to the kids is a very controversial subject because of the many different types of friends that we each associate with. I again will offer only a couple of opposing views. Many single parents hesitate to bring dates home or take part in family related activities with different people because emotional bonds can very easily form and result in pain for everyone if the relationship fails. Some believe that this can create emotional callousing at a very young age and will eventually result in an uncaring, indifferent attitude where other people are concerned.

On the other hand, some single parents like to take part in family related activities with a series of different people. This illustrates to the kids the importance of meeting other people without forming a quick, emotional bond and by introducing the kids to a wide variety of different people, you help prepare them for their future.

<u>Discipline</u>

Statistics show that in single parent homes controlled by mothers, the delinquency rate and overall rebellious attitudes of the children are much greater than in the homes where the father is in charge. It's very difficult for a one-hundred and twenty pound Mom to sternly threaten her one-hundred and eighty pound, half-back of a son with any degree of credibility. There are a couple of ways to combat this problem, however. You can try to outsmart your incredible hulk through psychological manipulation, based upon years of your experience. Or if this fails, you can resort to a physical means of manipulation. Does this sound absurd? Well, bear in mind two things.

1. Your child does have a tendency to be intimidated by you. This is a result of his past programming from infancy, to respect and obey you. This tendency may no longer be readily apparent. However, it is still there, buried somewhere beneath his new desire for independence. This new position that he is trying to maintain is more than likely based on bluff.

2. The other thing to bear in mind is based on the old principle

that "Hell has no fury like a woman, scorned!"

Regardless of the method that you choose to adopt, kids do need discipline and supervision. Without it, they form life-ties and traits that they feel are correct but which are actually based upon inexperience and immature reasoning. Studies show that kids do crave discipline. It confirms the fact that the parent does know best and does care enough about them to take charge. Curiously, it also provides a feeling of security. Whatever form of discipline you choose (psychological, physiological, or both) you will lose control without it.

The responsibility of shouldering all of the blame for the way our kids turn out causes a tendency in many single parents to refrain from making or enforcing many important decisions. This lack of trust in our own judgements and the fear of making an irreparable mistake causes many of us to try and pawn these responsibilities off on our kids. That way, if we goof up, they won't hate us and if they grow up wrong it won't be so much our fault. As a result, some of us allow them to make their own decisions, which are based upon illogical and emotional principles only, and cheat them of our own hard-earned experience and wisdom. The thing we have to understand is that we cannot shirk this responsibility by ignoring it or passing it off. The kids won't hate us for guidance and discipline if we use it with some good old-fashioned common sense. They need it and will love us for it even though they do seem to fight it.

To help in this burdensome responsibility of making correct decisions, there are many parents out there who are literally panting for the chance to exchange ideas and discuss childrearing issues, so use them! Childrearing friends, neighbors and singles abound everywhere. You dodge them on the freeways, race them for the bargains and sleep with them through P.T.A. meetings.

The P.W.P. (Parents Without Partners) organization is nationwide and is comprised entirely of singles who are aware of single parent problems. In conjunction with their enlightening meetings and family oriented get-togethers, they have a nationally distributed magazine virtually exploding with good advice and supportive comments.

If you are fortunate enough to have parted wedlock as friends with your Ex, rely on him or her for their share of the responsibility. Go ahead and discuss parental problems with friends, neighbors and relatives.   You don't have to take their advice but look for insights that might help in your concept of parenthood and child pslychology. The problem with child pslychology, however, is that quite often the child is pslyer than the parent.

Consistent with our pre-discussed subconscious desire for pain and self-inflicted torture, many single parents tend to hang on too tightly to the children and some are a little over-protective.   On the other hand, some single parents seem to care too little about their kids.   It's difficult to determine how strict or how lenient to be, and walking this thin line is complicated by the fact that each child is different in these needs. The best advice is to accept the responsibility and follow your own logic and instincts.   Enforce your decisions, keep your promises and fulfill your threats.   Try never to back down from an ultimatum or promise.   If you promise discipline for certain actions, follow through.   If you don't, you lose their respect and your control.

The biggest damper on this philosophy is the fact that kids never seem to be at fault.   Just when you're sure you have them in a spot where they can't get out of something, they come up with an excuse about as tangible as worm fingers and you believe them!   Ironically, the excuse is usually so bizarre that you can't possibly question it!

It really is a two-way street, however.   I'm certain that my kids often feel that I'm hopeless, also.   Like the time that I insisted that Tif raise her grade average and then made a scene when I found out that she got an A in her Human Sexuality class.   Or like the time I told Brady to stop running from the big kid down the street.   "If you have to, pick up a board or something but don't run from him," I said, "that just gives him more courage!"   The very next day I had to reprimand Brady for wrapping a heavy, lead battery cable around the big kid's neck and almost killing him.   It all worked out okay, the x-rays showed no broken bones and the big kid referred to Brady as sir from that day on, but from that day on I began to be more specific with my advice.

The Survey
I have dedicated a great deal of my time in the past three years going over surveys for this book.   I have come to the conclusion that you can make a survey say just about anything you want it to, and that the results of many reflect the personal attitude of the surveyor. Many single parents dwell so heavily on depressing statistics that they

feel defeated before they even start. For this reason, it might be advisable to forget about the problems of the national average and concentrate on our own. Knowing how singles love statistics, however, I am going to include a page offering results from a few of the more dependable and accurate sources.

It is an established fact that children from broken homes do suffer, although the extent of their suffering is debatable. Some confirmed studies show that children in single parent homes survive better than in a two parent home where severe marital problems exist. The greatest majority of these surveys, however, do indicate that children from broken homes have a much greater tendency to lean toward delinquency and poor scholastic performances. A national survey conducted by the Kettering Foundation of Dayton, Ohio, and the National Association of Elementary School Principals, indicate that children from broken homes are nearly twice as likely to drop out of school and are eight times as likely to be expelled. Further surveys indicate that fatherless boys are four times as likely to drop out of school, six times as likely to have a juvenile court experience and eight times more likely to be institutionalized. Delinquency among fatherless girls is even greater than among fatherless boys.

Statistics from an inner city survey conducted in Washington show that out of two hundred delinquent children, one hundred seventy-five came from single parent homes. A San Francisco survey indicates that even though children from single parent homes may suffer more in growing up, as an adult they are more self-reliant and succeed in life better than those from the traditional, two-parent homes.

The debatable nature of this subject tends to be due to the location (inner city versus rural) and the great diversity in methods employed by the many different single parents, in bringing their children up. According to noted authorities in this field, another reason for this confusion is due to the obsession our media has to report only the bad news pertaining to divorce. Surveys showing improvement in kids as the result of divorce have been suppressed to some extent.

Now that we have the national average out of the way, we can turn to some of the least discussed problems of single parenting.

Cooperative Parenting

There are many psychologists and experts in the field of single parent families who believe that problem children are not necessarily the result of divorce; but, in fact, divorce is often the result of problem children.

The diversifications and opinions in parenthood are as broad as they are in religion, politics and morality. Finding two parents with exactly the same concepts in childrearing is difficult to say the least. The big problem usually occurs in the fact that each parent is certain that his or her concept is correct. Instead of pulling together, many parents pull in different directions until the strain literally tears the marriage apart and the problem child still remains problematic.

Surprising as it may be, divorce actually brings many parents closer on childrearing issues and creates a greater incentive to work together for the good of their children. Many states are encouraging a teamwork incentive for separated parents called "Joint Custody" or referred to on a less legal basis as, "Cooperative Parenting." The concept behind this is that divorce need not mean the end of a family but merely the reformation of it. The divorce law gives you the right to create your own custody agreement, provided it is in the best interest of the child. Many parents are now putting aside their personal differences and are unselfishly agreeing on a cooperative parenting plan that will benefit their remaining bond; their children. Some of the terms for this agreement are:

1. The degree that each will help in making daily decisions.

2. The degree of authority each will have in major decisions which affect the children's future.

3. The amount of financial and emotional help each will provide.

4. The amount of time each will have the children, whether on an equal basis or sole custody with visitation rights.

5. Decisions regarding insurance, college savings and the children's savings.

An equally fair agreement between two jealous parents is not an easy thing to accomplish. Problems will also more than likely arise after the agreement has been drawn. There is, however, plenty of help out there for those who want it. Agencies such as the Conciliation Court, Family Counselors, Divorce Clinics, Parental Workshops and Appointed Mediators can help a great deal.

Another helpful hint is to leave a little verbal space in your agreement for changes, as it will have to be adjusted from time to time in order to meet continually changing needs and circumstances. Don't be too stringent regarding the agreement. You may not be able to work together as lifelong mates but that doesn't mean you can't work together as human beings with a tremendous common goal.

The High Cost of Leaving

Custodial parents don't usually have the problems in adjusting to single life that non-custodial parents have. The basic reasons are probably two-fold. First, they just do not have time to dwell on their problems, and second, they have managed to keep their own little world with them. They use the frustrating problems of dating, etc., as diversions rather than a way of life.

The non-custodial parent (NCP) has been ripped from the warmth of family and home, and cast adrift, completely alone. Adding to their grief is the fact that many have way too much time to think about it. Surviving this lonely existence often becomes their only goal in life. They often feel that they have nothing left to work for and no goals left to achieve.

I have heard many divorced wives complain that their Ex has gone off the deep end, drinking; spending money, sleeping around and acting like a sex-craved adolescent that has just discovered puberty. Contrary to logic, however, the NCP may not be doing all of this for the fun of it. Many are just trying to survive. The custodial parent should honestly put themselves in their Ex's space for a while and take an objective look at his or her present position. NCPs have lost almost everything, both emotionally and monetarily, that they have worked for over the past years. They can see their own children only as the courts decree. They are not present during their children's sickness, they can't help with their immediate problems, and they often have little or no say in their upbringing. Indifferent attitudes often develop as the result of shutting off pain. They usually try to fill the cavernous void with the less significant things life has left them. They have to stand by and watch helplessly as other strangers step in-and-out of their former position as parent and spouse. The tremendous, new financial responsibilities from the divorce can also create weird side effects.

The NCP usually has to take over someone else's family in a remarriage while a perfect stranger takes over his or her family. Children, in this case, often feel a form of rejection and alienation from their NCP, especially when they see the parent taking on someone else's family.   The kids don't realize that there is little say in the matter.   It is one of the most hopeless and helpless situations that loving parents can find themselves in, regardless of whose fault it is.

I have also heard custodial parents say that their spouse did not care for the children before the divorce and consider the present behavior as just an act.   Well, based on the NCPs that I have talked with, I can say that it is seldom an act!   The pressures and responsibilities of providing for a family and being a good parent in this day and age can be very confusing and oppressive.   Quite often we become so saturated with our worldly problems that we forget how much our family really means to us until we lose it.   I believe that such is the case with a majority of the divorced, including non-custodial parents.   I sincerely believe that the pathways to their present circumstances were built, to a greater extent, on confusion and oppression than on selfishness or indifference.

Childish Attitudes

The divorcing of parents affects children in different ways. The reasons for these emotional differences are broad; ranging possibly from behavioral chemistry to individual upbringing.   The major contributors for different attitudes and emotions, however, seems to be related to age.   Younger children often have more feelings of guilt as though they were the cause of the divorce. They often feel very insecure and behavior patterns can change radically.   They can either become very withdrawn from guilt or very aggressive in their craving for attention and security.

Kids from about 8 years to adolescence are often sharper than parents think.   They usually feel that they are caught in the middle and have to make a choice.   Their guilt feelings now are manifested in the parent they did not choose, or betrayed (usually the non-custodial parent).   Confusion abounds as fighting parents seldom discuss the divorce with their kids except for the lousy qualities of the other parent.   The kids are confused and may often withdraw from the parent that they betrayed.   The love they had can turn to hate through their feelings of guilt.   Or they can pull wild, desperate stunts in hopes that parents will reunite to help them.

Adolescents, ah yes, they are different!   They generally feel that their problems are the only important issues in the world.   They often feel that parents have no right to intrude upon their own growing pains with something like a divorce.   Adults are supposed to have it together!   A divorce often results in insecurities, resentment and doubts towards parents.   The realizations that divorce brings can result in a shorter adolescence and quicker maturity but it's not an easy transformation.   Younger adolescents and pre-adolescents usually resent their parents dating others.   It's usually against everything they were taught.   Mom and Dad, dating other people when they should be together?   Older adolescents, in their quest for truth, become very curious about their parents' dating routine.   They often look to Mom and Dad for an example and for wisdom, when the parents are often as confused as the kids!   Mom and Dad would probably resent this statement, claiming that they are much wiser as the result of their past and this is true.   But parents do not always follow their own wisdom initially and are prone to as many mistakes as an adolescent!   Maybe even more.

Child Warfare
In a divorce, children's loyalties are usually torn between Mom and Dad.   The pressures which are heaped upon the kids are horrendous.   One or both of the people that gave them life and provided a stable foundation of impeccable advice and authority to grow on...is/are wrong.   Too often each parent tries to persuade the children that it's the other.

Mom says it's Dad; Dad says it's Mom.   Which one is it?   Maybe it's both!   This affects the credibility of everything the parents have taught the kids.   Children think in absolute terms.   If Mom and Dad are wrong about this, what's to say they are right about ethics, sex, drugs, religion or anything else?

Divorced parents almost always have the tendency or desire to savagely use the children as a weapon against one another to vent their hostilities.   This is often done on a subconscious level with no great amount of thought about what it does to the children or what the consequences will be.

This tendency for child warfare is another fine example of "perpetual emotion."   The tendency is self-perpetuating because each parent often feels that the other is slandering them.   The main reason for these suspicions can have little to do with the other parent and is often due to the child's attitude.   For an example, a child may return to one home or the other with feelings of withdrawal or nervousness.   They may have problems eating or sleeping and may appear angry or indifferent.   The paranoid nature of the average divorced parent may click in and say "what has my Ex said to turn my child against me now?"

The children's behavior is not necessarily a good indication of indignation on the part of the wrathful Ex.   Studies show that children, going through a major transition like this, have a tendency to act weird and this is their right.   Further, I believe that, in an attempt to win a dwindling parent's affection, they are capable of saying just about anything that could help them in their cause. They may tend to be on the parent's side that they are with at that particular time, and say anything to win some affection or security.

The one thing that is most important to remember, is to refrain from running down your former spouse and their parent.   It not only creates animosities that you may eventually pay for personally, it tells them that you have bad taste.   It usually tends to hurt and confuse them for a while, but seldom affects the ultimate extent of their love for the other parent.

14
CHAPTER
How To
Speak Single

Chapter 14

How To Speak Single

Torso Talk

Torso talk is a method of communicating our interests, emotions and desires without having to commit ourselves. It's sometimes referred to as Non-verbal Communication and can be considered the art of speaking without speaking. This paradox has a very prominent place on the single scene, as many singles seem to have forgotten how to speak.

Have you ever attended a dance where the guys seem to congregate on one side of the room and watch the girls watch them from the other side? The guys are drawn to the girls, the girls are drawn to the guys, but there is a barrier between them called "The Fear of Rejection." The safest method of crossing this foreboding barrier is with the utilization of Body Language. There are thousands of subtle little messages constantly being sent across this barrier but unless you understand them, they will do you no good.

Body Language has been around longer even than words and is almost the exclusive form of communication in the animal world. Some experts believe that it is a product of our primitive past and as such, works on the principles of instinct.

In the civilized world of the modern family, and with the refinement of verbal communication, the need for sign language or non-verbal communication has subsided. As a result, our understanding of the art has lapsed. But the instinct is lying dormant somewhere within our subconscious minds. If you are in "the Jungle," (a term sometimes used to describe the single scene), it may be advisable to develop these instincts as you may have to deal on an animalistic level a great deal of the time.

Private Zones

Most members of the animal family draw seemingly invisible boundary lines which define their own personal territories. If another animal encroaches upon this territory, under certain circumstances, a fight for the custody of this area can ensue. Similarly, people also have a tendency to establish boundaries which define their own personal "Private Zones." The area of this private zone will vary from a radius of thirty feet for highway driving, to as little as a few inches in a crowded singles' bar.

These private zones are very personal and important to us and as such, they are generally considered worth defending. Experts agree that this is a significant cause of fights in bars and other crowded areas. Prison studies show the "intrusion panic" (a term used to describe the violation of private zones) is the main cause of violence in prisons resulting from no apparent reason. Further studies show that the more violent inmates have a private zone four times greater than the less violence-prone inmates.

Encroachment

One way of determining how responsive another may be to you is to encroach or intrude upon their private zone. If they accept this intrusion with a smile and hold their place, this is an indication that they are responsive to you. If they spit in your martini, this is usually a hint for you to back off! Other more subtle indications are the positioning of a glass, book, arms, legs or other objects directly between the two of you. For an example, if the intrudee holds a glass or another object in front of them, particularly between the chest and face area, or clutches a book or other object tightly into the chest area, this can be an indication that you are either moving too fast or that they are not comfortable with the situation. If a glass, book or other object is not readily accessible, a step backward or arms folded across the chest can be an indication. An arm held horizontally across the mid-section supporting the other arm which extends toward the chin or a middle finger extended vertically can also send the same message.

Encroachment is a good way of determining responsiveness. However, it's advisable not to trap someone between you and another object. Always provide the other person with a way of retreat or any positive feelings they may have could abruptly change to negative feelings. They may consider you as pushy and too aggressive. Negative responses do not always mean rejection. A negative response may simply mean that the other party is not comfortable with the situation as it presently stands. For an example, it could simply mean that they don't want you that close until they can get their breath mints. It's very important to remember that in order to tell exactly what's on the other's mind, you have to be able to read and decipher a series of messages.

Facial Language

It has been said that the eyes are the windows to one's soul. Whether this is true or not, it remains a fact that a large degree of body language is expressed through the use of our eyes. We are all familiar with the signs of anger, expressed by lowering the eyebrows and squinting of the eyes, and the message of surprise from the arching of the eyebrows and widening of the eyes, etc. There are, however, a great many more subtle reactions, expressed by our eyes, that often go unnoticed. For an example, women have a tendency to move and blink their eyes more slowly than men do. When a women looks at a man with a quick blink, it can be a flirtatious signal. A glance out of the corner of the eye sends the same message, especially when accompanied with a smile. These signs are psychologically designed to communicate a message without the risk of commitment and are, therefore, very, very, subtle in their delivery. The smile that can accompany an eye signal from a man or woman may be nothing more than a quick twitch of the lips and the entire glance may slide away before it can be answered. On the single scene this is often referred to as "A Whiff" and may consist of nothing more than a split second glance without any accompanying facial expression at all. This is also referred to as "making or establishing eye contact."

Men usually have a tendency to look straight ahead while blinking or to blink just before changing eye direction. Women, on the other hand, can blink while the eyes are in motion and it is considered to be a seductive signal. When this is done to a higher than normal degree, it is generally referred to as "batting of the eyes." Several quick blinks aimed in the direction of a male can also say "Hey there, my contacts are slipping."

Men also find it admissible to glance out of the corner of the eye; however, it's not used to the same extent as with women.

Generally men have a tendency to establish eye contact by looking straight ahead or slightly off to one side.   The glance can evolve into a quick wink and/or can be accompanied by a smile or a split second twitch of the eyebrows or lips.   The raising of one eyebrow can, of course, relate the fact that the sender approves of what he or she sees.

A longer than normal glance is a very assertive signal and can actually develop into a stare, lasting for several seconds.   This type of eye contact demands an answer or response and can cause an uncomfortable feeling on the part of the target.   This is an effective way to get someone to notice you but it is risky.

In some cases, a sizing up of the complete torso is very acceptable and projects an unmistakable message of sexual interest. This routine is no longer limited to men only; and women who use this signal are very liberal and assertive.

Some women wear fashions more seductive than a Jacuzzi full of Jello!   If a person dresses in like manner, they generally want to be sized up and contrary to old beliefs, a person can allow themself to be caught in the act.   If a woman is wearing a low cut, very thin or otherwise revealing top, the average male has a tendency to restrict his gaze to her face.   If she looks away he may sneak a quick peak but his eyes will quickly return to her face.   The man considers this as a polite respect of her privacy when the woman, in fact, is saying "Looky here at what I've got."   I have had several women resent this supposition, stating that they object to being _viewed_ as a sex symbol just because of the way they dress.   It is obvious, however, that they do not mind being viewed.   I do agree though that you can't _always_ judge a women by her clothes because quite often, it's a case of insufficient evidence!   At any rate, the reluctance on the part of the male to invade her privacy can send the message that he just does not care about her cleavage when, in fact, he is about to come unglued.

Anything can be overdone and consequently it is NOT advisable for the man to stare down the front of her blouse with his mouth hanging open.   A slow, sliding glance now and then will suffice very well.

Our eyes also have a tendency to send a very profound, physiological message that few of us are aware of.   This interesting effect is the dilation of our pupils when we look at someone that we like.   In this case, our pupils actually have a tendency to dilate or grow larger.   This startling new discovery has actually been around for centuries.   Women, aware of the fact that large pupils indicate a sexual interest, have tried for years to dilate their pupils with the use of various drugs which is not recommended.   The most commonly used drug has been Belladonna which contains the same Atropine that opticians use to dilate pupils.   This is a rather deceitful practice as it announces to everyone, "I like what I see in you," whether it is true or not.   This practice has met with a great deal of success which illustrates the fact that others are usually receptive if they feel that you are.

I feel it is necessary at this point to stress the importance of good eye contact while talking to someone else.   It goes without saying that if someone is continually looking around the room while speaking, they could be considered as disinterested.   Similarly, if a person avoids eye contact by looking down during a conversation, they are considered to be shy or inferior.   On the other hand, as pointed out previously, there can be too much of any good thing and an unbroken stare directly into another's eyes can cause the other person emotional discomfort.   It is important to break eye contact now and then by glancing at the nose, chin, mouth, hair, etc.

Another very provocative facial signal is the wetting or licking of the lips.   This is used by both men and women but men do not generally expose their tongue to the same extent that women do. This gesture is usually subconscious although some movie stars such as Marilyn Monroe have been known to accentuate it.   This courting gesture, as a rule, simply resembles the act of cleaning the lips with the tongue after a tasty meal; however, the more accentuated the tongue movement, the more provocative the message.   Women also utilize a similar gesture by exposing the top, front teeth and running the tongue over the bottom edge of them.   A lip signal widely used by women is accomplished by dropping the lower jaw slightly with a moderate pucker or protrusion of both lips.   Men and women alike use the lips in body language but men usually protrude only the bottom lip and generally refrain from the slight pucker.

Studies show that nodding of the head in an affirmative manner during verbal conversation has a tendency to keep the other party reassured that you agree with and believe them.   There are many other helpful little hints such as laying of a finger alongside of the nose can indicate that a lie or preposterous statement is about to be made and that a women is generally perturbed when she lowers her eyes and looks away.   Another indication of indignation is the proverbial tongue in cheek routine where the sender pushes out a cheek with the tongue. Just about any method of primping can be considered a seductive signal such as straightening or fluffing of hair, the one contrariety being the feminine act of twisting or playing with the hair which usually indicates indifference.

Hands

Hands are probably the best medium for delivering messages, next to the face. When someone uses a great deal of hand movement in conveying a message, it generally means that they are trying very hard to bridge the gap of understanding and consider you worth the effort. This does not constitute a courting gesture, however. Courting signals conveyed through the exclusive use of the hands are generally feminine. The most common is the repetitive exposure of the palms and inner forearms. Also, a man can let a women know that he is starved for her affection by gently taking her hand into his mouth.

Another direct line of communication through the use of hands involves other objects. Primping gestures such as the straightening of a tie, the adjustment of clothes, the handling of cuff links, etc. can tell you that the other person wants you to like their appearance.

You can also tell what someone is probably thinking by the way they handle or touch objects while talking to you. It goes without saying that if someone hammers on the table with a glass they are angry, but the reverse applies also. If they fondle the glass, caress it or run their fingers delicately around the rim, it conveys an almost undeniable courting message. They may, in fact, be using the glass as a substitute for you!

Touching your own body in specific places often provides a clear courting picture as well. When a man places both hands on his hips with the fingers pointing down to his crotch, he is usually subconsciously drawing attention to that particular area but this can also imply sexual dominance. Women often use the same indicator with one or both hands but generally tip the pelvis somewhat. When a women fondles a button on the front of her blouse or plays with a necklace or charm at or near bust level, she is generally drawing attention to a certain area of herself and it isn't her ankles!

LEGS

Probably the strongest signal involving legs on the part of either sex is the direction in which we cross them. When the top leg crosses and points in the direction of another person, it generally indicates acceptance. If it points away it generally means rejection. One thing to bear in mind is that a person's legs tend to get uncomfortable in one position and when this happens we rearrange them. For this reason the leg crossing signal may only apply at the initial seating.

Women who draw their legs up on the seat and pull them in tightly are generally receptive if the knees are pointed in the direction of the other person. If she sits on her legs with the knees pointed down and toes up, it can mean that someone has had too much to drink

Our Physiological Fountain of Youth

Another very interesting tidbit is the incredible physiological reaction that the act of courting subconsciously plays upon our bodies. Similar to the pupillary reaction of our eyes, it causes certain facial and body muscles to tighten. Bags under the eyes as well as facial lines and wrinkles disappear or are minimized. Jowling decreases, the blood rate is increased to the face and the skin tone improves. Chests expand, bellies tighten, the torso becomes more erect and posture improves.

Sum Total

In closing the Torso Talk Chapter, I think it would be wise to cover the dominating role in this interesting art. The dictators of the art are, of course, the so-called "weaker sex." It is the woman that almost always dictates with "nonverbal communication" whether or not a conversation or meeting should transpire, and when. This is often accomplished with only a quick glance which can be interpreted as permission to start the conversation.

Generally if the woman does not initiate the meeting or conversation in some subtle, feminine way, nothing will transpire.

Studies also show that woman's instinctive understanding of body language is much greater than that of a man's. Futhermore, the first touch, whether a hand on the arm or an accidental brush, is usually initiated successfully by the woman. If the woman makes the first physical contact, she will generally make more. If the man initiates   physical contact, the woman will often refrain from further touching.

As pointed out previously, there are many facets to this interesting art that are not covered in this short chapter. Becoming really proficient in the art requires study and practice, so don't disappoint yourself by reading signs that are not there. Practice what you have learned here strictly for the fun of it. If you want to learn more, buy a book written on this specific subject. In the meantime, go out and have a good old-fashioned nonverbal talk with a stranger.

<u>Speaking Single</u>

Singles generally like to have an edge. They like to know something that no one else knows. Many like to appear mysterious and deeply intellectual or intimidatingly witty, honed to a razor's edge. This not only impresses others, it serves to intimidate their rivals as no one wants to start something with a human razor blade!

As a result, most singles pick out three or four super impressive words, one or two really impressive places, two or three witty and provocative sayings or cliches, three or four famous designer names and one or two famous quotations. Add to this the names of five or six good wines and you have an arsenal of impressive verbosities that constitute a "Bluffer's repertoire to single survival." To illustrate I have created a sample word guide below.

IMPRESSIVE WORDS

PROFOUND: (1) Having a tremendous intellectual depth and insight. (2) Being somewhat hard to understand. (3) Very deep seated. (4) Extending far below the surface. (5) Not average. (6) All encompassing and complete.

Note: <u>Words with several meanings like this are handy for any repertoire.</u>

INCREDULOUS: (1) Not disposed to believe. (2) Showing unbelief. (3) Being skeptical. Spin-off words are: CREDULOUS, CREDULITY, CREDULOUSLY, and CREDU-LOUSNESS.

Note: <u>Words with spin-offs help to increase your repertoire</u>

ATTENSUAL: (Can mean anything as it is not even found in the dictionary but sounds great anyway.) Spin-off words can be ATTENSUATING, ATTENSUABLE, ATTENSUALITY and ATTENSUATED. Every single has one or two of these words for an emergency. It's okay to use it anytime you want because few singles would ever admit that they didn't know its meaning. If someone does ask, you can make up your own meaning anyway, thereby protecting your profoundly attensuating reputation against those with an incredulous nature.

OTHER GOOD SINGLE'S WORDS ARE: Surpass, Incredible, Extraordinary, Sufficient, Affirmative, Negative, Exuberant, Incontestable, Inculcate, Decadence, Ignominious, Augmented, Sublime, Profuse, and Prodigious

Learning to speak single is only half the battle. Understanding single is a whole new ball game. This is due in part by the average single's tendency to relay messages without actually saying anything. It's sort of like non-verbal communication relayed through the use of voice. Sigmund Freud was surely thinking about singles when he told us that when we jest, we are saying humorously what we are forbidden or frightened to say seriously. In other words, when a single tells you that you have a smile as natural as the great outdoors, it may mean that you have parsley stuck between your two front teeth. Similarly, if a single infers that your moon is rising, you need not check your buttons. They are probably just referring to your Astrological sign which is a favorite topic in the science of single talk.

Other favorite topics include contemporary music, participant sports, vacation villas, movies, plays, trivia, eating establishments, bars, nightclubs, fun things in general, and...themselves. The single that learns to listen and take an interest in the other single is a successful single.

Some singles are reluctant to talk to people they don't know, but they talk to their pets, plants and refrigerators. On the other hand, many singles are very bold. I used to shop with a girl who would always hand the grocery store manager a list of musical requests before shopping.

One of the biggest problems in speaking single appears to be in the literary gap between men and women. For an example, surveys indicate that women with a profuse vocabulary of profane terms tend to turn men off. So what do a lot of single women like to do? They like to show the men that they are tough, world-wise and self-reliant by talking like a drill sergeant! Similarly, in a survey conducted recently to see what turns women on or off, it was determined that witty ice breakers are one of the major contributors to a cold reception. So what is one of the greatest desires men have in wanting to approach women? They all wish they could come up with something really witty and provocative to break the ice with!

As a result, some guy's interest in rejection and public humiliation goes far beyond the realm of a simple hobby, it becomes a whole way of life! What are some of these provocative ice breakers? Well, ten of the virilest of these verbosities are:

1. "Tell me, do you have any interests?   I'm into feathers"!

2. "I can get you on T.V. As a matter of fact, if you sign up now I can get you On T.V. at a reduced rate!"

3. "Why don't we go over to my place and discuss our future. We can practice making Our bed!"

4. "Why don't we go somewhere more private? I know a little place where there's great music, good wine, a crackling fireplace, Wesson oil and plastic sheets!"

5. "Hi There! I'm an alien. Would you like to see my ray gun?"

6. "Excuse me! I'm a C.I.A. agent in trouble. I was wondering if I could crawl under the table and hide between your thighs?"

7. "I don't have much longer to live and just one night with you would give what little time I have left such meaning!"

8. "Pardon me. Did you happen to see my keys anywhere? They have a Rolls Royce emblem and they're on a gold

Krugerrand key chain."

9. "You have very beautiful skin. Tell me; do you like to roll around in margerine?"

10. "I'm leaving for World War III in the morning and I desperately need something to remember. Something that will give me purpose, an incentive to live and something to come back to. Will you please come home with me?"

And, after the inevitable rejection:

"I'm sorry you feel that way! I guess that means oral sex is completely out of the question then?" This simply illustrates the #1 Male Law of Sex which states: "If at first you don't score, act like it doesn't matter anyway!" What is the female's #1 Law of Sex? How about "When there's a will, there's usually a won't."

Singles change their vocabulary as often as they do their relationships, so a regular dictionary of single terms would be archaic before this hits the press. For this reason, I have included only a few of the more popular terms being used at this particular second to illustrate the hidden meanings behind the average single terminologies.

AIRHEAD (ar-head) n. Someone who keeps their nose so high in the air they become starved for oxygen.

DINGY (ding'gi) a. Someone with a screw loose in the head. It's usually the screw that holds their tongue in place.

DOORMAT (dor-mat) n. Someone that just lies there and takes it.

DORK (dork) n. Someone who does not know the meaning of a word that you learned yesterday.

DUMPING (dump'-ing) v.t.   The act of someone else leaving their emotional garbage on your doorstep.   It's similar to you complaining to a friend only this is called "looking for support."

FLAKY (flak-e) a.   Someone with emotional dandruff.

FRIEND (frend) n.   Someone that never tells you the truth, even when you ask for it.

FRIGID (frij'-id) a.   A girl that has found something more important than sex.

HARD CASE (hard-kas) n.   Someone that has a mind of their own.

HARD CASE (hard-kas) n.   Someone that you resent, dislike, are jealous of or will not loan you money.

HUNK (hunk) n.   A living mountain of male hormones.

KINKY (king-ke) a. Someone with odd twists in their sex life.

NERF (nurf) n. Someone who's nervous energy is exceeded only by their ability to drive others up the wall. Highly strung;   wired;   chronically   crazy. (French. nerveux, nervious)

ONE NIGHT STAND (one nightstand)   A dormant object of convenience, specifically made for the bedroom.

SCORE (skor) v.t.   To achieve a goal in the great football game of sex.

OUT OF THEIR TREE (Lit.) Someone that must have sustained brain damage from the resulting fall.

SPACE CADET (spas Kadet) n.   An earth dweller whose mind is still in interstellar space.

STUPID MIND GAME (stu'-pid mind gam)   A game of wit that someone else has beat you at.

TOOSH (toosh) n.   The extreme southern extremity of a northbound object of sex. Buns, derriere.

CHAPTER 15

Meeting Singles

Chapter 15

MEETING SINGLES

The How To's

There is a great deal more to meeting singles than just discovering where, so we will save the where to's for later. The How To's are what we are going to examine right now. One of the first steps might be to <u>de</u>-establish some of our preconceived ideas for the type of singles we want to meet and where to meet them and then re-establish some new ones.

We are far more successful when we accept others for themselves instead of looking only for the ones who fit our own specific designs. Granted, we will usually develop stronger relationships with those whom we have something in common with but we can often learn from those with opposing views.

Our tight-fisted compulsion to retain and confirm <u>only</u> our own attitudes and beliefs has produced a world where races have to depend on nuclear annihilation to protect them for other races. Where Catholics and Prostestants are killing one another (both in the name of God) and where a world of lonely singles who need each other are staying...Lonely.

<u>Most</u> of us desire friendships and relationships but we really don't know how to go about finding them. For instance, we may want to find a meaningful relationship with someone who is sincere, sophisticated, sharing, honest, strong, mentally awake and morally straight. We have approximately ten different places to look:

1. The American Scouting Program (boy scouts or girl scouts).
2. Single's ads.

3. Meetings, through friends and work.
4. Chance meetings (store, laundromat, neighborhood, etc.)
5. Single's discussion groups, meetings, seminars, etc.
6. Planned diversions (school courses, charity work, telethons, health spas, jogging, travel, etc.)
7. Organizations (P.T.A., churches, hobby and special interest groups).
8. Dating services.
9. Single's organizations and clubs.
10. Single's bars.

Many of us immediately rule out sharing groups, churches, and special interest groups. We have heard somewhere that most of the guys in these areas wear white sox and even though we may not fully understand the stigma of white sox, we know it's bad. Further, the women in these organizations are of the bleeding heart majority, or they are only out to nab a husband. Besides, everybody knows that these singles are unsophisticated and a little too open with their feelings.

The thought of answering or placing an ad in a single's publication or hiring a dating service has occurred to us, but the only people who do this are desperate and even if we are, we don't want others to know it.

Relying on friends, work and chance meetings requires a lot of time and Lord knows, we can't maintain control over our thigh problem or receding hairline forever...time is of the essence!

Planned diversions sound about the best so far but they also require a great deal of time and they tend to put our fate too much into the hands of chance.

Single's organizations and clubs sound pretty good but they are probably not for us. Everyone says that all members of these organizations are overweight, alcoholic, too old, unsophisticated and otherwise uninteresting.

This leaves us with two choices: single's bars or the scouts. Most of us would have some problem in qualifying for the scouts so we choose the bars. We put on our sexiest clothes, rehearse a witty line or two, memorize the name of a new drink we just heard of and embark in a search for Mr. or Ms. Sincere! Now I'm not implying that we will fail to find anyone of sincere worth in a single's bar. After all, you're really a super type of person and you may go to one now and then and this maybe is true!   I have met some really super singles in these places.   I will say, however, that due to the wide diversification of people there and in considering the average motive for being there, our chances of finding a sophisticated scout on the premises are about one in five hundred.

Men generally frequent these places looking for _physical_ love. Women often go in search of _emotional_ love...possibly with some physical overtones.   A guy will walk up, make her an offer that she can't refuse and when she does, he says, "Why in the hell did you come here then!!"   She will make trip after painful trip, turning down offers and then maybe accepting a few but always wondering why she can find no good in men.   The men, on the other hand, will walk away burning with rejection and wondering why they can find no good in women.

Why do these men constantly let her down?   The answer is, they don't.   Not any more than she has let most of them down.   If she is looking for something more profound than a one-night stand, she is going to have to reform her opinions and look elsewhere.   On the other hand, the guy has no right to be bitter simply because she exercised her freedom of choice in deciding that his desires did not fit hers.

There are a great many women that understand the requirements of the bar scene and go there for the same reasons that most men do.   The problem is that many other women, looking for emotional fulfillment, are so confirmed in their theories on where to look and what to look for, they refuse any new approach. It's much easier to stay in the bar rut, and blame the guys for their disappointments.

At this point, I can feel the fur of feminine hackles rising in indignation across the nation.   I am not just picking on women and I really am trying harder than anyone might realize to hold a "middle-of-the-road" perspective.   So, in an effort to be honest and fair, I will regretfully admit that guys also have a similar problem with this form of environmental deception.   For instance, when I find a liberal type of gal in my favorite bar that's there for all the appropriate reasons, and when the lovin' is over, I'm still in love but she isn't, I will also feel used and cheated and will maintain there is little good to be found in the female expression of humanity.

The disappointment that we can experience here is our own fault.   In the first place, we all too often do our emotional grocery shopping in the wrong market. Secondly, whenever we form expectations, or place demands on others, particularly strangers that don't owe us a thing, we are setting ourselves up for disappointment and pain. It's not their fault if they don't meet the demands and expectations that we have set upon them.

Generally, those of us who have been married are the ones most prone to establish demands on others. I believe this is true, in part, to the fact that in a marriage, we do have certain obligations to our spouse and vice versa. Quite often in a marriage, we have to fight in order to collect on the obligations that we feel are due us and this can become very habit forming. We may divorce our spouse but not our habits. As a result, we keep on trying to collect from those who have no obligations to us at all.

There are also many singles (I can relate to this) who have experienced a good marriage, full of sharing and openness. As a result, we run right out of our marriage into the carnivorous jaws of single life with our arms out- stretched, expecting to be greeted in like manner. What happens? We run SMACK right into a solid wall of emotional callouses. The resulting pain from our broken egos and swollen pride is due to the expectations that we had no right to place on others. Singles do like to have friends but usually maintain more space in their friendships than others do. Single's friendships are generally not quite as intimate. Learning how to establish and maintain this new type of friendship can be somewhat difficult. Singles generally have a unwritten code which, if it were written, would read:

> "If I have expectations of others,
> my disappoinntment is my problem."
> "If I fail the expectations of others,
> their disappointment is their problem."

The only hard part of this code is remembering the first part! Now this doesn't mean that all singles are cold and unfeeling. Some are just cautious and uncredulous. The Single Code is merely the end product of some painful experiences. The rewards of love or profound friendship are worth almost any price to many who honestly appraise their own needs, but some consider the price of pain (which inevitably results from any love) too high. For those, that is their problem!

Many refuse to dedicate any more of their life living up the expectations of others, but when they become certain that these others will accept them for themselves, without demands, they will then accept the others also. This has been a very bad pill for me to swallow. But the loss of friendships and relationships as the result of my own impatience has taught me to respect the attitudes of others and to seek intimacy at a slower pace.

Differences of opinions and attitudes do not necessarily mean that the other person is wrong, it's just that they may think and feel differently than I do. Genes play a large part in our individualities but we all do leave the womb with the same basic philosophy of life (although I can't remember for sure what it was). It's the circumstances that we each experience in life that forms our fears, expectations and hangups. It is no small wonder that we all end up different. Add to this the "Sexuality Gaps" between male and female and it's a wonder that anyone is born into this world through any means other than artificial insemination.

Another problem in establishing preconceived designs for friends and fiancees is that it can cause us to assume fictional roles, ourselves. To illustrate how fictional roles can adversely affect us, we will take a hypothetical look at a conventional single, named Clem (his friends call him "Ho-down"). He is really a nice guy down deep but somewhere along the line, Ho-down decided to try out for the traditional image of an ideal, all American, single male. He cashed in his securities (which left him broke), and bought a fantastic car and wardrobe. He practiced his new role until he really had it down to a science. Suave, sophisticated, debonair, handsome, intelligent and successful. He sold his dog to buy a new haircut, changed his name to Clemont (pronounced Clay-mont) and dashed out the door to make friends and influence women. He was certain that when he found his perfect partner (beautiful, kind, loving and giving), she could not possibly resist him. What about his financial state? Well, if she was his kind of woman, she would understand when he told her that his last big investment sort of crashed and burned.

Ho-down's first big mistake may have been that he practiced his part too well. His perfect image had a tendency to intimidate potential pals and perfect partners, as no one else thought that they could keep up with him, and the only women he influenced were out for the bucks that he didn't have. After experiencing disappointment after disappointment, he concluded that all women were the same. They were all out for a free lunch and if you didn't have the bucks, they'd drop you. The question here is: Who was it that really let H<u>o</u> down?...

Oh well, moving right along, it should be pointed out that most of us have a tendency to take on fictional roles at times in an attempt to make or maintain friends. This is particularly true with the new single who feels little in common with single peers and wants desperately to fit in. Not really knowing what is expected of them compounds the problem, making the situation appear more confusing and at times, totally hopeless.

At first, I tried very hard to impress others and make them like me. In an effort to be physically desirable, I made sure that I never had a hair out of place, my clothes were always just so (and from you know who), and I invariably took on the personality that I felt was best for the group I was with. I made plenty of new acquaintances but no new friends. The reason being, none of these acquaintances knew me well enough to be my friend. They only knew the false image that I was showing them.

Another obstacle in the way of successfully meeting other singles is our tendency to form preconceived opinions. We often know, instinctively, what kind of jerk or castrator someone is even before we ever meet them. We too often base these preconceived opinions on a person's sex rather than their personality. A few examples of these preconceived sexist opinions are:

Most men are out for nothing but sex.
Most women are out for nothing but an all-expense paid party.
Men are nothing but users and liars.
Women are all self-deceivers and lie to themselves.
Few men, if any, have feelings, ethics or compassion.
Almost all women are out for sex but refuse to admit it.
Men can't accept women for their emotional beauty.
Women always try to remake men to suit themselves.
All men are anti-committal and make nothing but idle promises.
Most women are just out to snare a husband to take care of them.

With opinions like these, some of us tend to seek out friendships and relationships with all of the warmth and sincerity of an untamed shrew.

A guy might spot a gal across the barroom and think to himself, "A woman that attractive is probably a real snob but I have to give it a try." He knows that she can cut him down with a quick flick of her tongue, and past experience assures him that she probably will. As a result, he might take the attitude that he is doing her a favor by even speaking to her. That way, the inevitable rejection won't be as painful. As he approaches, she looks up and thinks, "A man that attractive can only be out for one thing." He nonchalantly pauses at her table and says something like, "Are you waiting for me?" She smiles graciously and says something like, "No offense, Pig Parts, you're just not my type." Both, without every getting to know one another, can become very smug in the confirmation that they were each right about the other. The lesson to be learned here is, never underestimate the power of "negative thinking."

Painful experiences and the fear of rejection have a lot to contribute to these attitudes, but another equally vile villian is environmental influence. That is to say, most of us are influenced tremendously by our surroundings. If these two people had met at a local caring-sharing group, church, P.T.A., or bar mitzvah, they may have really got it on. When we are in an emotionally dangerous environment, our psychological defenses are usually working at peak efficiency. We might go there to meet others but we are often too apprehensive to succeed.

Now, on the other hand, I will admit that there are some real throwbacks out there. People that are so out of phase with our own convictions and interests that there is absolutely no hope for a relationship, friendly or otherwise. Recognize this fact and accept it, but don't dwell on it.   Don't look so hard for these people that you see them in everyone. Not everyone is a scout at heart, but believe it or not, the real degenerates are the minority, not the majority. Be aware of the fact that they do exist, and that you will undoubtedly meet a few, but don't look for them, just look out for them. Quite often the people that we consider degenerates are just good ole' folk, with different views.

<u>The Where To's</u>
There are literally thousands of places where you can meet singles. Some are right for us, some are not. The hard part is

sifting through, filtering out and discovering where to start. Once you get into the "mainstream" of things, the hardest part is over. Singles generally like to talk single. They discuss parties, associations, establishments, travel groups, clubs and organizations. By becoming involved in an organization, (whether it's perfect for you or not), you will discover an inexhaustible source of new opportunities.

It's a good idea, initially, to base your choice upon your own interests rather than a desire to find a relationship. If you join in an activity that you have no particular interest or ability in, your lack of enthusiasm can make a bad impression on the rest of your would-be comrades. A good example would be the cross-eyed guy that joined a single's archery club in order to meet women with well-developed pectorals. He didn't make very many friends, even though he <u>did</u> manage to hold everybody's undivided attention!

<u>Single's Ads</u>

Most regular newspapers offer information on single's activities in the entertainment section or Sunday supplement but the best source of single's news and activities can be found in single's newspapers and publications. Most of these are distributed on a bi-weekly or monthly basis and there is more than likely one or more such publications within your area. You can check newsstands, corner vendors or the yellow pages under newspapers and magazines. These publications usually contain information on single's activities, workshops, encounter groups, special interest groups, dances and single's bars as well as personal ads and advice.

There are two distinct variations in single's publications. There are relatively hardcore publications which advertise somewhat kinky ads and articles. Then there are the ones which are accurately referred to as respectable publications.

Some singles still consider the personal ad routine as degrading. They have the attitude that it is a desperate and somewhat perverted way of finding sex, when it is not! This seems to stem from the stigma produced by the underground type of publication which advertises strictly for sex and usually of the perverted variety. A great majority of the single's publications are now based upon integrity and reasonably moral values. Most reply letters are scanned before they are forwarded to the advertiser; the moral content of each ad is carefully considered before publishing it.

(200)

The fast growing acceptance and changing attitudes toward these personal ads are based largely on the success rate of its followers. It is a reasonably safe, inexpensive and very logical approach to meeting singles with the same views and interests.

In answering an ad, the letter is usually sent to the publisher where it is screened and forwarded to the advertiser. Most letters are accompanied by a photograph (ranging from photobooth to studio quality), a quick rundown on the sender and a telephone number. If the advertiser is impressed, they usually contact the sender by phone. If both are impressed after the phone conversation, a meeting can be arranged in the safety of a public place. It is a quick, safe and often very successful method of meeting others. Still in fact, don't be disappointed if the first few meetings fail to produce successful results. Statistics generally indicate that, even under the best conditions, only one out of four (25%) of our encounters will produce a reasonably close acquaintance and less than one out of 50 (less than 2%) will produce a worthwhile friendship or relationship.

One fear, shared by a great percentage of advertisers, is that of trying to talk to a complete stranger on the phone. There is no sound more deafening than the silence between two strangers that can think of nothing to say. Add to this, the feminine insecurities of calling a man, and you have a problem. It might be comforting for the female readers to learn that in a recent survey taken to determine what turns men on or off, it was proven that men seldom consider a lady caller as being too forward. In almost every case, the men stated that they really liked it and considered such a woman as emotionally together. It has also been proven that a great many women are calling men and the number is increasing rapidly. Once the telephone contact is made, regardless of who calls whom, you will more than likely find that there is too much to talk about and too little time to do it in. You will both probably be very receptive and the mutual desire to impress one another can work miracles.

Before making the call, you might want to jot down some interesting topics for discussion such as:

> What do you like to do?
> Do you have any hobbies or interests?
> How long have you lived here?
> Did you go to school here? If so, where?
> What do you do for a living?

In what area of town do you live?
Have you seen any good movies or plays recently?

Try to find a subject that sparks mutual interest. Some examples are: recent movies or plays; trivia; contemporary music; participant sports; eating establishments; funny dating experiences (good sense should be used); singles activities; pets; children; camping; hobbies and interests of almost any kind. Try to avoid subjects pertaining to ex-spouses, divorce and leprosy.

Meetings Through Friends and Work

What can I say about this form of potential danger except that it can be very tricky? If the rendevous does not go well, it can cause pressure between you and your friend and we all know the pitfalls of mixing emotion with business! If the meeting has been set up by a friend (or perhaps ex-friend), there is a good chance that it is a blind date. If so, you will probably be required to meet said person in a public establishment somewhere. Now all you have to do is figure out how to recognize them. Generally, this is very easy. Guys, your blind date is probably the one with the orange hair. Gals, all you have to do is look for a short, fat, bald-headed guy, standing on the bar, giving Woody Allen impressions. Have fun!

Chance Meetings

You can meet singles in malls, grocery stores, laundromats, department stores or while washing your car, looking for your contact lens or walking your pet feugit. If you would like to be more assertive in meeting others but have trouble building the confidence needed to take that first step, begin at a level that you can accept. Start with just a simple smile at someone or a hello. The first person you pick need not be a movie star look-alike. Choose an older person, possibly of the same sex. Later as your confidence builds, you can graduate to speaking to the person waiting in line beside you at the checkout stand.

There are many subjects you can use to break the ice. If at a grocery store you can comment on the rising food prices, the slogan on their T-shirt (that's probably why they are wearing it), or even on the weather. Common sense should be used, however, in picking the subject. For instance, it would not be a good idea to approach someone with, "Excuse me, I couldn't help admiring the handsome enema bag you just purchased."

Once in a while, you will probably make an innocent blunder like spotting a sixpack of uncola in an attractive stranger's basket and advise them of a sale on Squirt in the ten-ounce bottle at the precise second that they lay the proverbial enema bag on the checkout counter.

If something like this happens to you, just turn red, forget about it and wear a disguise the next time you go to the store.

Discussion Groups

Discussion groups are a fantastic way to meet singles. There are some white sox and bleeding hearts in some groups but if this bothers you, there are many others with red sox and hard hearts. I have met doctors, lawyers, executives, nurses, business owners, policemen, construction workers, cowboys and Indians as well as welfare recipients in these groups. Certain groups seem to draw certain types of people and the only way of finding out which one suits you is by trying them all.

People in discussion groups tend to drop their walls, break through their emotional callouses and let it all hang out. This tends to create a very friendly, open atmosphere where we can view one another as honest-to-gosh human beings with very similar problems and feelings. It allows its participants to relate in humanistic terms rather than the animalistic terms that many other sources demand.

Discussion groups are predominantly patronized by divorced and widowed; however, I know a great many "Lifers" that also attend regularly.

Here's how they work. The group leader usually presents the subject or calls for a vote on the subject to be discussed. He then leads the discussion by calling on people who want to express their views. Later on, in some discussion groups, the body is broken up into smaller groups for additional discussion, which gives the shyer people a chance to talk openly.

The main thing in a discussion group, encounter group or single's seminar to beware of is accepting <u>psychological</u> advice from leaders who have no formal training in this area. Generally, the leaders simply offer practical advice on single issues and coordinate activities. Some, however, develop a great deal of self-confidence and eventually feel that they are experts in the area of mind readjustment.

This type of organization was initially developed for those who are desperately looking for help and those who are newly divorced or widowed, although the friendly atmosphere and the desire we all seem to have to relate in human terms is drawing singles of every stage at an increasing rate. The point remains, however, that many of the people who attend these functions are extremely vulnerable and confused. They can definitely profit from these groups but it's important for them not to rely too heavily or form a dependency upon one individual who seems to have all of the answers.

Planned Diversions

As mentioned previously, self-improvement is a natural prescription for what ails the average single, and many instinctively turn to classes and activities which provide the means for this. You can enroll in a class that teaches art, business, auto mechanics, human sexuality, etc., etc., etc. The sky is the limit! All you have to do is decide which field to explore. If it's mental improvement you want, you can check with local universities, colleges and high schools within your area for the adult education classes offered. Chess clubs and tournaments are also a good way to meet the intellectual set.

If you are into athletics, try health spas, aerobic classes, bicycle and hiking clubs, or contact your local Y for information on interesting groups. Your local parks and recreation department might also be able to give you information on interesting groups and activities. Classes in tennis, squash, racquetball, martial arts, etc., are a good way of maintaining health, venting frustrations, improving appearance and meeting singles at the same time.

Health spas and gym clubs are a big thing with many singles, and one of the best sources for joining a physically attractive set. Many executive and professional people also use this type of service in order to keep fit.

If you like to dance, enroll in a dance club or sign up for lessons. One word of caution here! Many dance schools try to capitalize on the single's loneliness in an attempt to hook them on an exorbitant contract. The dance instructors attempt to establish an emotional dependency on the part of the student through praise and intimate contact.

Travel is one of the most enjoyable ways to meet singles but it is also one of the most costly ways. In order to get around the cost somewhat, many singles travel in pairs. This is because ocean cruises, hotel rooms, etc., are often as expensive for one as for two. By doubling up you can share the expenses. You can also look into single travel groups which get a quantity discount. You can inquire at travel agencies, watch for advertisements or listen for single gossip. Single's cruises and resorts are fast becoming a favorite form of entertainment and they are a great way of meeting some financially successful singles. Enterprises such as Club Med schedule world tours, and many resorts are sponsoring singles weekends, which are based upon a quantity discount.

The American Youth Hostels (A.Y.H.) offer an inexpensive, no frills place to stay en route. Singles of all nationalities often travel via the hostel rooms and there is nothing like it for meeting interesting people of many different countries. Hostels are primarily a supervised place of lodging for youth groups such as bicycle clubs; however, people of all ages are now using them. They are usually located within urban centers but most are found in an area of natural, scenic beauty. They provide shower facilities, private kitchens and a common social room. Information on hostels can be found by contacting the Chamber of Commerce within each city that you plan to stop in.

When traveling alone, one of the biggest problems for a single is not knowing anyone when they reach their destination. When planning a trip to another city, many singles spread the word among friends and working associates who can offer names and telephone numbers of acquaintances living within that city. Probably the best way to insure yourself of companionship during a trip is to take part in a club, pre-organized group, or plan your trip with a friend.

Organizations

There are many special interest organizations such as political groups, social clubs, hobby clubs, ethnic groups, religious organizations, etc., which offer excellent opportunities for meeting singles. Many of these organizations do not cater specifically to singles but you might be surprised at the number of singles that cater to these organizations. Realize that in a lot of cases, the single is the only person with enough time on their hands to take an active part in their interests.

The aforementioned "Encyclopedia of Associations," found in most public libraries, is a good place to start looking. Also, most major cities have a community service that you can call for information. If you can't find the community service number, call your local Chamber of Commerce for help.

Churches and religious organizations are an excellent way of meeting ethical singles. The term "ethical," when applied to this division of our single society, rarely means radical. Because of the unique problems that most of us face in single life and because of human weakness, there are few morally <u>stringent</u> singles to be found, even in most churches and religious organizations. The main differences are generally confined to the reduced participation in drugs, casual and kinky sex and the <u>extreme</u> use of profanity. Many religious singles will have one or two...or maybe three or four drinks but generally stop short of being totally "ripped." Generally, they are as human as other humans but manage to maintain a slightly higher expression of morality. Right or wrong, the fact remains that in some of our religious institutions, the degree of physical fellowship is higher than Mother Rucker's House of Oars! This may be due in large to the fact that the average person feels less threatened in this type of atmosphere and is more receptive to others.

A large church will, of course, provide a larger spectrum of potential friends to choose from. The larger membership also allows for different divisions and programs, based upon age and special interests.

<u>Dating Services</u>

Dating services are generally expensive, ranging in price from $25 to over $1000 depending upon their mode of operation, the extent and quality of their service or the greed of their proprietors. These establishments differ a great deal in their operations but the end result is usually the same. Some dating services utilize computers and are called, of course, computer dating services. Other establishments use no computers whatsoever and are called, of course, computer dating services.

The concept behind computer dating is fantastic and if you listen to the glittering propaganda put out by these businesses, the results are always equally fantastic. The problem is that despite the extremely high cost, there are usually no guarantees.

Probably the most successful type of C.D.S. utilizes a videotaped interview with each selectee to be played back for the selector. Photographs are generally kept with each file in order to make choosing easier.   Computers, as well as being very bad judges of character, are also very naive.   They believe whatever anyone tells them and many applicants stretch the truth somewhat when filling out the program questionaire.

I can find no documented statistics on the success rate of dating services; however, the success is approximately the same as for single ads (around the magic twenty percent range).   Other information that I have collected seems to indicate that the less expensive dating services have as high of a success rate as the more expensive ones. In dealing with a dating service, beware of any pressuring or hard-sell tactics.   If a C.D.S. sales person tries to pressure you, go elsewhere! You might also be well advised to check out any such agency with the Better Business Bureau.

Single's Clubs and Organizations

There are "North-town Singles," "West-town Singles," "South-town Singles," "East-town Singles" and "Downtown Singles."   There are the "Bachelors" and the "Bachelorettes," the "Single Nonsmokers,", "The Nicotine Ninety," "The Under 30 Club" and "The Senior Swingers."   Somewhere within this mass of organized mess there is a club that will more than likely meet your needs.   Single's clubs that are dedicated primarily to card playing and sorted conversation are fast becoming the thing of the past.   There are a great many very lucrative singles clubs that offer gym facilities, racquetball and tennis courts, swimming pools, dancing and bar facilities, lounges, computer game rooms, saunas, hot tubs and almost everything imaginable.   These clubs are usually very expensive; however they offer the members a whole way of life, rather than just a diversion.   Club comaraderie is generally very high and emotional defenses are at a minimum.

Regardless of the club, an annual membership fee is usually required and it is proportional to the benefits offered.   Some have monthly or bi-monthly publications which outline special events, and offer insights and advice.   Smaller club functions often include discussions, dances, potlucks, picnics, participant sports, trips and so forth.

In most clubs and group associations, there exists a real, down home, family type atmosphere which sounds great but does have one drawback.   Similar to most large families, there are few secrets. Everyone knows everyone else's business and if someone has no interesting business, others might end up making something up. For this reason, if you join a club, it might be advisable to keep your personals...personal.

<u>Single's Bars</u>
From my own standpoint, single's bars defy all human reasoning. In the first place, they are usually so crowded that unless you are extremely near-sighted, you couldn't find anyone to be compatible with anyway.

It's very difficult to dance at a single's bar because the dance floor is usually about twenty feet square and there are eight hundred singles trying to dance on it.

So what's left? Talking, of course. The only problem here is trying to compete with a two hundred and fifty watt, quadraphonic sound system that was specifically designed for volume! As a result, the typical conversation between two potential would-be's often goes like this: (at the top of their lungs)

Guy: Hi there, my name is BILL!

Gal: Oh, I don't work here. If you want your bill, you'll have to see the Waitress!

Guy: Oh! I'm sorry, you weren't in uniform. How long have you been a waitress here?

Gal: No, don't tell her to bring me a beer, I'm not sure what I want next!

Guy: You WANT WHAT! DID YOU SAY YOU WANT SEX!

Gal: WHAT!

GUY: WHAT!

GAL: You can order me an ORGASM!

GUY: What! YOU WANT WHAT!

Gal: AN ORGASM!   O-R-G-A-S-M!

Guy: Oh, you bet!!!

The possibility for problems in this very short relationship should be apparent.   So if we can't dance and can't talk, why are bars so popular?   Maybe it's the desperate anticipation that, miraculously, something might go right and a worthwhile meeting might accidentally occur.

Single's bars are exciting, challenging, glittering and plastic. They are also magic!   They are a place where we meet one another at our worst; where thousands meet every weekend night in an attempt to create and live an entire relationship with a complete stranger in the space of one night, and where few can really be themselves.

It's a place where hearts beat to a rhythm of pounding music and minds reel from the effect of alcohol and drugs.   It offers an escape from reality and the chance to find what some believe is love.   It's a place where two, new found, potential lovers are constantly looking around for someone better, while talking to one another.   A place where the "quick-score frenzy" reaches panic proportions by midnight and the atmosphere is heavy with sweat, perfume, cigarette smoke and desperation.

The single bar scene is a fantasyland for the desperate and a supermarket for social disease.   The majority of its patrons have become hard, cold and indifferent as the result of many bad experiences, and from giving of themselves with only the recollection of someone's first name to show for it the next morning.

Now you may have come to the conclusion that I am somewhat biased in my opinion of single's bars.   This is not completely true. Once in awhile they can provide a very significant service for some, if they are used in the context for which they are designed.   Many of the singles that I have talked with, however, do their emotional, as well as their physical shopping here and get very little back for their investments.   It's easy to get caught up in the conventional single bar rut of feeling that this is the only place to meet singles--but it isn't.

16
CHAPTER
Sexwar Syndrome

Chapter 16

THE SEXWAR SYNDROME

The Sexwar Syndrome is a relatively new expression of an old term, "Battle of the Sexes." It is a modern analogy of the incredibly cruel games that people play with one another and can be perpetuated only in the atmosphere of today's liberal society. The Sexwar Syndrome is the product of three emotional elements prevalent in our contemporary, single society which are:

Emotional Callousing (the emotional defenses that we sometimes erect between ourselves and our feelings)

Self-Deception (our uncanny ability to believe everything we say or want to believe)

Sexual Misunderstandings (biased prejudices and emotional ignorances that we often have with regard to the opposite sex)

These three elements result in "Sexuality Gaps" between men and women and these gaps grow wider with each painful experience. There are no statistics on the percent of singles per capita that have joined the Sexwar movement; however, the percentage is high. Most, thankfully, are not Sexwar Extremists (which will be covered later).

So, how do you join the ranks of thousands who propagate the Sexwar Syndrome? Easy! In fact, if you have been single for at least six months, have need for love and have had at least one painful experience in dating, you are probably already enlisted. Here is how it works.

First, we will take a look at Sally Snibbles again, in the basic training program of the women's corps.   She is unhappily married to a real Clod that has neglected her, bored her, possessed her, cheated on her and/or beat her.   This basic training is necessary to inflict the psychological wounds needed to start an emotional scarring process. The abuse that Sally endured has convinced her that old Clod is the epitomy of male chauvinism so she files for divorce and emerges as a Private in the Sexwar Syndrome.

On her rebound and in search of a new, perfect mate, Sally meets Joe Snurps, a dashing, young Corporal in the male corps which immediately takes her to the battlefield.   He charms her, lies to her, lays her and leaves her. With this necessary amount of new emotional scarring, Sally is promoted to Private First Class.   During the next eighteen months, she falls for a Sergeant with sexual perversions, a Lieutenant that is alcoholic and a super-neat Major that loves her but hates her kids.

Now decorated with scarred hashmarks of a Full Lieutenant, Sally walks around the corner one day and runs into Private Marve E. Lous, a cute recruit, fresh out of bootcamp and created just for Sally. Now Marve, being new on the scene, is somewhat lonely and naive. His sincere honesty is now so unique to Sally that she mistakes it for weakness and abnormality; however, a relationship somehow manages to develop. She considers it simply a physical and friendly relationship but Marve believes it to be romantic and is deeply involved emotionally.

The relationship blossoms until Sally begins to feel emotional commitment.   Instantly, her defense mechanism is activated, the relationship is broken and presto, we have promoted Marve to Private First Class. At this point, Marve himself is well on his way to becoming a trainer of young female recruits.   Sally, on the other hand, has become a "lifer".   Her emotional callouses have started to crust over and she may grow old and lonely under the pretense that she just never could find the right man.

So how can you tell if you're ready for the "Sexwar Syndrome"? Well, let's take a look at the qualifications.

<u>First Stage.</u> You have to acquire a sufficient degree of emotional callousing which results from painful experiences (in most cases, divorce will do).   You have to be able to convince yourself that love may not be worth the risk.   You have to let your fear of emotional pain rule you to the extent that you will sabotage your

relationships before they can hurt you.   It's okay to secretly hope for an intimate relationship, but you should doubt its eventuality.

<u>Second Stage.</u>   You have to convince yourself that you are the only one that matters and looking out for Number One is where it's <u>all</u> at.   You have to be able to use others mainly to fulfill your own physical and monetary desires. What about emotional desires?   There is little room in the Sexwar Syndrome for emotions.   The philosophy is that emotions just cause problems and pain.

<u>The Sexwar Extremist.</u>   If you are bucking for a high rank as a Sexwar Extremist, you have to nurture and cultivate your pain in order to develop enough callousing to <u>completely</u> isolate yourself emotionally from the opposite sex.   You have to become totally self-sufficient in the traditional human needs for intimacy.   You have to become less human by developing your barriers against human emotion.   It helps to tell yourself that love is just a euphoric fantasy that exists only in the minds of poets, insecure adults and small children, and you must live these convictions to the fullest extent, even subconsciously. You cannot even in your most subterranean thoughts hope to find love or someone to share with.   You have to remain "safe" and the joy of love is simply not worth the risk!

Now the extremist group of the Sexwar Syndrome is very much the minority when compared to the "silent majority" of our total single populace.   The fact is, however, in a fit of vulnerability (a state most singles find themselves in from time to time), it's very easy to get sucked into it.

<u>Emotional Callousing.</u>   We have already overdosed on most of the aspects of emotional callousing, so we will skip this for now except to say that grief associated with divorce, the sting of rejection and the pain of broken relationships has a tendency to create a defensive attitude in many singles. As a result we sometimes want to show the world how much we are hurting. We often abuse ourselves physically and emotionally in the subconscious hope that mom, dad or someone will come to our rescue, just like in days past.   At the same time, many of us try to protect ourselves from any additional painful experiences.

<u>Self-Deception.</u>   The sexwar attitude often starts off as an aloof, indifferent act which progresses to <u>habit</u> and then to a <u>doctrine of life.</u>   Many Sexwar <u>Extremists</u> deny their natural cravings for intimacy and love by telling themselves that these emotions produce unhealthy complications such as possessiveness, insecurity,

(215)

immaturity and jealousy. As a result, they often try to fill the emotional void within through a physical means--emotionless sex!

Extremists or not, most of us at times try to fool ourselves and others into believing that this is where it's at!   We tell everyone that the concept of love is fine but does not work.   That emotionless sex and no commitment is the only way to go!   Then, like all of the others, we go back to our empty apartment and tell ourselves that it's working for everyone else, so it has to work for us, too.   It's the biggest con job in the "free society" and everyone involved is the con artist as well as the victim!

Self-deception is a funny thing. You can take three happily married men or three happily married women and put them in a room together.   Let one of them start griping about his or her spouse and before long, the other two will join in, each griping about their own spouse.   Inside of an hour all three of them will be ready for a divorce!   This is a perfectly human trait, inspired by the desire for comaraderie, the need to let off steam and the compulsion to relate. If we break this one-hour segment down, it might start out as an act, develop into a conviction and progress to fact. This just substantiates the old theory that if we tell ourselves something long enough, pretty soon we believe it!

Sexual Misunderstanding

I have spent a great deal of time wondering why men and women have to be so different emotionally.   I mean, I really approve of the physical differences and aside from the limited amount of Orgasms Per Hour (O.P.H.) a man can have, I wouldn't change a thing.   But sometimes the extent of our emotional difference is downright nauseating!

The only plausible explanation I can come up with is that in considering the pure pleasure of sex, this old earth would probably have standing-room-only by now if both sexes were emotionally compatible!   At any rate, it is a fact that there are a great many emotional differences between men and women and there are few of us, if any, that will claim to fully understand the opposite sex.

One of the main problems with these emotional differences is that each sex tends to judge the other from their own emotions.   Men judge women from a man's point of view and women judge men on feminist terms.   The emotional ignorance that each sex seems to have about the other is complicated by the fact that as a result of our emotional callousing, we often lose all desire to understand our sexual counterparts. As a result, many of us give up, crawl into our lonely little shell and blame the opposite sex for not being compatible enough to allow us to find someone to love.

It's true that the Sexwar Syndrome has resulted in more liberalized views regarding sex. Victorian philosophies have been trampled down. Purist views have been squelched; sexist roles re-evaluated; taboos forgotten and sex has been defined as the fulfillment of a natural, biological desire instead of a filthy game, perpetuated by evil. This is a definite improvement until it's overdone, but then you know how singles are! In place of antiquated sexual hangups, the Sexwar Extremists are contracting chronic forms of emotional impotency and intimate frigidity.

Most of these hardcore extremists refer to their form of mutual masturbation as simply "casual sex," and it is. It can become so casual in time that the act loses almost all trace of sex whatsoever. Participants indulge in a mechanized ritual, usually with no concern for their lover's feelings, and the emotional vendettas between men and women grow larger and more destructive with each experience. Lovers become nothing but trophies and sexual encounters are quickly forgotten. Men remain animalistic beasts in women's eyes and men look at women as monetary leeches and castrators. Each sex forgets and denies the human need each has for the other, aside from the physical aspects. "Sexual Burnout" resulting in impotency and frigidity is but one price many extremists are paying for free sex.

Sexwar Casualties

The effects of the Sexwar Syndrome are beginning to surface on a grand scale. Its Extremists fill the couches of psychiatric offices and the small rooms of behavioral institutions across the country. These casualties of the sexwar have many of the same symptoms. They are withdrawn and cold, impotent or frigid. Many complain that they are unable to feel anymore. Emotions like remorse, happiness, joy, pride, passion, shame, etc. have become nonexistent. They have no worthwhile goals and nothing seems to have meaning or reason.

So where can you enlist in the Sexwar Syndrome if you don't want to be recruited out of a broken relationship? Just about any single's bar will do. As a matter of fact, more singles have enlisted through this recruiting office than by any other means. Sex is easy to find and the emotions that are said to "complicate sex and create problems" are minimal.

They offer the easiest method of recruitment as the only thing that's really required is a desirable body, void of emotion and one's self. There may be a small degree of depersonalization, disappointment and maybe even shame, the first few times that one experiences sex with a stranger; however, with a little work, one can become a sexual robot in no time at all.

The Sexwar Code

The code of the Sexwar extremist is simple. You can lay together naked, get acquainted physically and share sex but you <u>cannot</u> share private thoughts or emotions. Sharing feelings is just too personal!

Extremist or not, all sexwar veterans have one common philosophy. They all believe that love is not worth the risk of pain and view their fear of intimacy as strength; referring to it as independence! They consider the basic human need for love as a bi-product of antiquated, social programming. The question is...Is it?

Are we actually denying an important, deep-rooted, human need or are we simply shedding some insignificant desire that was inspired by social programming? Do we really need on a humanistic level or a <u>lower-classed</u> animalistic level? I said "lower-classed" animalistic level because a number of the higher-classed animals are monogamous and seem to experience love. Whales have been known to starve themselves to death and actually die of grief when they lose a lifelong mate. As far as I know, a whale's need for love cannot be inspired by social programming. In cruel, medieval experiments, babies who were given everything needed to sustain life except for human touch and voice, died! Dogs will wait for hours underfoot for a loving pat on the head and perhaps our ability to relate to this is why we refer to a dog as "man's best friend." The point that I want to make is that babies and some higher-classed animals seem to have a critical need for love outside the pressures of social programming! What makes us different?

I am not trying to change anyone's life by forcing my own philosophies on them. I am simply trying to provide some "food for thought" for those who might be looking for some different answers.

The next "food for thought" question will be: Is love worth

the risk of pain?   Again, I will leave you with your own convictions but from where I stand, anything fantastic enough to cause this much trouble as the result of its absence has to be fantastic enough to find, whatever the cost!   I don't recommend commiting emotional suicide but there are ways to minimize the risk of pain which will be covered in the "Relationship" chapter forthcoming.

The last casserole for contemplation involves the question: Does love rob us of our independence?   In my book the answer is NO! Our lovers, in a desire to control us, can take our independence if we let them but the only reason that we would have for allowing this is if our love for them was greater than our desire for independence.   If this were the case, our fears are unsubstantiated.   Granted, if we have to struggle with a lover to maintain our independence, it IS a big hassle, but I don't intend to become related with someone that I would have to fight with for control over myself anyway.   There are some women out there who would love me for me.   I will settle for nothing less.   Some singles feel that love will rob them of their new feelings of self-worth but love, if it's right, will not rob us of our self-worth. It will substantiate it.   There are obligations in love but if love is right, they stop being obligations and become a means to fulfill our desire to make someone of great worth happy!   The trick is in finding the right love and this will be covered in the last chapter.

So whatever happened to the blushing virgins and the guys in white hats?   The truth is, they all died in the middle nineteen-sixties, right?   The only things left out there are sexual degenerates that are interested only in getting into our pants for our money or other things!   Right?   The funny thing is that probably everyone of us, male or female, feels or has felt the same way at some time. Have you ever been considered a sexual degenerate?   You can almost bank on it!   Now there really are plenty of degenerates out there but the majority of them exist only in our minds.   Just like all lawyers are money-hungry - legal thieves, politicians are all crooks and Russian communists are all war mongers; all members of the opposite sex, at some time, become degenerates.   This pure human tendency to stereotype has created one of the widest "Sexuality Gaps" between the sexes.   It was only when I realized things would not improve for me until I re-formed some opinions, that I stopped stereotyping and started understanding the opposite sex as well as my own attitudes. In other words, I did not make the all out attempt to swim until I was on my way down for the last time!   Suddenly, I realized that if nothing was working for me, it had to be, to some <u>small</u> degree, my fault!

Before this happened, I would pick myself up by the collar, reluctantly drag myself back out into the single world and make still another painful attempt to find some good in women, other than their physical attributes. My first stumbling block was that I was so defensive and prejudiced, I wouldn't have seen a good woman if I had fallen over her (and I'm sure that I did on occasion). My second problem was that I was looking in all the wrong places, and third, my imagination was working overtime! I would light a cigarette, she would cough with allergies and I would say, "AHA! A CASTRATOR! SHE WANTS TO CHANGE ME! Case closed. A girl would say, "Call me?" I would say, "AHA! GLOMER-ONNER! SHE WANTS TO OWN ME! End of talk. If a buddy was to tell me <u>all</u> women were not out for a "free lunch" or cunning and conniving or self-deceivers, I would think, "I'm right, you're Wrong!" End of discussion. Since my emotional modification, however, I have found that there is a tremendous amount of good in the average woman and some have even become my very best friends.

I still have bad experiences and even as I write these words, I'm trying to recover from another one. It is painful out there and this pain can result in a total social withdrawal where singles just don't even want to meet singles. We all go through it from time to time and in some cases, it becomes a way of life. Bad experiences and pain have convinced many of us that there is just nobody out there worthy of us, so why try? We shed the responsibility of our own failures and say, "What's the use?"

After an extended period of social regression, we might go back out again with the same attitude that all members of the opposite sex are retarded throwbacks from an unsuccessful gene experiment and whaddaya know? We come back home, alone, with the reaffirmed conviction that we were right! When we look for and expect to find the bad in others, that's what we will see.

Each sex has a tendency to carry this proverbial chip on their shoulder and as long as it exists, there will never be any significant degree of agreement. Ignorance of the emotional machinery that makes each sex tick, and our human desire for sex at any cost, will continue to perpetuate the "Sexwar Syndrome." How it affects us, however, is up to each one of us...individually.

The Sexwar Liberation Movement

At last, with the development of women's lib, ever changing social standards and new sexual concepts, we find ourselves in an exciting era of social reform where antiquated rules have been phased out and <u>new</u> <u>rules</u> <u>are</u> <u>completely</u> <u>non-existent!</u>

Now I'm all out for equality and I definitely believe that ability and ambition should govern a person's place in society rather than nationality or sex. I do feel, however, that <u>some</u> Libbers have a chauvinistic appetite that far exceeds any desire for sexual equality and their ultimate goal is to plunge ahead, at any cost to others, until they either cause an international nervous breakdown or get their busts placed in the great Hall of Fame.

Meanwhile, the innocent bystanders, which are not actually involved in this contemporary battle of the sexes, stand by in a state of bewilderment, wondering what is expected of them. Women truly have come a long way but as the result, most of them have absolutely no idea where they are, much less what is expected of them. To add to this mass hysteria is the confirmed fact that men are as confused as the women are and a great glob of this confusion seems to have concentrated itself in the area of the single dating practices.

The SWLM is a terrorist organization comprised of a small band of feminine sexwar guerrillas who get their <u>personal</u> power by establishing vendettas between men and women, creating sexuality gaps, and pitting each sex against the other. This small group of female war guerrillas capitalize on the fact, which history has proved, that the most vicious wars occur where vendettas and personal convictions are the cause.

For years women have had to be content with social celibacy and men have had to endure the sting of sexual rejection. Those were the days, my friend. I can remember when the most traumatic decisions of the evening were whether or not the guy should try to kiss the girl good night and whether or not she should let him. Each sex followed social standards to a T and confusion was minimal. The finely set rules were that:

1. Girls did not want sex.
2. Guys were obsessed with it.

Things were easy and simple before women's lib bared the truth that gals also desire sex. Before this the only a thing a guy had to worry about was being considered a sex-crazed pervert. Now if he is not considered a sex-crazed pervert he may be thought of as an impotent disappointment. On the other hand, a woman is considered easy if she does and frigid if she doesn't. No one is considered normal any more!

Traditionally it has been the man's responsibility to brave the horrors of rejection, make the initial move and ask the woman out. He then has been expected to pick the time, place and form of entertainment, open doors, light cigarettes, provide all transportation, pay for the entire evening and then again face rejection and scorn by determining whether or not to push for sex.

It's rather hard to understand why women would want it any other way, except for the possibility that they may now be experiencing some form of the sexist pride that has caused the male gender to act so funny for so long. To this, I can honestly say, "ATTA GIRL!"

One thing that bothers me, however, is why I have to be one of the singles caught up in the confusion of this social reform and how do I cope with a social structure that has no rules or guidelines to go by. The only plausible answer is to perfect my abilities in the methods of communication, period classification and to develop a superhuman ability to comprehend, analyze and ad lib.

<u>Sexual Finances</u>
One of the biggest sexuality gaps between men and women seems to take place in the area of sexual finances. To illustrate we will again turn to the subject of dating. Women can generally assume that a man is attracted to her if he asks her for a date. But a man should never make the assumption that she is interested just because she accepts. The man would not invest a chunk of money entertaining someone that he was not attracted to but traditionally, women have little to lose. Gals are usually willing to go out for an expensive evening, just for the platonic fun of it. The woman generally feels that he is reimbursed by the presence of her company and companionship. The man generally feels that the only reward for his time, energy and investment is rejection and often an insulting judgement. He feels that he has been lied to, led on and conned. Just as some women feel that all men are out for sex, some men feel that all women are out for a "free lunch." Both of these conclusions are correct in some cases but they do not necessarily make the rule. Unfortunately, these are the types who make the heaviest impression

and are, therefore, the dates that we are more apt to remember and draw our stereotypes from. Only by becoming more aware of what makes the opposite sex tick, can we ever expect to get along well together.

The basic male view is that it's okay to pay for something as superficial and fun as a role in the rack but friendship and companionship should be free. Entering this area of sexual finances, many (not all) men feel that if they make a financial investment in the evening, they should be entitled to get their money's worth. Many men would not dream of putting a monetary worth on something as valuable as friendship or companionship and most would gladly date women on a "dutch" basis just for the friendship involved.

The philosophy here is that companionship or friendship is not worth anything if you have to buy it. It should be a gift. In the traditional bread-winning world of the male, when someone takes your money, you are supposed to get something for it. If they take your money and don't deliver, you have been screwed...<u>financially!</u>

This, of course, is not the basic woman's point of view at all. Generally, women tend to put a great deal more emotional worth on the act of sex than men do and feel that men sometimes try to purchase their intimacy for the price of an expense-paid evening.

The typical female point of view seems to be that due to sexist biases, discrimination or just plain fate, men have more money than they do and if anyone is going to take anyone out for any reason at all, the men are going to have to pay the way. The women just flat cannot afford it!

Now the woman could say, "Save your money and we can have dinner at my place," but this might have sexual implications. She could say, "We don't have to do anything expensive," but that could imply she thinks the man is cheap. Besides, with today's high cost of dating, what's not expensive? It all boils down to the fact that the expense-paid evening is the price that men are going to have to pay for their company and that men, in truth, insult them by thinking that there is a monetary price tag on their physical affections.

The general assumption is that a woman usually gets more emotional gratification out of sexual gratification than a man does. When she entrusts a man with something as precious as her emotions and he says, "It was great, see you around," she feels she has been screwed...literally! The man's conventional "wham, bam, thank you ma'am" type of attitude toward sex is only about 180 degrees out of phase with the woman's "woo me" attitude. As a result, many men go ahead and woo the woman, just like it's set up in our finely set book of nonexistent rules, and when he doesn't follow up with at least a phone call, the day after the night before, she feels that she has been used and conned. What does all of this lead up to? Sex war vendettas and hard feelings between the sexes!

Men feel that they have been conned out of their hard-earned money and women view themselves as a commodity on the open market. Both sexes want to meet and date each other and yet we create attitudes which prevent this. Not all guys see women as a piece of meat hanging in the great single's marketplace, and many of those who do were forced into this attitude by sexually biased opinions. A guy has no other way of meeting a woman than to approach her. Once approached, however, a woman often takes the attitude that she will not be used as a receptacle for male lust and immediately assumes her vendettas by reducing him to a rejected pile of emotional rubbish, right there, on the spot. Consequently, he decides to answer his vengeance by using all women, and the beat goes on!

The only way to effectively bridge these sexuality gaps is through honest and open communication, but with our society's anxieties regarding the discussion of sex, before sex, our chances of achieving a successful, platonic pow-wow are minimal. Not only that, communication would probably take all the of the challenge out of dating anyway.

The one rule that society has managed to maintain down through the years which states that two potential lovers should not discuss sex until after they have done it, has to be maintained at any cost. Can you imagine how boring it would be for the woman if she knew that there was no need to sit on the edge of her seat waiting to be mauled the second the car stopped. and what if the guy already knew the answer and did not have to make the adrenalin-producing decision of whether to be called a sex-crazed pervert or an unmanly nurd. Male pituitary glands could become obsolete!

17

CHAPTER

Dating Disabilities

Chapter 17

DATING DISABILITIES

One of the biggest and best dating disabilities one can acquire is in the obsession to date outside the realm of our own generation. Now there are dates, within this realm, that may definitely be worth the risk; however, it might be advisable to take a short class in period classification in order to view some of the generation gaps before falling into one.

In order to provide an accurate picture of today's dating scene, it is necessary to divide this somewhat risque rendering into three basic generations. The problem is, some singles take offense at being classed by vintage so I searched for something else that had a significant effect on singles, other than age, and I came up with...SKIN! Astounding as it may sound, different skin types seem to make different singles act differently.

Now it's very true that there are rebels of every skin type which do not necessarily conform to the generalities of their generation. Generally speaking, however, dating practices seem to follow the following patterns.

Tight-skinned Singles

This generation is generally very active, honest, intelligent, spontaneous and about as stable as an antique egg. Their honest search for truth and their obsession to say it as it is often has a tendency to get under the wrinkles of those singles whose skin is not so tight. Not all tight-skinned singles are into drugs, free sex, mind games and emotionless relationships, but the largest bulk of these subversions are propagated by members of this skin type.

Tight-skinned singles are often more liberal with sex, free with

(227)

four-letter words, honest about socially suppressed topics, open to the use of drugs and reckless with money, emotions and social disease. As a matter of fact, most of the best Herpes jokes are spread by tight-skinned singles who usually consider social disease just a minor, recreational hazard.

Many tight-skins come in second only to rabbits in the art of emotionless sex. And to go with emotionless sex, they often have emotionless relationships. Many of the tight-skins I have talked with have a completely different concept of the term "meaningful relationship" than do other skins. That is to say that some view a meaningful relationship as something that would traditionally be referred to as friendly sex, with no possessiveness, jealousy or other humanly frail characteristics whatsoever.

Tight-skinned girls generally open their own doors and tight-skinned guys are generally broke. For these reasons, tight-skinned girls sometimes go after looser skinned men who usually oblige because they have a fantasy about tight-skinned girls, which really bugs looser skinned ladies. As I stated earlier, however, tight skin has a tendency to get under looser skin, which causes an irritation in the emotional wrinkles and as a result, relationships of this type are often very short. This is due to the fact that people's wrinkles, which are formed over a long period of time, become very comfortable in their fixed form and any deviation in them is very uncomfortable. These deviations or incompatibilities take form in many ways, such as:

1.   Youthful games vs. seasoned wisdom.
2.   Youthful spontaneity vs. seasoned ruts.
3.   Youthful energy vs. seasoned exhaustion.

There is also a theory in sexual physics that states "For every deviation, there is an opposite and equal counter-deviation" and this deviation is that loose skin can have a tendency to cause premature wrinkles in tight skin. So what does all of this boil down to? Simply that:

1.   We have fewer skin problems if we stay within our own generation.
2.   Gallant, tight-skinned guys with bucks really have it made!

<u>Loose-skinned Singles</u>
Loose-skinned singles often reach their state of singlehood with

the conviction that they still have tight skin.   As a result, many go to the single bars looking for another tight-skin, of the opposite sex, who is as wise, refined, stable and secure as they are.   Once in the single's bar, however, they are usually surprised to find that it is occupied almost completely with teenagers and upon further examination, they are even more surprised to find that most of these teenagers are in their early to mid twenties.

Loose-skins generally try out the single's bars at first and then retire to a more restful and refined interest such as sky-diving, jogging or racketball.   Loose-skins are very athletic.   This is often the result of trying to displace the wrinkles with muscles.   Loose-skins are into community activities, travel, church, occupations, reading, education, health spas and in short bettering themselves emotionally, spiritually, intellectually and physically.

It's rumored that loose-skins are more mature, secure and much wiser because as the skin loosens up, it frees the blood flow to the brain.   I am secure in the fact, however, that many loose-skins suffer from an over-oxygenated narcosis as a result of the initial rush.   For instance, there are a lot of loose-skins walking around on tight-skinned nudist beaches that look like they're wearing a long suit of wrinkled underwear, and their main complaint is that they have nothing in common with the other singles.   Of course, it's the tight-skins fault for not conforming to loose-skin philosophies.   Now I know of many loose-skins who get along famously with tight-skins in spite of their incompatibilities.   The fact remains, however, that if you are a loose-skin on a tight-skinned beach and nothing seems to be working, you might consider checking out another beach...closer to home!

Baggy-skinned Singles

Baggy-skinned singles tend to be a little more conservative and reserved than the other two skin types, but they do have their times. They rarely swing, take part in cooking oil parties or share in group sex; however, many enjoy a good sexual fling now and then, on a good old-fashioned one-on-one basis.   A great many view this varicose virility with a humorous attitude, like there's nothing really wrong with it when you get older, because you do it more for the nostalgia than for passion.

There are a few of my closer, baggy-skinned friends, though, who have confided a well guarded and very profound secret to me. The secret is that sex gets better with age. In fact, it gets so good after a while that you can't stand it more than once or twice a month!

Baggy-skins are usually on very close terms with God, ride three-wheel bikes, golf a lot, play cards, shoot pool and take time to enjoy life and things around them. Baggy-skinned singles love each other's company almost as much as they love their own solitude and privacy. These are fantastic singles who are generally very much in touch with themselves and it can really be a beautiful time for coming to terms with life!

Masochistic Motivation

There is nothing like writing a book of this type if you really want to get to know yourself. I began this chapter by honestly looking for one or two slight dating disabilities that I might have. By the time I finished the rough outline, I had discovered twenty-seven! As a result, I have become more tolerant of others, more analytical of myself, more self-tuned and have developed a s-stutter. I plan to perfect these disabilities just as soon as I find someone who will go out with me!

In previous chapters we have discussed, to some degree, the subconscious desire some of us have to sabotage our relationships. THIS PORTION IS DESIGNED TO HELP!!! We will probe the powers of "negative thinking," study the wisdom of "masochistic motivation", research the "requirements for rejection" and learn how to develop the "dynamics of depression" in such a way as to enhance our chance for complete failure! In short, we will learn how to select the dating disabilities that are best suited for our own particular set of incapabilities and weaknesses.

There are several motivations behind our subconscious desires to destroy our dating relationships, so in order to fully develop our dating disabilities to maximum efficiency, we are going to pull each one of these motivations out of our psyche and study it.

Many singles, in their infatuation to hate the opposite sex, have created certain dating disabilities. These dating disabilities are subconsciously designed to make the opposite sex reject them and this confirms the fact in their own mind that:

a.   As usual, they were right all along about the opposite sex.
b.   It's the opposite sex's fault that nothing works out.

c.   They are so much better than the opposite sex that they will
     probably never find anyone else that deserves them.

Motivation Number One

This deals with the very prevalent desire some of us have to
sabotage relationships before they sabotage us. It is still another
classic example of "perpetual emotion" and it can become an
"Emotional Masochist's" best friend. How does it work? Simple!

A relationship of any type requires some vulnerability.
Vulnerability often results in pain.
Our fear of pain causes us to destroy relationshps.
Our loneliness causes us more pain.

It's FOOLPROOF! We can hurt while in love, or out of it!
Because we have it, or because we don't! What more could one
want? Well, if you think this is the extent of its perfection, you're
wrong! IT GETS EVEN BETTER!
Another delightful dilemma of this aspect is that we can't
correct it because we don't know what to blame it on. We don't want
to take the credit for our romantic failure ourselves so...

We blame our pain on others and they blame it on us.
Our friends blame it on fate.
Ministers and priests blame it on the will of God,
And physicians blame it on gas!

With all of these other elements to blame it on, we never have
to realize that it's our fault and therefore we never have to correct
it!
In order to utilize this delightfully devastating motivation to its
full potential, we simply have to convince ourselves that if we allow
ourselves to love, we will eventually lose it and the loss of all that
bliss would be too painful to chance. Hence, we can hurt from not
experiencing love at all and we don't even have to take the chance
that we could be wrong.

Motivation Number Two

Motivation Number Two deals with the subconscious belief that
we deserve whatever we get. Most relationships (marital, passionate

or friendly) provide a fantastic opportunity for letting us really beat ourselves up. The average relationship is full of manipulation and guilt is the greatest manipulator of all. As a result, many of us leave a relationship with an exaggerated and very defeating sense of guilt.

Psychologists tell us that when we have a healthy guilt complex, we often develop a subconscious desire for punishment. Now we can definitely turn to ourselves at just about any time for punishment, but it just isn't as effective as when we have help! There are plenty of people who would be tickled to help us, but finding them is the problem. Many singles are so busy beating themselves up that they don't always have time for us. Oh sure, if you tell them you're a creep, they'll generally agree with you but if you want a really first-class emotional mugging, you have to be a little creative! You have to use your imagination a bit! If someone has other plans, you can look it as a rejection. If someone fails to call, it's because they don't like you. If someone doesn't smile, it's because they think you're ugly. The extent of your grief is limited only by the lack of your imagination! When a relationship fails, you have to let the estranged other convince you that it's all your fault. The masochistic possibilities here are phenomenal. Never will anyone else have more incentive to help you create guilt and develop a destructive self-image than a scorned lover.

Motivation Number Three

This motivation concerns itself with the greatest lie-ability we have--the ability to lie to ourselves. For instance, we may have become fairly well content with the freedom of our single status but if we manage to maintain our old obsession to be paired, we can prevent ourselves from acknowledging this contentment. As the result, we can continue our search for Mr. or Ms. Wonderful, while our suppressed desire for single freedom ruins any potential relationships and our false desire for commitment can keep us convinced that we are unhappy.

Similarly, and in retrospect, we can suppress our desire to be paired by telling ourselves that we are happy being single when we are not. This way, we can openly and knowingly sabotage the relationships that could make us happy.

Regardless which version of these motivations we might have, the only way to maintain these "dynamics of depression" is to refrain from making a choice between single freedom and love. When this is accomplished, we can again be depressed with freedom or without it, in love or out of it!

Motivation Number Three deals with our subconscious desire to stay where we are, whether we like it or not. (Perhaps you can see the possibilities here already!) Whenever we remain in one certain environment for a period of time, we all have a tendency to become bogged down in it. This is called a rut. The biggest problem in adapting to single life is getting out of our "commitment rut." The biggest problem in finding a relationship is getting out of our "single rut." The thing to do here is to convince ourselves that we _are not_ in any type of rut and that the causes and cures of depression are out of our hands.

Regardless of what subconscious motivation we have for wanting to sabotage relationships it is necessary to become somewhat neurotic. Now don't worry. All singles are neurotic. If you're not, you're weird! So how can you be neurotic and average? Simple, have a few bad experiences and convince yourself that love is not worth it! This neurosis that I call emotional deceptionitis (hereinafter referred to as E.D.) is not just a dating disability, it's often a way of life. Just about any single who has experienced the effects of the sex war syndrome, for any duration, has developed a dose of E.D.

As with any dating disability, the cause of this effect can be traced to one or more fears that form a group called, "the neurotic nine." These are:

1. The dread of emotional pain.
2. The fear of repeating old mistakes.
3. A subconscious desire for punishment.
4. The apprehension of rejection.
5. The effects of becoming bogged down in an existing rut.
6. The dread of being committed to an imperfect person.
7. The schizophrenic desire to keep our freedom and be committed, too.
8. Hatred for the opposite sex.
9. The desire to please our society.

Now comes the fun part! Choosing the dating disabilities best suited for our own incapabilities.

<u>Sexist Hateyouitis</u>
This is one of the most delightfully destructive dating disabilities one can have. It combines loneliness with hatred for the opposite sex and...WOW! I'm sure you can see the possibilities already! The best way to acquire this type of dating disability is to:

a. Get yourself into a relationship.
b. Heap on plenty of demands and expectations.
c. When it crashes in a flaming display of emotional fireworks, blame the other person for your pain.

What should you blame the other person for? For not living up to the demands and expectations that you placed on them, of course! For not wanting the same things that you want; for not investing in the relationship to the extent you wanted them to, and for considering their own desires before yours. The best thing you can do is to pick an argument about anything. If logic is against you, argue emotion. If emotion is against you, argue logic. If logic and emotion are against you, throw a tantrum! It also helps to tell yourself that they deceived you, whether they did or did not!
If we are really creative, we can utilize the principles of the sex war syndrome to the fullest extent and hate everyone of the opposite sex. This hatred will inevitably ruin relationships and create bad dating experiences which you can also blame onto the opposite sex. In short, you have to believe that it is their fault that you hate them and the results of this hate will confirm your reasons for hate. Pretty foolproof, huh?

Favorite topics are:

a. How the opposite sex has taken advantage of you.
b. How much someone else reminds you of your ex.
c. How hard you have tried in the past.
d. What you demand in the future.
e. How the opposite sex is all the same.

Telephone techniques are:

a. I'm too busy to talk.
b. Okay, but make it quick.

c.   What's your motive?
d.   (Burrrp!)
e.   You are all alike and I know what you're after.

Allergenic Rejectionitis

This dating disability is generally diagnosed by the reluctance to speak. It is an emotionally allergenic reaction to strangers and it works on the concept that you reject all others before they have a chance to reject you.

In order to induce this disability, you have to convince yourself that others will not see your full worth and will reject you on the basis of some imperfection that they will more than likely make up. In order to attain a desirable degree of rejection, you have to become certain, in your own mind, that you will be rejected. When you are, try to convince yourself that it is painful, destructive and not worth the risk. It is an indication that others hate you and it is your problem. Don't ever consider the possibility that the other person's actions are the result of their own problems and hangups and tell yourself that the rejection is because of you. In order to maintain this disability it is advisable to:

1.   Never establish eye contact with anyone. Always look just to the left of their head. If you are forced to look at someone, don't focus your eyes.

2.   At parties, it's a good idea to enter the room staring at the ceiling. If anyone asks what you are looking for, just say "cobwebs". It's also recommended that you study all of the pictures on the walls, books in the bookcases and record albums by the stereo. If you run out of pictures, books and albums, you can spend the remainder of your time in the bathroom.

Favorite topics include:

a.   Uh, Er Um, Gulp, Uh...
b.   Why you hate parties.
c.   The fact that you don't have friends.
d.   What you did wrong in your last relationship.
e.   Your worst qualities.

Telephone techniques. You can begin by saying:

a.   I know that you're too busy to talk.
b.   I'm sorry to bother you.
c.   You probably don't remember me.
d.   I don't have anything to say. I just called, umm...
e.   Before we go out, I want to explain about this rash on my
      groin.

Beauticious Rigor Mortis

   The single world is full of fives who would not be caught dead with anything less than a nine. Generally, these beauticious rigor-mortis subjects develop the philosophy that physical appearance is all that they have to offer and once someone finds out what they have hidden under their thin sugar coating, no one will want them anyway. For this reason, it's best to go for short, physical relationships which result in an extremely high turnover rate of adequate dating material. One other thing to remember is: Whenever you do something wrong while on a date, act like it was on purpose!

   Rigor Mortis aspects of this dating disability, of course, result in the stiffening of emotional responses, causing the subject to maintain a very rigid, cold state of...affairs.

   If you would like to become a beauticious rigor mortisian, it's best to date only the rich nines and tens of the opposite sex. Let everyone else know you are not emotionally vulnerable and that they have little chance with you. Forget about love and look for the monetary beauty in people. Convince yourself that money can buy happiness and that love buys only pain.

   If you should accidentally fall in love (perish the thought), keep the other person hanging for as long as possible by making promises like "I promise to fall in love with you by February 3rd." But don't ever give them emotional nourishment by exposing your inner self and don't let them know that you love them! If you do decide to get involved emotionally, try to do it on an unemotional level. If you meet someone who is genuinely interested in you, nice (ugh), thoughtful and considerate (heaven forbid), reject them on the spot! Anyone like this has to be very weak and naive to overlook your surface qualities expecting to find something of worth below. Convince yourself that they are on a different plane than you. Look for the surface people who will mistreat you. This way, you will always be the good guy in broken relationships. How could you compete for good guy with someone who is genuine anyway.

In order to maintain this neurosis, it is of paramount importance to keep you walls up and never let any of your inner feelings pop out for others to stare at unless it's someone who will not appreciate them.

Interests should include:

a. Money.
b. Vacation villas.
c. Sports cars, limousines and mansions.
d. Staying away from swimming parties, campouts, hayrides or anything that could detract from your personal appearance.
e. Looking for rich tens.
f. Researching fashions and memorizing designer's names.

Favorite topics are:

a. The people who are infatuated with you.
b. The speed with which other people fall in love.
c. Money.
d. Vacation villas.
e. Sports cars, limousines and mansions.
f. The faults of others regarding dress, conduct, worth and social ignorance.

Telephone techniques are:

a. You won't exactly win any beauty contests but I guess we could sit in a dark corner.
b. If nothing better turns up for me by Saturday, we'll go out.
c. I just called to get someone else's phone number but while I have you...
d. Bugabugabuga, guess who this is.
e. Hi there, "Sweetcakes." This is your lucky day!
f. Someone has been trying to get in touch with me and I figured it was probably you.

Delayed Reactionary Narcosis

This dating disability is diagnosed by the overwhelming tendency to fall asleep emotionally, during a date, particularly if the date has significant possibilities. It can be caused by a low self-image (where you don't want to expose your inner self), an over-abundance of emotional callousing; an inflamed pride (inflammatory prideritis), or any other insecurity that you might happen to catch.

In order to be a successful D.R.N. neurotic, you have to be able to put everyone of significant potential on hold and forget them. It's best never to commit yourself to anything and offering any type of encouragement to a date is completely out of the question. You have to appear enthusiastically deficient and dead to desire. While making love, it's a good idea to yawn.

If any relationship does accidentally occur, it's best to fall in love, unemotionally. If you keep it very cool and logical, it won't last long anyway. It's best to become involved with dating material and relationships that are so emotionally void that they let you sleep in peace. While asleep, however, it's okay to dream about the emotionally stimulating experiences that could have been. (This increases your heart rate and cleans the cholesterol out of your arteries.)

It's recommended that you remain in this emotionally comatose state until you are subconsciously satisfied that all chances for subsequent dates are satisfactorily squelched. Then you can sit up, rub your eyes and say, "Where did everybody go and...why?"

Interests are:

a. Going out with the same sex.
b. Breaking dates.
c. Complete involvement with business.
d. Making excuses not to go out.

Favorite topics include:

a. The last person whom you rejected and how badly they were hurt.
b. The things you demand from others.
c. The reasons for abstaining from any kind of relationship.
d. Logical approaches to human emotions.

Telephone techniques:

a.   Who did you say this is?
b.   Oh (as in, Oh, it's you), I was just getting ready to do something
     else.
c.   I'm busy, but I guess I can take a minute or two.
d.   Well I'll go if the other thing I want to do falls through.
e.   When I got home I found this tongue in my collar and was
     wondering if it was yours.

Massive Depressionitis

This dating disability is characterized primarily by the "depressionate profile."   It takes time to perfect this profile so it's recommended that you practice it three times a day, in front of a large, clean mirror.   First, everything about you has to be influenced greatly by the law of gravity.   Comb your hair down over your eyes, pull your shirttail (or blouse tail) out, untie your shoe laces (if applicable), let your hands hang down to knee level and touch your chin to your upper chest area.   Stand sideways to the mirror and look at yourself.   NO!   DON'T LIFT YOUR HEAD!   All upward glances are accomplished without moving your head!   There you have it, depression in its purest form!   Last but not least, you have to learn how to shuffle your feet when you walk, act very tired and talk without moving your lips.

If you should choose this disability, your favorite interests will be:

a.   Abstaining from exercise.
b.   Waiting for the phone to ring.
c.   Mass inhalation of alcohol.
d.   Watching CARE films of starving people.

Your favorite topics are:

a.   Ex-spouses.
b.   Bad dating experiences.
c.   Loneliness.
d.   Gonorrhea.

Telephone techniques:

a.   Answer the phone in the lowest, gravest tone that you can--
     (hullloo).

b.   Let callers know how depressed you are. Cry if possible.
c.   Don't answer it when it rings and ask yourself who in the
world would call you!

Lethargic Acceptamania

Lethargic acceptamaniacs are similar to the previously discussed depressomaniacs except that they are more selfish with their grief. Many acceptomaniacs are almost normal. They go through the motions of holding down jobs, eating without assistance, and many even date occasionally (very occasionally). They are all extremely dedicated to a defeatist attitude and their tendency to give up makes this the safest dating disability in the world. If you are interested, give it a try!

The first thing to do is to sit back and wait for something to happen. When it doesn't, you get up and shuffle across the floor to your mirror. Next, make a big sigh and sadly say, "Well...I guess it just wasn't meant to be!" Then shuffle slowly into your bedroom and take a nap. Simple, safe and depressing! What more could anyone want? The acceptamaniac attitude is also easy to live with because you are never at fault. The world is at fault! Nothing ever happens and it has never given you anything! Right?

If you choose this dating disability, your interests should include:

a.   Whatever happens to be in the fridge.
b.   Whatever happens to be on TV.
3.   Waiting at home, in case Mr. or Ms. Right accidentally
drives through your front room wall.

Favorite topics will be:

a.   Whatever happens to be in the fridge.
b.   Whatever happens to be on TV.
c.   The time the cat missed the sandbox.

Telephone techniques are:

a.   Hi, do you play double solitaire?
b.   There's nothing on TV but you can come over anyway if you

c.   want.
     Did I ever tell you about the time my cat missed the
     sandbox?

Advanced Pessamania

Any type of pessimism is great for defeating our desires but "advanced pessamania" is an art form of defeatism in its purest state. We can anticipate failure even before it happens! We can be miserable without even a reason.

It is a psychotic form of emotional S & M. Before asking for a date, convince yourself that the other person will say no! If your date wants to go to the toolies, tell yourself that the car would probably break down in route. If someone gives you flowers, it's probably because they know about your allergies.

Your interests could be:

a.   Dating only the misfits because people of true worth will reject you.
b.   Watching the tens and wishing you were good enough.
c.   Fantasizing about rejection.

Telephone techniques are:

a.   I wanted to ask you out but...
b.   I know that someone like you probably wouldn't be interested but...
c.   I know that you're very busy but I'll just take a second.

Obsessed Perfectionitis

This has been one of the most defeating disabilities that I have ever experienced myself. I am a pro on obsessed perfectionitis. You have to tell yourself that you have never met anyone who fully deserves you. Convince yourself that your failures are the result of others' shortcomings and try to dwell on the imperfections of others.

If you can't find a bad habit or an emotional problem in someone, look for a physical imperfection. Chubby feet, a crooked tooth, a weird finger, an appendectomy scar or anything of a significant defeating value. If you fail here, put your creative ability to work. Tell yourself that this seemingly perfect person will probably get ugly, lazy or otherwise imperfect after the commitment. There are literally thousands of imperfections that can be found or otherwise created in others. If you have trouble maintaining this disability, just try and remember what would happen if you fell in love, became hopelessly committed and then, by some miracle, a real, honest to gosh, perfect person showed up! It would just be your luck, right?

Obsessed perfectionitis will almost invariably result in the pain of others, which can also be used in a delightfully destructive way. Tell yourself that this pain, which you have inflicted on others, confirms the fact that you are not ready for a commitment and therefore you should not become involved with anyone of emotional worth. It helps to become interested in those who abuse you and use you. You would not want to hurt anyone that really liked you and besides, anyone who really liked you would be so naive and dumb, you couldn't become interested in them anyway.

Topics, interests and telephone techniques, in this case, are the same as for Premature Infatuitis, below.

<u>Premature Infatuitis</u>

This is a unique type of dating disability, inasmuch as it allows you to make critical designs for your perfect partner before you ever meet them. The chances of finding your one and only are infinitesimal but it still gives you a good reason for waiting and rejecting. Who knows, if you let yourself really fall for your date, you might actually get married someday. Then what would happen if your one and only true love showed up? You would be up the proverbial tree of matrimony without a ladder.

If you want to start drawing up your own specific designs but you don't know what you want, just base them on the one special love that you had, and make some minor improvements. You know the love I'm talking about, we've <u>all</u> had one!

It's good to hold out for someone who is:

a.   Rich and yet generous.
b.   Dependent but independent.
c.   Physically fantastic yet humble and modest.
d.   Sophisticated but uninhibited and down-to-earth.
e.   Sexually liberated with deep religious convictions.

(242)

f.   Sharing but not demanding.
g.   Considerate and yet aggressive.

Whatever you decide to look for in people, make it impossible to find.   You will never find your perfect person but make up your mind not to settle for less.

Interests include:

a.   Looking in singles bars for sensitivity.
b.   Searching churches for casual sex.
c.   Comparing people to your checklist of human imperfections.
d.   Complaining and crying because you can find no one who deserves you.
e.   Embarrassing your date in restaurants.

Favorite topics include:

a.   The imperfections of others.
b.   The dates that could have been.
c.   I'm looking for someone who is more...

Telephone techniques:

a.   "Buzz off, Dog meat!"
b.   No, I won't go to a movie but if you want to take me to that new play, I'll go!
c.   If you were just a half an inch shorter, I'd ask you out.
d.   Obesity really turns me off.   How much do you weigh, anyway?
e.   The only problem with you is...
f.   Try not to embarrass me in front of my friends, o.k.?

CHAPTER 18
Sex & the Single

Chapter 18

SEX AND THE SINGLE

Well, here we are, the BIGGIE!   The one we've all been waiting for!   Assuming that you haven't cheated and skipped ahead to this chapter, and taking for granted that we all know where everything goes, we will begin with the whys--the motivations behind "sex and the single."

Our State of Averageness

There are two things in this world that are universal: hydrogen and the desire for sex.   Unfortunately one of the biggest voids in the life of the average single is sex and it is, without a doubt, the largest source of confusion!   The most significant question burning in the mind of the average single is, "How many others are really getting it regularly?"   I suspect that at least ninety-eight percent of the singles in this country feel that they are _below average_ in the amount of sex they have (the remaining two percent feel that they are barely average).   This is another example of the single's passionate infatuation for statistics.   Why do we like statistics? Because we want to compare ourselves to others in an attempt to see how average we are and where the competition is!

In anticipating the importance of this question (how many others are getting it regularly?)   I have spent a great deal of time pouring over statistics on the sex life of singles from all age groups. The answer comes from seven different sources, each one confirmed and documented (by whom, I don't know) and no two were exactly alike.   They ranged from 51% (probably taken at a grade school for girls only) to 96.7% (probably taken at a motel down on Canal

Street). This would give us an average of 73%; however, the largest bulk of statistics presented an average of 88% for those in an age bracket of 25 years to middle age that do actively engage in sex. Does this satisfy our burning desire for statistics? Of course not! Now we want to know how active is actively.

It wouldn't be as much fun, but it would be much easier and less confusing if we could just measure and take sex in prescribed dosage but I guess it probably wouldn't help the average single anyway. If the average dosage was 200 milligrams of sex per day and we forgot ours, we would just get sick with worry! I have often thought, if the Russians were really smart, they would print and circulate statistics showing the U.S. national average for sexual intercourse at five times per day. Within a week, there would be no one left strong enough to fight.

In an effort to further clarify the extent of our averageness, I would say that the average veteran single does not get it as often as the average majority thinks. The main reason is that singles who have been around for awhile learn the difference between good sex and simple screwing.

Good sex is like a wedding cake! It's composed of two separate properties--the icing, which is similar to the physical pleasure, and the cake itself, which represents intimacy. The icing on a wedding cake can become pretty thin as time passes which, of course, sparks a desire for more icing. As for the younger, never married generation, it's generally believed that one can survive on sweets alone. It is only after someone tries to sustain life on icing by itself for awhile, that one realizes the need for the nutritional benefits of the cake. Generally, singles in the under 25 group are gobbling up all of the icing they can find, in an effort to acquire their daily, recommended requirements of emotional nutrition (which the icing doesn't have). The veterans who have become somewhat selective about whom they are ultimately intimate with, just do without and feel inadequate much of the time! It's really a matter of choice but when the veterans hear how everybody else is doing, they often feel that it's out of their control, that something is wrong with them or they worry about not getting their daily dosage. Then there is always the old "what does everyone else think of me" neurosis!

The main reason behind this neurosis is our public media's obsession to project images of a cornucopia-type sex life for the single world in general where an abundant, emotion-free, uncomplicated sexual utopia exists for all who want it. For the many singles with feelings of failure, this can produce an exaggerated sense of inadequacy and undesirability.

When you consider our social conditioning, it's no small wonder that many of us are slightly neurotic when it comes to the subject of sex. We have all been raised in an atmosphere of ever changing social standards and pressures. The rules and attitudes instilled in us during our childhood tend to stay with us throughout our lifetime and are generally the very foundation of which we build our lives.

Many of us were raised in the belief that sex outside of marriage is unethical to say the least. Mom, dad and society placed this simply super sin right under murder on the great list of don'ts. If a bolt of lightening didn't get us, the revenge of the stork would and then there was always "vulnerable disease" to watch out for!

On the other hand, we now find ourselves in a sexually obsessed society where music, movies, plays and the mass media in general portray a clearly urgent demand for our extramarital participation. You show me a soap where Bill's wife isn't in bed with Fred and I'll show you a soap where Fred's wife is in bed with Bill! Everyone from the "President's Mistress" to x-rated cartoon characters are doing it and if you don't, <u>you</u> <u>are</u> <u>weird!</u>

Sex is used to sell everything from Mom's apple pie to plumbing fixtures. Do we look for the suntan lotion that will protect us best from the sun? No, we buy the brand which suggests that a physical masterpiece will walk up and give us an erotic rubdown with it. Do we guys buy "the breakfast of champions" anymore? No, we buy concentrated litharge and glycerin in the hopes that Ms. Marathon will bring us breakfast in bed. And I still haven't figured out how a guy could smell the essence of a flower-scented douche, three blocks away, or what on earth would motivate him to jump fences and run through hedges to present the feminine user with a fresh bouquet of flowers.

Do we ever see rejection on TV? No, but we see plenty of it in our own life! Do the hero and heroine on the screen become hopelessly bogged down with the problems of jealousy, insecurity, possessiveness and final rejection as a result of sex? Not as a rule! He usually takes care of the bad guys, she takes care of him and they both go on their separate ways as lovers and lifetime friends, with no commitments, hangups or ill feelings whatsoever. It works for them, why doesn't it work for me?   Everybody else is enjoying _free_ sex, why can't I?

This social programming not only makes unfulfilled promises, it has a tendency to put our need for sex on an urgent level.   Sex plays such an important part in the style of our present society that it often makes us think that if we don't get it, there is something wrong with us and to complicate matters, society has programmed us with the belief that this is a healthy attitude.

I wish there were some accurate statistics available on the number of abortions performed, lives ruined and social disease spread out of the assumption that we _need_ sex and that we should perform sexually in order to fulfill our social responsibilities.

Now don't get me wrong!   I think sex is the best thing to come around since protoplasm.   It's just that I have come to the realization that I don't _have_ to have it, I just like to have it! Contrary to some beliefs, I have found that sexual organs don't wither and fall out from lack of use; that celibacy does not cause warts, rotten teeth, baldness, blindness or insanity, and that unless someone psyches themself into believing otherwise, it cannot produce impotence.

Another big factor that contributes to my list of insecurities is the apparent ease with which _free_ sex can be found by everyone on the screen.   For years now, I have diligently searched my bathtub, bed and shower when returning home, and I have yet to find a beautiful, strange lady lounging in any of them!   There have even been extremely hard times when I have searched the closets!

I have also found it a big mistake to base expectations and plan strategies on incidents that I have seen on the screen.   The following is a very true and accurate account of one of my (formerly personal) adventures.

I had waited anxiously for a certain very pretty girl to convalesce from an operation so that I could get to know her better. At last, on a certain romantic fall night, we found ourselves seated together on the veranda of a single's lounge, enjoying our wine, fried mushrooms and each other's company.   Suddenly, she downed her half full glass of chablis, planted it firmly on the table, stood up and said, "Why don't we go to my place for a nightcap?"   Fully forgetting the half-eaten basket of fried mushrooms, I arose with the sexiest smile I could muster and said to myself, "This is it!   Just like the movies!"

When we reached her apartment, she said, "Why don't you fix us a drink while I slip into something a little more comfortable?"   Well, if there were any doubts in my mind at all, they were completely obliterated by that line!   Visions of sheer lingerie and satin sheets merrily danced through my mind as I nervously mixed the drinks.

Suddenly, she was there, standing before me attired in the oldest, baggiest, terrycloth bathrobe I had ever seen!   Convinced that we had probably just seen a different movie, I walked her to the divan and we sat down.   I took a sip of my drink and set the glass on the coffee table to clear the field of any obstacles.   She did the same!   "You're very beautiful," I said, lifting her chin tenderly and kissing her soft lips.   She responded!   Wow!   I have to tell you that it was just like the movies!

I pulled her body close to mine in an uncontrollable display of passion.   "Ow, hey, what are you doing!" she shrieked.   "I've only been out of the hospital a week and I don't even have my stitches out, so don't get funny!"   Acting somewhat indignant at her sarcastic reaction to my inconsiderate display of stupidity, I said, "I'm sorry, I didn't even think about that."   I laughed and said, "In the movies, when a girl tells the guy to mix drinks while she slips into something more comfortable, it means only one thing."

"A terrycoth bathrobe?" she grinned.   What kind of movies do you watch?"   She went on to explain that due to her condition, she was very uncomfortable in her dress and she wanted only to come home and get into the most comfortable thing she had.

The misunderstanding was also her fault to a large degree and I'm convinced that I was caught in one of those games some singles play.   It would have been just as easy for her to let me know where she was really at, if that's where she really was.   Where was I at? Quite frankly, Scarlet, I didn't give a damn!

The Basic Female Attitude

Social programming has succeeded in putting undue stress on both men and women, and has created still another sexuality gap between us as a result.   Traditionally, society has demanded that a woman has to be in love before sharing sex with a man.   Because of this, many women have to fool themselves into believing that they are in love before satisfying their sexual desires.   As pointed out previously, it's very easy to fool oneself if it's convenient to do so, and this one factor, in itself, has produced many painful relationships and fruitless marriages.   Women often sacrifice their own identities, self-respect and independence for what they feel is love but what may be, in fact, just a strong urge to justify sex!

Not all women are that way, just most women, particularly those brought up in the post-Viet Nam era with the free sex fallacy. In short, there are many women these days that are long on sharing sex just for the pure pleasure of it...but wait! There's this weird-looking little guy with a set of wings and a bow who resides in the heart of <u>almost</u> every women and he keeps "harping" on the concept of love with regard to sex. Can you hear him? He's the little guy with the voice that's telling you that there is no little guy! He's a liar, just like all men...right? Well, what about men? These animals who demand sex only for their own selfish pleasure?

The Basic Male Attitude

Men generally believe that sexual intercourse just feels good and is a fantastic answer to sexual gratification and a sound's night sleep. Right? Sure, most men enjoy some degree of emotional intimacy from the act of sex but not even close to the degree that most women do. The basic male attitude seems to be that any woman is bound to want something that feels so good; however, social programming prevents her from admitting it. Because of this, some men feel that women sometimes need to be talked into it. This clears the female conscience and lets the woman do it in the name of love.

Even when a guy tells the woman that he loves her, she knows better but it clears her conscience for bigger and better things, while this verbal virility helps to enhance the act of sex at the same time.

So us guys really have it together. Right men? We do it for the pure, physical pleasure, with no emotional hangups...but wait! In the heart of <u>almost</u> every guy, there's this raspy little voice that says, "You've got to do this and do it well, in order to prove your manhood!"

But it still boils down to the fact that women do it primarily for emotion and guys do it most for the physical pleasure...right?

Well, here comes Catch 22!

In recent interviews, taken with a group of well-known sex therapists, it was determined that the main concern of the female participants, during the act of sex, was connected with achieving an orgasm. What were the men most concerned about? Their emotions, connected with pleasing the lady, of course! See how complicated this simple biological urge is? Women, who are in it for emotion, are concerned mainly with pleasure and men who are in it for pleasure, are concerned mainly with emotion! So what does all of this boil down to? I don't know! Could it be that everybody really digs doing it but our fear of society gets in the way?

Women are urged to deny their sexual desires outside the realm of love, while men are actually encouraged to grope for it. This is just one example of the morbid sense of humor our society so often displays.

The point that I'm going to try to make is that:

1.   Women should not be slandered for being overly emotional and neurotic about sex because men are just as emotional, neurotic and socially controlled as the gals are!
2.   Men should not be slandered for coming on strong, because they are simply answering society's demands to get all they can, the same way women do when they say, "Oh no, you can't!"

Now men generally realize why many women are so possessive in regard to their ovaries but I have found that most women (and some guys) refuse to believe that man's uncontrollable quest for estrogen is a product of social programming. Well, it's not! The big problem is "male pride." Social programming simply establishes the guidelines for it. The male image, associated with machoism, has changed a great deal in recent years, allowing men to feel and otherwise project a more humanistic attitude. But in its place, we are finding an equally devastating condition of mind called "male scorn" which is a by-product of the sex war syndrome. This can be a hard thing for some women to believe but it's even harder for some guys to admit. Generally, however, after a few drinks and some good old "buddy to buddy" talk, even the most avid sex seekers will admit it, even the Incredible Hunk his self!

He had a reputation of being the greatest lover around and I was told that some of the more liberal women would literally wait in line on the Hunk's couch for their turn. In my quest for facts, I approached this mountain of male hormones and struck up a conversation with him. He told me a story that would put Branigan's Bull to shame!

He said that in one certain night-time ordeal, he had serviced seven different gals effectively without even a coffee break! I asked why? He looked at me in complete disbelief. "Why? Because I love it, it feels good!" he laughed.

"Come on,", I said, "I know sex is great, but seven times in one night? That has to surpass all human desire for sex."

He looked at me with a slight grin and said, "Yeah, I guess it does. I guess I just wanted to prove something, and I did!"

I still have to envy this guy. Not so much for his experience but for the ability to do it! Why do I envy him? Sorry gals, you would have to be a guy to understand.

Society has saturated the single male with the attitude that sex is probably the most important thing in the world and any guy that does not exist entirely for its fruits is fruity! One of the heaviest burdens on the average single today is the attitude that we all have to perform sexually. With the male, this burden demands an essential type of conduct that will substantiate his sexuality.

It's true that if a woman refuses to perform sexually, she can be considered frigid or lesbian, but she always has the traditional rationale of chastity to lean back on. Not so the guy! If he doesn't perform, it can be considered an indication of homosexuality, impotence, weakness or stupidity. Why do so many men come on like sex-crazed perverts? Well, many of them are "performing" because they believe that this is what society demands of them.

Guys often act funny as a result of other emotional motivations as well. Some believe that a girl might feel inadequate if they didn't make a pass at her. If the guy just dropped his date off at her place and said "Goodnight," she might feel that he didn't like her. Why? Because, traditionally he is expected to come on strong. To this, most women say, "Ridiculous," but in discussing it further, they usually admit that certain insecurities do prevail when this happens.

<u>Sex in a Nutshell</u>

The subject of sex is so intriguing that one could expound on the philosophies of it until one became completely neurotic. How to act before, during and after, if and if not. Where to put it, when to put it, how to put it, how to put it off, how to achieve, how not to achieve. Then, after writing thirteen extensive volumes on the subject of sex, the average "professional" sums it all up by defining it as a "simple biological function."

For this reason we are going to skip the how's, where's and when's and go directly to the simple concepts which are seldom covered. In a nutshell, there are essentially only four basic kinds of sex and it all boils down to choosing a type that fits each one of us best.

MMaaas Uh Maastureaaa Uh M-Masturbation

I always have trouble with that word.   It's probably the result of some kind of Freudian guilt trip.   I really believe that society has christened it with this formidable sounding verbosity in order to keep everybody in line.   It sounds like something that would be associated with the satanic rites of an unwilling virgin.

Anyway, maa-hasturbation occupies a very significant place in a sex life of the average single, and therefore therapists tell us that we should not feel guilty about it even though many of us do.   Mahast, Mahastur...Self-gratification, often reaffirms the fact (in our own minds) that we are a sexual failure.   It can convince us that we have failed society's plan to be successfully paired and it can hint at the assumption that we are undesirable.

Ma-hasturbation occupies a very prominent position in the life of the average single. In fact, I was told by one sex therapist that there are essentially two types of singles with regard to this subject; those who m-masturbate and those who lie about it!

The D & D (Down 'n Dirty)

The D & D, otherwise known as free or casual sex or the one-night stand, is probably the most prevalent sex in the single world. The main qualification is that it has to be void of all or almost all emotion and intimacy, which is much easier said than done.   Many relationships often start off with the D & D, proceed through friendly sex and eventually end up with the real earth-shaker: emotional sex. Most new singles tell themselves that they can handle this type of emotionless sex but when everything is said and done, they are left null and void.   With the D & D, there is nothing to fall back on "after the lovin'."   It takes time and work to be able to function as a successful sex machine, and emotion has a tendency to rust up our joints.

As pointed out, good sex is comprised of two basic elements: emotion and physical pleasure.   The problem with emotionless sex is that when the physical passion (the only significant element in the D & D) is expelled through orgasm, there is no emotion to fall back on. The physical passion is gone and the remaining void is often filled with nothing but guilt or emptiness.   These lovers can quickly become two naked strangers that suddenly awaken and find themselves lying next to each other.   You have no respect, love or intimacy to take the place of passion, and the act of sex itself can become very animalistic and depersonalizing. In many people, especially women, this depersonalized void creates a feeling of rejection and of being used.

The D & D serves five basic functions.

1. It is a step above masturrrbation in achieving physical pleasure and relief.
2. It serves to convince us that our sexual machinery is intact and functioning properly.
3. It confirms the fact that we are somewhat desirable physically
4. It shows others (in our own minds at least) that we are normal and average.
5. We can sleep better in the knowledge that we have answered the demands placed on us by our society.

The D & D provides very little of the emotional sustenance that we crave.   This type of emotional vitamin is supplied only by relating to someone else in human terms: an overpowering elixir called intimacy.   The problem is many singles overdose on emotionless sex in a frenzied attempt to get their daily recommended dosage of the companionship, love or intimacy that results in emotional gratification.   As a result, most D & D enthusiasts just end up emotionally undernourished and physically depleted.

Now I'm not trying to say that emotionless sex is bad. However, it can be bad for some people, particularly those who use it:

a. In an attempt to find intimacy
b. To prove their sexuality
c. To satisfy a vendetta against the opposite sex
d. To answer social demands.

The D & D is a step above m-masturbation in achieving orgasm and if used within this realm, with some degree of good sense, it can serve a worthwhile purpose.   If two horny people who want absolutely no type of commitment, accidentally run into each other, the D & D can be just the ticket.   The important thing, however, is to know exactly where you stand and what you want.   The only way that you can be sure is through good, honest self-appraisal.   Don't fool yourself or anyone else into thinking that you can handle a D & D if you can't, because you will be the victim.

How do we go about finding a D & D? Bars, parties, grocery stores, schools, they abound everywhere. How do we act? Stay loose and free from intimacy. Don't talk about the kids, the Ex, religion, morals, feelings, attitudes or anything that might confirm the fact that you are human. You can discuss trivia, current affairs, contemporary music, sports, travel or anything that is governed by logic rather than emotion.

The D & D fan club is comprised mainly of new singles, trophy hunters and the very young. Veterans sometimes try one on now and then even though they know it won't fit. The D & D often has a tendency to inflate one's ego while deflating their subconscious sense of self-worth. Many constituents complain that the physical aspects of a D & D are barely worthwhile. Emotional benefits are virtually nonexistent, the psychosomatic aftermath is often unpleasant, the apprehension of having sex with a stranger is high and the possibility of contracting social disease is definitely worrisome. Add to this the numbing effects of emotional callousing caused by the need to stifle our emotions and we have established some of the price tags that free sex can have on it. Now and then you can find a pretty good bargain on sex, but it is seldom free!

Why then is the D & D so popular? Two reasons:

1.   This type of sex is readily available
2.   It is free of commitment and most of the hangups that other sex is noted for.

When the one-night stand runs into two or three nights standing, it leaves the realm of the Down 'n Dirty and generally becomes ...friendly sex.

Friendly Sex

This passionate paradox is basically a D & D but with some humanistic overtones. NO COMMITMENTS, mind you! Just some good old-fashioned, friendly sex. You scratch your friend's back, they scratch yours. The theory behind friendly sex is perfect. It contains intimacy, you can both perfect your techniques through repeated sex in order to achieve maximum pleasure, and you are allowed to please one another with no commitments or emotional hangups. Sounds perfect, right? It's extremely difficult to achieve an emotionless type of emotional sex and this is exactly what you have to do. You have to become involved in an emotional type of sex without emotional commitment. And few there be, if any, that can do it without making enemies.

Now I'm not saying that friendly sex does not exist. I will say, however, that I sure haven't found it and I've searched everywhere, including the Encyclopedia Brittannica.

The little green twirp most responsible for failure is, of course, Jealousy...the result of possessiveness. It's sometimes difficult to share a plain old platonic friend with their other friends, but when sex is involved, the twirp definitely has an edge.

The problem with friendly sex is that it is generally very good sex. It has emotion, continuity, the rewards of giving as well as receiving pleasure and consequently, as with anything really good, it can become very habit forming. Repeated sex has to be pretty good, in order to be repeated in the first place, but when it attains perfection through practice, and you both really start getting a bang out of it...(so to speak), it can become downright addicting!

Now, from the many singles with whom I have discussed this, I'm satisfied that some can experience a repeated, friendly type of sex and yet maintain the friendship. However, the mortality rate of friendships is admittedly high, even with the very best.... friendmakers.

The big hassle is in keeping friendly sex friendly and yet, not too friendly. The best way to do this is to use open and honest communication, eliminate all romance, agree to date others as well as each other, make sure that the frequency of sex doesn't become too frequent. Feel free to discuss other friends (but <u>do not</u> compare) and keep tab on your emotions. Don't look for problems but do look out for them. Anytime that one partner could not be happy for the other partner if he or she finds the perfect partner, their partnership is in trouble!

The main attitude, shared by most of these passionate companions, is that during the heat of this companionate passion, you should keep your cool, remember that this is <u>just a friend</u> but not someone whom you would want to marry and that if your companion screws up by falling in love, it's their problem and not yours! Your problem may be that you start developing a genuine like for your profound friend and even though you wouldn't want to marry them, you can't stand the thought of hurting them. Friend, this is when your heartaches begin.

There is nothing more self-defeating than hurting a friend, especially one you really like. What do you do? If you decide not make the mistake of marrying them, you're going to have to hurt them and this is accomplished only by applying one more layer of emotional callousing to your conscience. Yet another emotional barrier between you and the ability to feel. If this thought stirs up some disgust or anger, ask yourself why?

Occasionally two sex war extremists will meet, fall into an unemotional type of love (if there is such a thing) and enjoy friendly sex repeatedly, without romance or the emotional hangups of possessiveness or jealousy. For two singles who can handle it, friendly sex is great. For singles who fool themselves and others into believing they can, when they can't, friendly sex can be very destructive. Consequently, it might be advisable to determine just how important your friendship is before getting overly friendly. Now for those, like myself, whose strength, in regard to desire, is sufficiently strong enough to enable us to withstand anything...except temptation, heaven help us, and our friends!

Romantic Sex

Now for the biggie: Super sex! The really profound stuff that'll blow your socks off! How do you know when it's romantic sex? Usually if you share it with one certain person consecutively and frequently, over a period of time, you start developing a feeling of possessiveness. How would you feel if this friend made plans to spend next Saturday night (all night) with someone else? See what I mean?

Casual sex, which is good and fairly safe, can develop into friendly sex, which is absolutely great but fairly risky, which can evolve into romantic sex which is really fantastic but usually final. Final because romantic sex generally ends up in one of two final ways: final commitment (marriage) or final goodbyes (dissension).

It might have involved a noncommittal type of living arrangement, somewhere in the middle and it might be dripping from saturated promises of eternal friendship, but one way or the other, romantic sex is almost always final.

Romantic sex is so fantastic that it is quickly addicting. Once addicted, a pair of "love junkies" enter a transition where they each become the most important person in one another's lives. They continue to support each other's habit forever, unless they split up and when this happens, the withdrawal usually creates dissension and broken friendships. One way or another, it is usually final.

This isn't always the case but it's hard to settle for seconds when you're used to firsts. It's really hard to be reduced from most important person to just plain friend without some feeling of resentment. You both vow to always be friends no matter what, you say your final goodbyes, part company and then the fires begin to smoulder. Your pain begins to build, your suspicions mount and if the little green twirp doesn't get you, the desire to replace love's pain, with love's hate, will! Romantic sex can be so earth shaking that it causes some of us to lose interest in any other form of sex. Consequently, we sometimes tend to fall in love with everyone we meet. New singles, in particular, have this tendency to try and make something profound and romantic out of any kind of sex, even something down 'n dirty.

Romantic sex is considered by some sex war extremists to have such a high price tag on it that they shrink into a corner and quiver at the sheer thought of it.

Many "unsingles" consider the devastation of divorce in an often futile attempt to find romantic sex.

Horny millionaires try to buy it,
Defeatists dream of it,
Self-deceivers search the bars for it,
All singles in one way or another, crave it
and
Those of us, fortunate enough to find it, often destroy it
through our fear of it.

Romantic sex has a power of two, squared by sharing. The joy that one experiences through physical pleasure is doubled by the joy that one brings to the other person as well. As a result, it's twice what any other kind of sex is. As with anything of great worth, it is exceptionally rare; however, it is not necessarily as expensive as it is hard to find.

The thing that drives up the price on romantic sex is the pain that we experience from our failures. The biggest reason for failure is our pure human tendency to force the issue: to take simple sex and turn it into romantic sex, at any cost! Intimacy is a natural thing and therefore has to evolve naturally.   It cannot be created or forced.

The Nutshell
Now the nutshell is the hardest part of this concept to swallow! Where does all this leave us?

Ma-hasturbating is self-defeating,
D 'n Ds are dangerous and unfulfilling,
Friendly sex can destroy friendships,
and
Romantic sex is very rare.

Our answers lie within each of us.   We all have to do what we have to do in order to survive.   I did not create this philosophy of "sex in a nutshell" in order to condemn single sex or to confuse the issue; only to unconfuse it.   Perhaps, with these considerations in mind, some of us can, more easily, choose the type of emotional discomforts that we will experience en route to finding romantic sex.

19
CHAPTER
Relationship
Operator's Manual

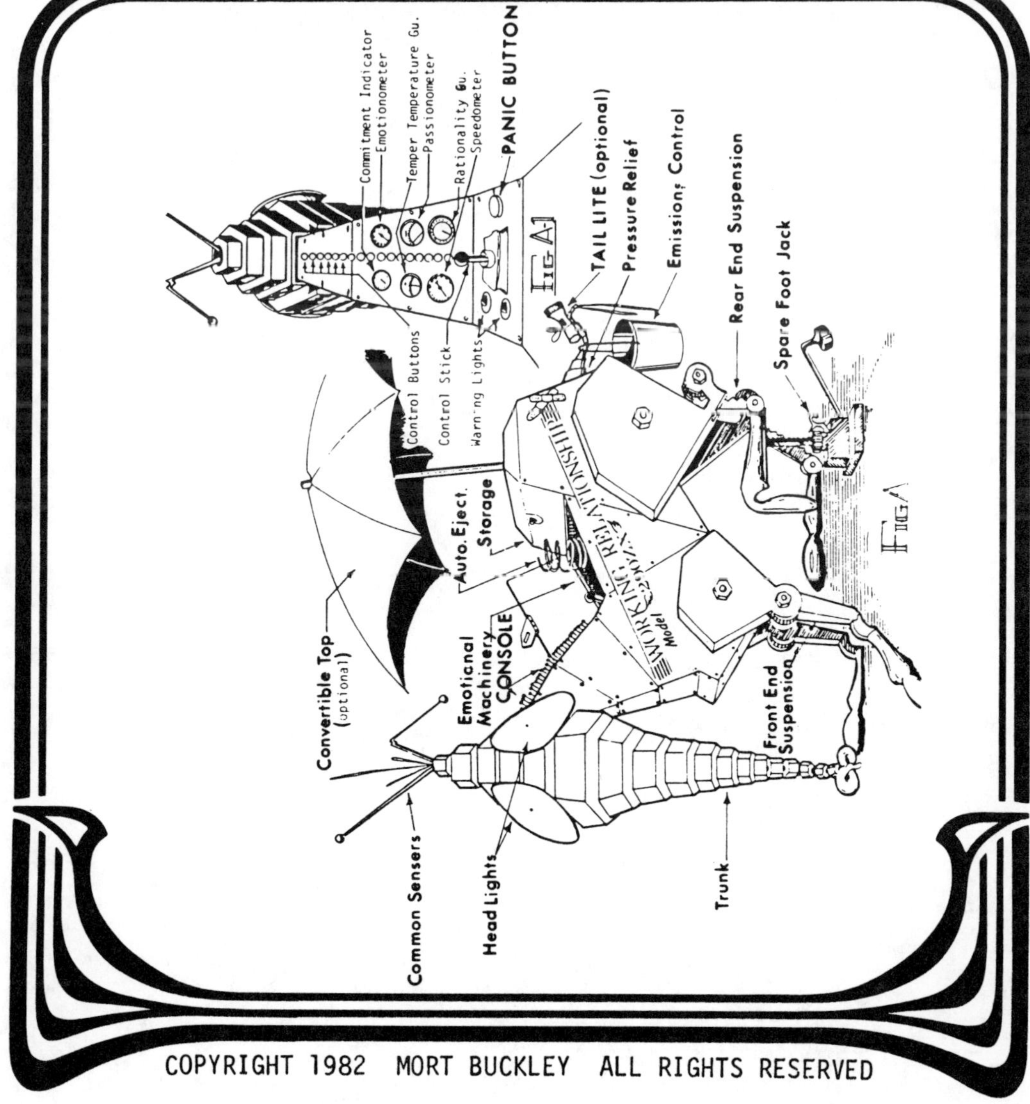

Chapter 19

RELATIONSHIP OPERATOR'S MANUAL

What is Love?

The definition of this four letter crossword puzzle has probably been debated ever since Gargo clobbered Garget with his club and dragged her by the hair, into his cave. Love cannot be defined by the number of orgasms a woman has, any more than by measuring the size of a man's club. However, these are bound to be factors!

Continents have been conquered in the name of love. Infants have died from the lack of love. Scriptures preach the divine importance of love and grants have been awarded for the scientific research of love. As the result of the latter, it seems that our tax money has produced one really profound hypothesis. This is that certain pituitary secretions within our bodies produce the essence of love...or that the essence of love creates certain pituitary secretions within our bodies! No one is really sure which way it is but they are working on it.

The Equity Theory

Poets, writers and composers have, for centuries, tried to express love in their writings. Debaters have debated, philosophers have philosophied and broken-hearted lovers the world over have tried to understand the meaning of love! The results all boil down to a mere fifty or sixty thousand different theories involving emotional responses resulting from glandular secretions and glandular secretions resulting from emotional responses. Probably the most sensible philosophy borne out of this bedlam of debate is the "equity theory," which is the notion that you get what you pay for. In other words, love is like money and a relationship is the bank.   If someone takes out more than they deposit, their bank goes bankrupt!   If your partner is happy, they will be more apt to make you happy.   If they are unhappy, you will be equally miserable.

The theory behind this theory is that the main secret to a successful relationship is to make your partner happy and they will make you happy and all this happiness creates an emotional dependency called...love.   Does it sound too simple?   If so, you can always go back to the physiological study of hormone-soaked lovers whose glands are dumping passionate secretions into their cardiovascular system by the quart and try to figure out why.

Now this might seem to contradict the previously discussed theory that you should not rely on someone else for your own happiness, but it does not.   Each partner in this hypothetically happy relationship gets happiness by pleasing the other. They still rely mainly on themselves for their own attitudes and happiness but they have learned how to get it from seeing their partner happy.   So what happens when you do something to please your partner and your partner doesn't appear pleased?   That's up to you!   You can choose to be unhappy or you can choose to pass it off, but your partner doesn't make the choice, you do!

<u>Counting Hormones</u>

In taking my simple-minded approach to the whole thing, I have come to the conclusion that many people can't fall in love because they don't know what it is!   We often associate love with fireworks, goosebumps, hormonal combustions or the fiery passion of a youthful romance, long past.

Many singles whom I have talked with have hinted that they would be more prone to a certain commitment if they just knew for sure whether or not they were actually in love.   But what is love! Is it a high degree of like...or is like a low degree of love?   At what stage does like stop being like and become love?

In order to understand the logical meaning of love better, we are going to start with the very basics of "puppy love" and research this complex subject clear through to the way that it affects humans. In order to do this, we are going to strike the word "like" from our vocabulary and insert in its place "fifth degree love" (which is puppy love).   Then we are going to progress down the list through "conjugal love" (the really profound stuff) and include the emotional properties that each degree is comprised of. To do this, I have devised a very simple chart (next page) that can put our emotions into a more tangible form so that we can see them better. In a sense, the chart will allow us to count our hormones, to see just how in love we might be.

In this chart, love represents the sum total (100%) of all the emotions listed. Fifth degree love, in this case, is comprised of 35% sexual passion, 5% companionship, 25% apprehension and 35% excitement, which totals 100%.

There are many properties within the concept of love, but they all seem to concentrate down to the four listed above. To provide a better insight, some of the by-products of the four main properties are also listed below.

<u>Passion</u>	<u>Companionship</u>	<u>Apprehension</u>	<u>Excitement</u>
Sexual desire	Commitment	Desire for freedom	Infatuation
	Contentment	Fear of pain	Anticipa-
	Possessiveness	Fear of rejection	tion
	Desire to please	Fear of failure	
	Respect		
	Admiration		
	Trust		
	Security		
	Sharing		
	Jealousy		

The hypothetical percentages listed in the chart are based on an average of my own physical and emotional patterns but each relationship and each person is different.

In filling out your own chart, I recommend using a pencil with a good eraser because, to fill it out correctly, you will be doing a lot of erasing and fine tuning.

OCCASION	DEGREE OF LOVE	PERCENT OF PASSION	PERCENT OF COMPANIONSHIP	PERCENT OF APPREHENSION	PERCENT OF EXCITEMENT
First Meeting	ZERO Degree	30%	0%	50%	20%
First Date	5th Degree	35%	5%	25%	35%
	4th Degree	50%	25%	10%	15%
Stage of COMMITMENT	3rd Degree	40%	50%	0%	10%
	2nd Degree	35%	60%	0%	5%
50th ANNIVERSARY	1st Degree	20%	80%	0%	0%

This simple chart is 100% foolproof, if it is filled out accurately; but your ability to fill it out accurately, is somewhat of a weak spot. In doing so, you will have to reject all desires for wanting your emotions to be just so, and work on your emotions and feelings exactly the way they are. This will also be a good exercise in the self-honesty concept that I have been harping on.

Emotion and passion fluctuate radically in the course of a relationship, so it is recommended that you keep check on them. Just because the emotional side of your chart is low at some certain point, does not indicate a cause for alarm. You have to base your conclusions on the average overall percentages.

This chart can also be used to determine priorities, as in your freedom vs. your profound partner, etc.. In other words, if your apprehension remains exceptionally high, it could mean that your freedom is more important to you than the relationship.

You might note that emotional dependency and need, which are usually significant emotions of love, are not listed in conjunction with the chart. This is because you can form an emotional dependency on someone as a result of desperation, without actually being in love. Since emotional dependency is generally a significant element of love, it makes this desperate need feel like love. It is very difficult sometimes to distinguish between the two. The only way I know to do it is by appraising your partner's happiness.

* Do you get significant pleasure out of just seeing your partner happy, through no doing of your own? If so, you are probably in love.
* Do you enjoy making your partner happy, primarily for the security you get in knowing that you can? If so, you may be needing, not loving!
* How do you feel when your partner is unhappy, through no fault of your own? Does it make you feel almost as bad as they do? If so, this is an indication of love.
* If you have little or no desire to share their sorrow or consider it too much of a personal burden, you may be more in love with the relationship than the person.
* Do you strive to please your partner primarily to get what you want (which is a perfectly human characteristic), or do you simply like to see them happy? Do you please them to keep them or please them to share their joy?

This chart has no way of measuring the intensity of love, only the significance of it. The best way to determine the intensity of love is by establishing how much joy you experience from seeing or making your partner happy, for the appropriate reasons.

The degree of giving or taking has little to do with it. I definitely believe that the world is split into two distinct groups here. "The givers" and "the takers." If someone is a "taker," it does not make them bad. It just means that they get more of an emotional high from accepting than giving. For this reason, "takers" don't give to a great degree, however, they usually enjoy seeing their partner happy.

So now for the bottom line. In using the chart, how do we know when we are ready for a commitment? It's when our COMPANIONSHIP (second column) equals the components in the other three columns. This phase is illustrated as third degree love or...love in the third degree.

I sincerely believe that this chart can also help one get in touch with the concept of love. From a man's point of view, I can at least assure you of this: true love is like a clitoris. It really does exist, it's just that it's somewhat elusive.

The Components of Love

Trying to keep an emotional entity, such as love, in a tangible form, so that we can see it better, is a little bit like catching a burp and painting it red, but here goes!

Love is strange! It does not consist of one feeling, but is comprised of many separate emotions such as companionship, fulfilled pride, sorrow, passion, contentment, admiration, trust, dependency, etc. Love is a combination of all our emotions which are focused upon one certain individual.

When we love someone, we divert to them most of the emotions and feelings that we are comprised of so, in a sense, we give them a portion of our selves. The effects of this strange phenomenon are amplified by the fact that pleasure when shared is doubled, but pleasure when not shared is halved and sorrow when shared is halved but sorrow not shared, is doubled. This makes for quite an incentive to look for love. On the other hand, it's no wonder that when we lose our special person, we seem to lose a great deal of ourselves, too, and the resulting pain can be quite an incentive to dodge love.

Each relationship has a different flavor. The flavor depends upon the degree of each emotion within it. One of love's most common flavors is "plumb painful" so we usually learn either to be cautious or we decide never to taste love again.

A relationship with a new love will be high in excitement and anticipation, but low in trust, respect and contentment of a seasoned relationship. As you can see, relationships change flavors as they mature. The longer love mellows and matures, the more profound and subtle its flavor becomes. Comparing a passionate, new love affair with a properly seasoned relationship of many years, is like comparing cherry soda pop to a well seasoned Pouilly Fuisse. Those who have never developed a taste for fine wine, would probably not enjoy it. On the other hand, the person who has a steady diet of Pouilly Fuisse for twenty years running, might long for a cherry pop.

Often when a relationship starts to change flavors on us, we detect the loss of one ingredient (excitement, maybe) and convince ourselves that the whole thing is going down the tubes. The conjugal love, which replaces passion, doesn't knock your socks off with artificial sweeteners and canned carbonation, but it has a quality that you could never find in a pop machine. It doesn't make your heart pound like the beat of thunderous music or fill you with the adrenalin-producing agents of a five o'clock traffic jam, but it can produce the type of security and peace that many of us only dream about. So when the pizzazz of passion starts to peter out, it can mean that your relationship is just changing flavors!

The Big Race

Many singles, starting a new relationship, expect both parties to advance at exactly the same rate of speed. When the hare progresses faster than the tortoise, he, for reasons of self-preservation, develops insecurities and bounds off. Or the tortoise, feeling pressured, becomes afraid, pulls in its head and goes back to sleep!

Both the tortoise and the hare in this case felt that if the other was not willing to meet their own expectations now, they probably wouldn't in the future either. They both looked for problems to develop in the third stage before they even reached it. The truth is, you will seldom find two potential partners who will progress in a relationship at exactly the same speed, unless they are both doing so out of desperation. Out of this desperation we often try to make love-type demands in the first two stages that these stages will not yet support.

Big Cass

In chapter nine we studied five different species of dragons. They all live on the emotion of fear, and our tendency to run from them is what develops them into the monsters they are. Now there is a sixth dragon that I have saved specifically for the subject of love. This is the dragon of romantic despondence, alias, Draconis Casanovas, or referred to simply as..."Big Cass"!

It's Cass's job to isolate us from love and with the ever growing momentum of the single movement today, Cass enjoys the ultimate in job security.

Some of Cass's weapons are, of course, the effects of "the sex war syndrome," "sexuality gaps," "emotional callusing," rejection, manipulation, emotional misunderstandings and peer pressure. All of these weapons boil down to one thing--pure pain and the fear of it!

Our pain can prevent us from making any emotional investment at all. We figure that we will do it eventually, but there is always tomorrow. The problem is, every time we put it off, old Cass grows one story bigger and becomes one story "fearsomer." By the time Cass reaches approximately 20 stories, we give up all hope of facing him. The truth is, however, that this emotionivorus giant is really just an "emotional squirt"! Like all of our other dragons, he is just an optical illusion. It is our fear of facing Cass that makes him appear to be the giant that he isn't.

Big Cass, like all other dragons, started off as no more than a microscopic spot in the back of our minds. Through our fear of love's pain, however, old Cass has evolved into one of the biggest emotionivorus in the entire single society. It's difficult to be associated with single life without experiencing some pretty significant assaults by Big Cass.

Love has had more of an impact on mankind than possibly any other thing, in any other form, on the face of this earth. Love in many instances has even surpassed our number one instinct; "our fight for survival." This is substantiated, not only by the many suicides as a result of lost love, but by the many lives that have literally been sacrificed for the protection of a loved one. Yet, Big Cass has actually convinced many of us, through our fear of love, that we do not need it.   That it is simply an unhealthy emotion, perpetuated by our social programming.

The Rut

One of the biggest problems that many of us have to conquer before finding a worthwhile relationship is that of digging out of our self-imposed solitary confinement, referred to in less descriptive terms as..."a rut."   Singles generally have very few of these emotional wrinkles, but the ones that they do have, are the grand canyons of the entire rut industry.

There's a fairly popular philosophy floating around that recommends marriage within two years after singlization.   The theory here is that some time after we have successfully escaped the rut of commitment and have adjusted to single life, we fall into the equally deep rut of single life, and can't adjust to the thought of a commitment.   Many of us long for it, but lack the strength to pull ourselves out of our newest rut.

Within the first two years of singlehood, most of us (not all) are most prone to commitment of marriage.   The main reason for this desire to be recommitted is because we are conditioned to live under the conditions that we've become accustomed to.   At this time, many of us take it to mean that we are meant to be married.

After a couple of years or so, the conditioning wears off and we become reconditioned to a new condition--<u>single life</u> and then we take it to mean that we are meant to be single.   It is believed that for every year a single is single, their changes for a successful marriage decrease.   This is because of the difficult adjustment to a recommitted life.   The longer we are single, the deeper our rut becomes and the harder it is to get out.   It does not mean that we would be happier as a single, but merely more contented in the environment that we have become accustomed to.

This single rut, in conjunction with our fears, often joins forces prior to a marriage and it creates a neurosis called "the prenuptual panics."   It is a perfectly natural phenomenon that plagues almost every single who approaches this final finale, or any other type of relationship for that matter.   It's good to remember that the First Single's Rule of Commitment states: "Those most opposed to commitment are often those most desperate for one."

This "single rut syndrome" can cause all kinds of problems and create all types of hangups.   Someone may have spent a considerable amount of time in a marriage just trying to figure out how to survive and make it work. The spouse may have been very assertive, making all of the plans and decisions in the marriage. It is very possible that this person is still in the same rut, and is now looking for another someone to dominate them and take charge of their life. The problem may be compounded by the fact that this domination was responsible for the initial divorce and may cause a second!

Women have been known to leave one wife-beater and marry another. Why? Because their subconscious rut was right for that particular guy. People have been known to be very shy and withdrawn in the company of the opposite sex because their Ex was insanely jealous. Other people have been known to divorce one alcoholic and marry another. Why? Because they had become subconsciously secure with a certain set of circumstances and had become bogged down in their rut.

We're going to cover one more rut before moving on--the rut of "thinking safe." As a result of the "sex war syndrome" and the effects of "emotional callusing," many of us have a tendency to go for a "safe relationship." The funny thing is, no relationship is completely safe.

One of the relationships that is mistakenly considered to be the safest, is with someone else who is married. They seldom start off as a relationship, but almost always end up that way. I have talked with a great many women who have experienced this backseat-type or romance and few, if any, would recommend it. It's a relatively easy situation to find because there are definitely as many husbands out there looking for girls as there are girls out there looking for husbands!

The girl, of course, figures that if he is married, he has to be a find and all she has to do is lure him away from his present person. The husband almost invariably assists the girl in her self-deception by telling her that he gets no love at home, his wife does not understand him and as soon as he gets the children and money thing straightened out, he will get a divorce. The irony that makes all of these relationships the same, is that to each single, their relationship is different! <u>Their</u> espoused spouse will really do it...but seldom does. Another emotional phenomenon is in the possibility of the person becoming involved again and again in other relationships of exactly the same type.

Initially, one of the main reasons that singles get tangled up with unsingles, is the subconscious conviction that it will be a safe relationship. If our person is already espoused, the relationship will simply result in a fun-filled, emotionless fling. The fallacy here is that singles like to have what they can't have. When we become involved with someone whom we can't have, we simply have to have them.

The Classic "Safe Relationship"

Our fear of feeling not only has a tendency to make us sabotage relationships with those whom we could really love, it can also cause us to seek out relationships with people who do not disturb our emotional chemistry in the least. The theory here is that if you get involved with someone who completely "underwhelms" you and where no love is present, no one gets hurt; Right? Wrong!

We often feel so contented and safe from emotional pain that we enter into a boring and unfeeling relationship or even marriage with our good buddy and every buddy gets hurt! One of the "classicalist" statements that I have heard on the single scene is that so-and-so is really strange. They never pick up on the nice guys (or girls), they always go after the creeps, and this is true! We often bypass the ones whom we could really get hung up on and go for the safe ones, we couldn't...but often do!

Types of Relationships

Essentially there are only two basic types of relationships to be found on the single scene. There are romantic relationships and friendly relationships. There are a very limited few which are comprised of both properties, but again, we are speaking in general terms. Romantic relationships usually end up in either marriage or in hard feelings. There is a quote by Colten that states, "Friendship often ends in love, but love in friendship never." Now, I disagree with the "never," however, I do agree that this is _almost_ always the case. For this reason, I seldom consider a romantic relationship with anyone, unless I am certain that it could end up in marriage. So this leaves me with friendly relationships for the most part.

Now friendly relationships are split up into two groups also -- sexual (which is not romantic) and platonic. If two friends can handle friendly sex, that's great; however, as discussed previously, friendly sex is often very hard to control and often ends up in unfriendly feelings. If both parties can't handle it, this leaves the platonic relationship.

Platonic relationships are also very difficult to maintain, especially if there's a physical attraction between the friends. If the platonic relationship is out of the question, that leaves...no relationship at all!

Romantic relationships (as with romantic sex) generally end up in either an ultimate commitment (unsinglization) or in ultimate scorn (hard feelings and pain). Granted, you both vow to be good friends but, as pointed out, it's very difficult to settle for something less than you had. The transition from number one person to good friend does funny things to any relationship.

There are many sub-types of relationships on the single scene, but for practical purposes, we are going to just look at two of the less discussed relationships.

Platonic Relationships

Originally, this contradictory concept of companionship was conceived by Plato as a practical joke! Surprisingly enough, however, it can and often does work. If there is a strong enough need, the human animal will find a way and the need for companionship reaches critical proportions in many parts of the single world. Needs for platonic relationships are predominant, mainly, with the male!   As a result of this statement, I can hear the rustle of fifty million eyebrows raising!   Why the male? Because many of us guys have a real problem with our sexuality!

Women seem to be the largest catalyst for the average relationship today. In short, women generally have more female friends and so do men. The latter is due largely to stigmas and beliefs that are linked to sex, from a man's point of view, specifically the fear of being considered homosexual!

I, for one, am a devout heterosexual, but I enjoy the close respect and companionship that only two buddies can share. I would like to establish many more male friendships but this is somewhat difficult. I can't walk up to another guy in a bar and say, "Hi there, my name is Mort. Can I buy you a drink?"

A lot of men share this fear and with many, it borders on the brink of terror! If buddies live together, or go out on the town together, it's often done in three's or more. This strong strain of sexuality between two buddies often prevents any close relationship at all. There is generally a barrage of male gestures and jive that lets each other and those around them know that they are each okay.

In cases where two buddies share the same living quarters, the residence usually turns into a house of male prostitution and the atmosphere is clearly heterosexual enough to ward off any assumptions of homosexuality whatsoever!

On an average, it is extremely difficult for two male friends to let down and really be themselves. To discuss intimate philosophies, admit certain insecurities and relate in intimate terms. This holds particularly true for the single male who does not have a spouse to help substantiate his heterosexuality.

So Guys, from an intimate point of view, what do we do? It's difficult to attain and maintain an intimate type of relationship with our buddies and God knows the problems we would have in platonic relationships with women! We can sop up some emotional sustenance from group activities or parties and we can fill our lives with an endless stream of one-night stands, but this does not begin to satisfy our needs for intimacy.

The only logical answer would seem to be in finding a meaningful relationship, but these are about as common as worm fingers. Many of us go out looking for intimacy in a series of physical relationships, but after the lovin', there's no feelin' and the would-be relationship crashes and burns! The women hate us and we end up right back where we started from, emotionally starved and physically depleted!

To say that platonic relationships are difficult to sustain is an understatement in its purest form; however, when the need is great enough, anything is possible. Sincere honesty and complete openness is required to make a platonic relationship work. You have to ignore social demands and your sexual desires. Ground rules pertaining to sex and commitment have to be established, and harder yet...maintained!

This type of relationship probably will not be free of sexual desire, however, both parties have to share the same nonsexual attitude toward one another, while at the same time care for and respect each other.

This is the heaviest problem that you will encounter, and sexual intercourse has been somewhat accurately defined as "an expression of affection." If you care for your platonic partner and if any sexual attraction exists, you will have a strong tendency to want to "express your affection." Unless the relationship has evolved to the point of a binding commitment between the two of you, sex can very easily blow your friendship into oblivion!

(277)

The most important tool that you will have to work with is communication. Don't be afraid to confront your friend with sexual or other problems and whatever you do, be honest with one another. The one secret that you may decide to keep from your platonic partner is the occasional one-night stand that you might choose in order to satisfy your physical needs. It's recommended, however, that you refrain from lying about it. If your friendship is strong enough, it will support the truth.

<u>Bi-Single Relationships</u>

The phrase "we are just living together" is gaining acceptance and is becoming more and more popular every day. Aside from being very long and having eight syllables, however, this sentence is often aesthetically difficult to say. For this reason, and for the purpose of this book, the term "bi-single" shall hereinafter apply.

In determining the possibilities for such an arrangement, it's advisable to come to honest terms with ourselves, regarding the motivations involved. Why do I want such an arrangement? How would it make me feel? And what are the legal consequences (yes, legal consequences)? In order to attain a clearer understanding of the bi-single living arrangement, let's look at some of the pros and cons associated with it. Otherwise you could find yourself unformally espoused to a human garbage disposal who talks continually, smokes while asleep and keeps their yeast collection in your half of the fridge.

1.	<u>Bi-single living is more economical.</u> This can be very true if your roommate carries their share of the load and if their idea of thrift is not limited to saving string and eating your yogurt!

2.	A <u>greatly reduced workload.</u> This can also be a very contributing factor, provided your partner is responsible. If not, your workload can be greatly increased. Men and women, due to their social backgrounds, generally have different household capabilities. By combining these different skills, it's possible that a household can run more efficiently. One of the main drawbacks is the failure of one party to live up to the expectations of the other. What might be clean to one, may not necessarily appear clean to the other. You could get stuck with a roommate whose underwear grows hair!

3.   <u>Sex acsexability</u>. If the choice of roommates happens to be a lover or sweetheart, the ready accessability of sex can be quite an incentive.

One problem is that this incentive is so enticing that many singles jump into it like they had springs on their socks, without even considering other considerations. What if a pregnancy occurred? Oh sure, there are precautions, but sperms have been known to have a few tricks up their little sleeves too!

This is a very important consideration, because any children that were born would be illegal unless you both unconditionally agreed on a forced marriage. The other option is abortion. Both of these alternatives are easily agreed to in the heat of passion but are hard to live up to in the coldness of reality. The fear of a forced marriage can be awesome and a woman may have second thoughts about destroying the marvel of new life once it is within her.

The one true asset in this type of arrangement is the ability to check each other out on an intimate, one-to-one basis if the ultimate goal is really marriage. I, for one, would not recommend this type of arrangement for any other reason. I also would not consider it unless I had known my prospective mate for at least six months prior.

Legalities of a Bi-Single Relationship

In a sexual, bi-single living arrangement, there are many legalities to consider. Depending upon the state in which you live, the first legality to worry about could be the lack of legalities. In other words, it could be downright illegal to do it. The only thing you have going for you in this case is the difficulty that the state would have in proving that sexual relations did occur. If, on the other hand, you are guilty of breaking the law, it makes it difficult to go to the courts in an attempt to recover the stereo which your prenuptual partner may have kept as a result of anger.

Some other considerations to be considered are the legal ramifications regarding common law marriages within your state. There can be few things so depressing as to wake up some morning to the realization that you are accidentally but very legally married to a sex object that you have nothing else in common with.

Rarely, but on occasion, a bi-single couple will live together for several years. They will work toward a common goal and she may help to educate him, make house payments and carry half of the load. Later, they split up and to her dismay, she finds that she has legal rights only to the clothes on her back.

A similar injustice can occur if the one who holds the title to the house and car should die. The entire estate would be left to the next of kin and the surviving lover can be left on the doorstep.

So why not put everything in writing and form a legal partnership? This is a good idea if you are 100% sure of your prospective partner. The problem is, however, if your partner is sued or decides to buy the city of San Francisco on an installment plan, you can be equally liable.

If you are really serious about this thing, there are two sound business-like approaches which can offer legal security as well as a terrific tax shelter.

1. Form a corporation. A trip to your local Corporation Commission to get advice on forming your own, can possibly save you considerable expense. Now, let's suppose that you have your corporation set up, the stock issued and it has been kept up to date regarding the investments in time and money, that you each have put into the arrangement. The records and minutes of your corporate meetings are up to date, the red tape and forms are current and now you decide to dissolve the relationship. You may find that coming to terms in a corporate settlement is like coming to terms in a divorce settlement. The good thing about it, however, is that you will each have a fair opportunity to retain what is rightfully yours.

2. The second business-like approach to living together is marriage. Most of us are well in tune with the requirements here, so I will say only that a prenuptial agreement is not a bad thing to consider. It can offer ample legal protection from each other from the time you say I will to the time you say I do. I realize that it's very difficult to walk up to your only true love and say, "Put it in writing, Sweets," however,

you both may be surprised at what the other expects when it is all laid out in black and white! The simplest truth is, if you can't come to terms on paper, you won't come to terms in life after the ceremony either.

Roommates

A prenuptual agreement is a good thing to consider even if you bunk with someone that you will not become nuptual with (a friend of the same sex). This agreement does not even have to be signed or notarized. Just list on paper your present agreements regarding household duties, financial responsibilities for rent, utilities and upkeep, dating and visitation limits, drugs, alcohol and tobacco limitations, parties, pets, privacy and other pet peeves. Refer to this list of agreements when disagreements occur. If you can't come to terms on paper, you might as well forget living together!

As far as legal requirements are concerned, it is recommended that you each make an inventory list of valuable possessions. Also, if you have your own home and are renting to someone else, make sure that the renter realizes that he or she is paying rent and is not making an investment in your mortgage. Further, be careful about allowing them to pay for house improvements and fixed assets. If you have any misgivings, it might be worth a consultation fee with your attorney to see how the law would apply to renting in your state.

Binding a Relationship

One of the most common insecurities that the average veteran single has, seems to surface in the phrase, "What's wrong with me? I just can't seem to find someone to love!" Contrary to personal feelings, this is a universal problem, shared by millions of singles.

Many of us feel that because of callusing we will never experience the hot, wreckless, fiery passion of a youthful-type romance again, and it is difficult to settle for less. As the result, some of us either quit trying, or we end up in a relationship borne from the bowels of desperation. From the many singles whom I have talked with who have found true love, I am convinced that this fiery passion is possible at any stage of the game. So why is the profound, romantic relationship so elusive? It's because people are similar to trees.

Life's windstorms cause our bows and branches to form in

certain ways and in unique patterns. Hence, we enjoy certain things and dislike others. These bows and limbs can be compared to our likes, dislikes, opinions, interests, behavior, ethics, beliefs, etc..

Once these branches are formed, it's very difficult to change their configuration and finding two people with exactly the same limb structure or emotional makeup is impossible, to say the least. Unfortunately, these differences in limb structure are the main problem in finding a relationship or making one work when we do. If these differences are slight enough for two people to accept, that's great! If not, you may as well forget the relationship.

It's bad judgment to enter into a relationship thinking that the other person will be okay once we change them or that traits we can't possibly accept will work themselves out. People are seldom that willing to be changed and once they are, they often become unhappy and discontent with themselves. If you can't accept someone as they are, it's usually best to never get involved.

So many of us find an appealing frog somewhere and try to change it into a perfect prince or princess. On the other hand, when we do occasionally find a perfect prince or princess, they all to often turn into a frog! These frog frustrations are often caused by our very own expectations. Most of us seek a meaningful relationship with others, even before we have time to see their warts. Many of us would deny this. However, the largest portion of the dating scene seems to be centered around the concept of establishing a romantic relationship, immmediately, if not sooner. In other words, many of us spend the majority of our single life on the emotional make, seeking the ultimate commitment from others who we may have never even met. The problem with this is that it causes expectations. We not only develop expectations that set us up for pain when our hopes fail, these expectations often create failure through premature demands that we heap upon intimate strangers. In antiquated terms, we often get the horse ahead of the cart. We set out in hopes of establishing a romantic relationship, with the belief that if it doesn't work, we will settle for just being friends. As pointed out previously, this concept rarely works. As a result, we create a deeply frustrating sense of hopelessness and failure and we continue to sabotage possible friendships.

Expectations also tend to create impatience. Developing even a class-two relationship is a painfully slow process and, because of this resulting impatience, many singles live out a whole relationship in the space of a few days or even hours.   Once in a while, we may fall into a really neat relationship that's just short of perfection. Instead of enjoying the relationship and letting it build, however, we tell ourselves that it would be perfect if only...!   As a result, we sell ourselves on the assumption that the relationship is not good enough in its present condition and consequently, we become dissatisfied with it and destroy it.

The answer that works best for me is to try and forget these expectations and date for the pure fun and the possible friendship involved.   If an ultimate intimacy transpires, that's fantastic!   If it does not, I may be able to keep my friend and a friendship is a pretty fantastic thing, in itself.   Not only that, my hopes and expectations won't come crashing down around my ears in a neurotic holocaust, shattering my fantasies and suffocating me with depression.

Now being a human being, it's somewhat difficult to attain perfection in this philosophy.   I'm still looking around for someone with the type of compatible chemistry that will trigger a hormonal combustion within me and make the earth move the second that we gaze into one another's eyes.   If this happens, I will more than likely throw caution to the wind and plunge right in with all of the wisdom and grace of a pimply-faced adolescent.

I have found that this hormonal combustion (sometimes referred to as "chemistry") is predominantly physical.   The few pituitary earth tremors that I have experienced have occurred with physically beautiful women which, so far, have failed to turn me on emotionally. When I have let myself create expectations and fantasize about this type of relationship, my desire to be in love mixes with physical desire and results in an emotional combustion, which feels just like love.   If it were not for warning lights, I would have surely become an "unsingle" by now and possibly married to a hopeless situation: to someone whom I was not right for and someone who was not right for me.

So is my singlehood the result of some kind of freudian hangup or is it the result of good sense?   Why is it that out of all of the women I have met in the past six years, I have not glombed onto one?   After a great deal of honest appraisal, I have come up with the theory that a good, first-class relationship is not that easily found, created or maintained.

According to professional pessimists, specializing in the field of human behavior, we are generally attracted, physically, to less than 5% of the people whom we meet. Sixty percent of these people are "unsingle" and 80% of the relationships that do transpire have little or no initial attraction at first meeting. Attraction is generally accumulative, occurring over a period of time, out of perhaps, several different encounters. I hate to get started on statistics again, but no matter how inaccurate these statistics are, they can serve to illustrate a point here.

A certain sadist got up on the wrong side of his bed one morning, did some quick calculating, and came up with the theory that we all have to meet several thousand people, of the opposite sex, before we find one that we can have a successful relationship with.

Hypothetically:
> 25% of the people we meet will reject us for any type of relationship at all.

> 50% of our encounters could end up in a casual friendship.

> 25% can end up in a romantic type of relationship.

> 95% of these resulting relationships will fail.

> Only 5% will end up in marriage

> and

> The failure rate of marriage is approximately 40%.

To add to this depressing dilemma, someone else figured out that only one person in 500 will truly accept us, just the way we are, for better or worse!

If these depressing presumptions are correct, there can be some good news here and some bad news. The bad news is that I may have to meet an awful lot of people before finding one of mutual acceptance. The good news is that I am not alone. Everyone has the same problem and is just as miserable about it as I am!

The point that I am trying to illustrate is that no matter how inaccurate these statistics might be, the fact remains that a super good relationship is not that easy to consummate! This bit of news can serve us in two ways:

1.   It can assure us that we are normal and average, in all of our previous failures.

and

2.   It can depress us to the point of forgetting our expectations and cause us to date just for the fun and friendship involved.

Another common cause of failure, associated with our incessant search for a perfect relationship lies in the fact that a perfect relationship, as with a perfect person, just does not exist. Furthermore, a good relationship cannot be found, it has to be created. Many of us find a relationship with someone who we feel hopeful about and when we discover that it's not perfect, we quickly give up and start our search all over again for one which is. We often create designs for our ideal relationship and then try to find people who will fit into our plans. If this has not worked in the past, perhaps a new approach might be to look for those who we feel really hopeful about and create the relationship to fit the people.

If we really care for this person, but have nothing in common with them (which is the most widely used cop-out), we should create some things in common. On the other hand, if there are adversities in the relationship that outweigh our love, it's usually smart to get out. But many of us, with our obsession to have it all our way, hang onto a hopelessly destructive relationship until it almost destroys us.

So far our study of emotional physics might seem confusing and somewhat contradictory.

*   We should not give up on a relationship too quickly, nor should we hang onto one too long.

*   We should not recklessly jump into love and yet we should allow ourselves to love.

*   We should not limit ourselves to looking for the worst in others but we should not fool ourselves into believing the best of others.

*   We should not prevent ourselves from feeling but we should not jump in and commit emotional suicide either.

(285)

    *   We should get our kicks from pleasing one another but we should not rely on another for our main source of happiness.

Nothing is contradictory. The secret is simply to hit a happy medium. Now this statement might seem superfluous but the fact remains that few of us ever do hit a happy medium. Singles (being singles) do have a tendency to overdo everything. If we benefit from making a right-hand turn somewhere on the road to happiness, we often form the opinion that right turns are the only way to go. If a little right turning is good, a bunch is great, so we continue turning to the right and wonder why we keep going in circles.

The best answer I have found to this dastardly dilemma is to clearly and honestly look for the effects and causes of my failures and modify my strategies to fit each unique situation. But instead of learning how to control our love and our quest for it, many of us learn only how to fear it and subsequently do without it!

There is no such thing as safe love. Love is vulnerable. We have to become vulnerable if we are to allow ourselves to love. The problem with many of us, however, is that we have allowed our fear of love to blow our perspective of it, completely out of proportion!

We also become vulnerable every time we use an electrical appliance, answer or unlock our door, eat something or step into our car. Life is vulnerable, but we don't stop living. In order to make life safe enough to live, we must establish certain precautions. That's why we have brakes, lights and horns on cars. Similarly if we develop certain precautions and safety features in our love life it can become as safe as freeway driving!

Love is Like the Automobile

The first few cars, like our first few love experiences, were somewhat deficient in their safety features. They had no horn, the candles in the headlights kept blowing out and the brake guarantee was based proportionately to the thickness of our shoe leather. Through research and experience, the greatest portion of risk has been eliminated in the car and the same holds true for love. There are many safety features to be covered in this chapter which will significantly reduce the risks of being hurt in love.

The first safety feature that we will look at are the warning lights. When we are driving our car and a light flashes on that warns us of low oil pressure, high engine temperature, bad brakes or a shortage of fuel, we usually acknowledge it and take appropriate action.   Once in a while, however, we may be so engrossed in getting where we're going that we ignore or overlook the warning light. This almost always ends up in regret.   So do we stop driving?   No!   We simply start acknowledging our warning lights!

Now, the same holds true in relationships.   We have all had warning lights go on in previous relationships and most of us will admit that we refused to acknowledge some of them.   After our emotional breakdown, we admit that we saw the warning lights but refused to believe them.   So, what do we do, stop loving?   Or do we simply start acknowledging our warning lights?

Now don't worry about not seeing them.   Most experienced singles are so good at seeing warning lights, that they imagine them coming on, even when they don't.   This causes a whole new problem. Many experienced singles are so paranoid about malfunctions within a relationship, that they don't even trust their own warning lights any more.   In a subconscious fear that our warning lights have stopped working, many of us keep turning out of relationships and pulling to the side of the road to check our emotional vehicle.   As a result, we never seem to get anywhere.   We forget that our original failure was due to our reluctance to believe the warning light when it did come on.   Many of us have learned this lesson of caution so well that it defeats its very own purpose.   All we really have to do is watch our warning lights, gauges and dials and act accordingly.   This emotional aphrodisiac called love can cloud our senses, but the risk of this happening is greatly reduced if we control our speed and follow our experience.   Remember, the <u>Single's #1 Law of Experience</u> states: "Only those who are unable to learn from past mistakes are condemned to repeat them."   The <u>#2 Law</u> states: "Experience never comes until right after we need it the most."   Object in point: You have paid a high price for your experience so use it, don't waste it! For every single, there is a different set of warning lights that can be tripped by our potential partners.   Some of these are:

Lack of consideration
Dissimilar ethics or beliefs on critical issues
Generation gaps
Infidelity
Reluctance to communicate
Selfishness

> Broken promises or lies
> Past records in relationships
>   and
> Incompatibilities in general

When a warning light comes on in a relationship, it doesn't necessarily mean "bail out before it blows!" It simply means, take notice and appraise the potential problem.

<u>Importance of Feeling</u>

Another one of the greatest safety features of love is our ability to feel. We have to feel before we can make logical decisions that will allow us to protect ourselves. Now it gets a little complicated here, because feeling is what many of us are most afraid of. The concept of feeling in order to protect ourselves from our feelings is more than some can understand. The fact remains, however, that if we enter the realm of emotional danger, without our emotional senses working at peak efficiency, we could be in trouble!

When we find someone that makes our torso titillate, we should lower our walls and go for it with all of our feeling and logic working at maximum efficiency. When we learn to do this, we can more easily spot the warning lights and if we are honest with ourselves, we can usually determine whether it could work or whether it would be just another painful experience. Similarly, some of us may be very unhappy but without the ability to feel, we cannot accurately determine whether it is due to love, loneliness or gas!

Contrary to popular belief, the pain that we may have experienced has not been destructive. As a matter of fact, if it is used correctly, it can be one of the most constructive assets in our lives. Pain does not eat its way through our nervous system, devouring our red "corpsucles" and any other cells that get in its way. Pain is the most constructive teacher the world has ever known. The experience we derive from pain is called "hindsight." The problem with many singles, however, is that they consider hindsight only as the posterior view of a tightly stuffed pair of designer jeans and they don't learn a thing from their past, they just fear its return!

The past is nonexistent except for the valuable lessons it has taught us, but many of us remain terrified of this nonexistent dimension. The first thing we have to do to whip this dragon is to stop telling ourselves that we just can't feel anymore and do it!

I truly believe that our calluses are created entirely by our subconscious desire to create them. It's only when we make the decision to control them that we can start feeling again.

Now the question for some is "How do we go about doing this?" Unfortunately, there is no one perfect answer to this question. Mankind did not invent hormones but since we all seem to be caught up in the resulting mess, it's up to each one of us, individually, to determine how we can best handle it.

Some of us are very talented in our ability to control emotion. This is because some of us are very self-persuasive and we believe what we tell ourselves (the rewards of self-honesty). For others, self-confidence and self-trust are things that will have to be learned, through the practice of self-honesty.

One of the biggest problems that some of us have in understanding our feelings and emotions, lies in the fact that they are invisible--we can't see them. The only way we can sense their presence is by feeling them. When we let ourselves callous over to the point of not feeling, what do we do?

The best answer I have found is to substantiate or confirm our feelings through a tangible means. If you find someone that you want to care for, take their hand, put your arm around them, give them a quick kiss, an affectionate smile, a funny little card, a hand on the shoulder, a small gift, a loving look, a compliment or you can share your pickle with them.

Let yourself talk in intimate terms about personal subjects. Concentrate more on their happiness. Force yourself to be considerate. Let yourself experience happiness as a result of their happiness and let your emotions react to theirs. If we allow ourselves to give and receive in this manner, emotion will inevitably follow.

This approach will work and most of us know it. For those of you who choose not to use it, that's okay, but accept the results of your decision. Don't tell yourself that you can't feel and that it's not your fault. Remember, every time you put love off or run from it, your subconscious fear of it grows one story larger and becomes much harder to face. If you put it off today, chances are you will put it off tomorrow.

Priorities

The average single spends a great deal of his or her life between a rock and a hard spot! Many desire love but are subconsciously afraid of it, mainly because they don't know how to control it. We may crave compatibility but cringe at responsibility. We may want someone to share with but fear the loss of our freedom.

Love is a decision and it boils down to the choice of priorities. Life is comprised of priorities. We are making decisions and choosing between priorities every waking second of our lives. When we come face to face with a difficult decision (the choice between two priorities), we often put it off for months or even years, and this is the worst decision of all. This indecision eats and gnaws at us and eventually evolves into a monster so big that we can't face it. One of the main reasons for our indecisiveness may be due to our lousy batting record regarding our ability to make the correct choices. Most of us would admit that if we had been COMPLETELY HONEST with ourselves in appraising the pros and cons, our batting record would be much better.

So it is simply a matter of choosing priorities and our ability to select the one most important to us. Only through honest and truthful appraisal of ourselves,   motives and desires can we come to terms with the indecisiveness that stands between us and what we want.

Emotional Investing

Previously, we discussed the concept of love in terms of the giving of ourselves, emotionally, to others.   When we give our love to another, it is similar to giving a part of ourselves and this depletion of our emotional resources is what causes many singles to stop giving, as it rightfully should.   The concept of giving is great, especially with regard to love and the emotions that comprise love.   There are many philosophies that lead us to believe that love is free, so we should give it freely and hope to be loved in return. Well, single life has convinced many of us that love is not free and when we give love without receiving it, we can become emotionally depleted.   The single world in general has a tendency to take all that one can give, but because of its fears and callusing, it often gives back little.

Most experienced singles don't just give strong emotions away. This is called "emotional suicide"! Many successful singles, however, have learned how to invest emotions. The neat thing about investing is that you do get something back in return.   When you give something away, it's a gift with no conditions, but not so for the investment. If we are a loving type of person, it's okay to entrust complete strangers or those that we don't know well, with a companionate type of love, or first degree love, but we can save the really profound stuff for those few who deserve it and have earned it.

The best way I have found to break into the world of emotional finances is by creating my own "emotional commodity exchange system" and trade emotions with people of my choice. In other words, I can trade you a half pound of my trust for a half pound of yours.

If my emotional associate is not agreeable, or is having a "trust flow" problem at this time, I can rescind my offer and try again later if I choose.

The initial commodity exchange should generally start with companionship. I have found that most singles have a surplus of this commodity, and it has a relatively low-risk factor.

Companionship is simply defined here as the pleasure that we each get from being in one another's presence. The par value is low and the investment is minimal. If we enjoy each other's companionship, we might try trading consideration and then intimacy, but I have to bear in mind that my partner has as much right to reject my offers as I do theirs at any point in the relationship. If they forget to call or show a half-ounce debit from some other inconsiderate withdrawal, I am usually careful of a future investment but I seldom withdraw my total investment because the relationship would probably go broke.

I just invest as they invest and adjust my deposits and withdrawals to coincide with theirs. I do not invest more than the other person, unless I'm willing to take the loss. This does happen occasionally, but only through my own choice.

Emotional Finances

From a financial point of view (particularly with men), it's best to gauge our cash expenditures (the high cost of dating) to a degree, proportional to the satisfaction and pleasure that we get out of it personally. I forget the antiquated theory that my cash pays for love in any form. If the pleasure of dating is not worth the expense, I usually find a more economical form of entertainment. If my date doesn't appreciate the 50-cent, all-expense-paid bus tour of the city, my warning light goes on and I may cancel the account with a minimum of loss. If I feel that my potential partner is worth the risk,

I hang in there but I watch the warning lights and accept the results of my own decisions. Unless it was agreed otherwise, my potential partner does not owe me a thing! MY cash expenditures are not an emotional investment.

The tendency that some (not all) women have to demand an initial expense paid fling might tend to make some men consider this theory as unfair, but bear in mind that we are talking "relationship," not a date or a one-night stand. If you want to enter into a relationship with this type of a woman, be prepared to pay for it, willingly and with the knowledge that you can't buy emotional love with cold, hard cash. Emotional love is a great deal more expensive!

Emotional Estimating

Now many at this point will say that the "emotional commodity exchange system" is an interesting theory but its application is impossible and this might be true. Everyone has a scheme that will not work and this could be mine! How do you plan and control emotion? How do you estimate love? The answer lies in our past experiences. Anyone with any degree of emotional callusing, at all, is somewhat of an expert on controlling emotions.

As pointed out, emotion, being a nontangible entity, is impossible to see and is therefore somewhat difficult to gauge. The easiest way I have found to keep track of it, is by putting it into a more measureable form. I can estimate companionship by the amount of joy that I experience when in the company of another. I estimate trust by the degree of intimate conversation that we are willing to share. I estimate consideration by the things that we each do to make the other happy, in the form of small gifts, fulfilled promises, favors, considerations and other emotional pickles that we choose to share. I estimate intimacy by our conversation, touch and body language (the way that we look at or hold each other).

To determine the amount of commitment, it's necessary to evaluate the sum total of all the emotions that have been invested to date. You might even give the love chart a try.

So how do we achieve perfection in estimating the amount of emotion that we invest? The answer is -- we can't. Complete control is almost impossible when applied to any driving force. As an example, we will return to the analogy of the car, as it is compared to love. We can steer a car to within inches of where we want it to go. We can brake a car to within inches of where we want it to stop.

<u>Complete</u> <u>control</u> of a car is virtually impossible. However, we have perfected the extent of its control to a degree of acceptance. If we miscalculate, the end result can be pain and the same holds true for our emotions.

This fear of feeling that many of us have stems from the fact that, out of impatience and lack of experience, we have let our emotions and love prematurely consume us at some point in time. As a result, we may believe that if we relax our emotional defenses, even a little bit, our emotions will consume us again.

We may never achieve total control over our emotions but by using some of the systems outlined here we can control our emotions, like the car, to an acceptable degree.

Again, the simplest way is by keeping our emotions in tangible form and limiting the degree that we substantiate or confirm them. We can use the experience that we have gained in limiting our emotions in the past, only this time, we can use it to our own advantage.

When we want to limit or control our emotions, we should limit the extent to which we share our emotional pickles (touch, intimate conversation, body language, gifts and so forth) to coincide with our partner or to coincide with our own logical decision for intimacy. We can let those emotional calluses work <u>for</u> us, instead of against us, for a change!

I have also found that it helps to avoid fantasizing about unobtained desires and it helps to <u>not</u> set future goals, until I reach the point of commitment. I try to keep the relationship friendly, with a minimum of demands and expectations. It does not pay to sit by the phone, expecting it to ring, and I seldom plan consecutive dates right off. I try to avoid blowing the relationship out of proportion to myself or to others. I enjoy the moments that we have together, but try to leave those moments on the doorstep at night until the relationship will support my bringing them in with me.

Now very few people, if any, are capable of blocking out all thoughts of human desire, but most of us can keep ourselves from dwelling on them if we try. We cannot <u>completely</u> control our emotions by limiting our desire to substantiate them, but it definitely helps. One other weak spot in this system can be our general lack of patience, but this is another problem that we can learn to control through past experience and the incentive to survive.

Because of impatience, some of us try to manipulate another into a relationship or control the amount of dedication another has. If, through manipulation, we do force the other person to progress faster or further into the relationship than they want, it will more than likely fail.

One of the most critical problems in establishing a relationship is in the fact that there are seldom two people who will enter into it at exactly the same speed. Invariably, one will invest more than the other and then make demands on the basis that the other "owes them"! Theoretically, by using the emotional commodity exchange system, both associates will be more likely to progress at the same speed, thus reducing this risk. If one makes a bad investment, that's their problem!

This system also reduces the tendency that many new investors have, to put every emotion they own into a relationship just because of a desire or hunch. This way you can watch the emotional market (or relationship), determine when to invest more or when to get out with a minimum of loss.

If you invest in a relationship only in relation to the progress of the slowest party, you will each have approximately the same incentive to make it work.

If we limit the amount of intimacy in direct proportion to the amount that the slowest party can invest, the chances of success are greatly enhanced. Both parties will have to refrain from fantasizing and adjust their degree of touching, intimate conversation, open displays of affection and their emotions in general, to coincide with each other.

Chemistry

If the "chemistry" is over-powering, and you end up investing the cat and the kitchen sink on the very first date, try to follow some patterns of good sense.

a. Try and keep the investment equal by controlling yourself, not your proposed partner.
b. Try not to go faster in the relationship than your ability to appraise it. It's hard to see something clearly when you are on a dead run.
c. Do not con yourself into believing in something that does not exist and don't fool yourself into overlooking a problem that does exist.
d. On the other hand, do not imagine danger signals that don't exist or subconscious excuses for terminating the

    relationship. Look for the good in it also.

e. Be completely honest with yourself in appraising the relationship at any stage of its progression.

f. Invest your trust, don't give it away. Don't trust someone with your personal expectations until you have some collateral to back it up. If we don't expect anything from others until we have good reason to, our chances of being disappointed are greatly reduced.

Finding a Relationship

Most of us should be self-confident in the amount of wisdom that we have gained from our past experiences and need only to apply it.

The first place to start is by forgetting the theory that a counter, genetic dimension exists in a perfect, perpendicular plane to our own dimension and that through the course of fate and destiny, a perfect counterpart was conceived, designed and built expressly for our own use.

Our search for the eternal fountain of love, through the perfect partner, governs the very existence of many singles. Decisions pertaining to jobs, residences, hobbies, vacations, friends and where to shop are often based upon the obsession of finding our one and only true love.

Somewhere, out there, we believe, exists one Mr. or Ms. Right, who was created specifically for us and no one else will do! When we meet this perfect partner, we will know it beyond any shadow of a doubt. Our pituitary glands will literally explode in a veritable volcano of hormonal eruption and we will be swept away in a raging sea of passion to make love for all eternity beneath the rockets' red glare!

Now it's easy to see that this type of relationship could work, but finding one like it is the problem, right? Right! You can search from now to the end of eternity and never find a relationship like the one above. It just does not exist. We have to choose a non-perfect person, design the relationship, culture it and build it around ourselves. Good relationships don't just mysteriously pop into existence by themselves by way of sheer accident. Nor do we accidentally stumble over one while jogging some morning. So, it's best to forget the idea of looking for one...if, however, by some sheer accident, some gal out there should accidentally stumble across a relationship like the one above, I only hope that it's with me!

Making it Work

As we enter the third degree of love (the stage of commitment), we have to reform our investment strategies. If two people make it this far, it's usually safe to assume that they can each be trusted and that they both want it to work. At this point, we have to step out of the business world of love and enter the emotional world of love. From the third stage on, any investments should be gifts, with no strings attached. From here on, if the relationship is to be successful, you will be making your partner happy by the gifts that you give them, getting your kicks from their happiness and vice versa.

As pointed out previously, we are all motivated by the desire for our own personal happiness. Our desire to make others happy is controlled only by the degree of happiness we get out of it, ourselves. We don't make others happy to make them happy, we do it to make ourselves happy.

If love exists in a relationship, it is based primarily on the amount of happiness that we each get from our partner's happiness and it is without demands. If we demand or trick our partner into making us happy, they will get absolutely nothing out of it and therefore we won't either. The gift of happiness is simply that -- a gift. We could not expect to receive happiness from giving a gift if someone held a gun to our heads and demanded it or conned us out of it. We have to want to make the other person happy and we get our own special rewards from doing it. This is love!

When we rely on our lovers to make us happy, we are placing impossible demands upon them. We have to get our happiness from making them happy, they get their happiness from making us happy and, as pointed out previously, all of this happiness creates an emotional dependency called love.

Again, we cannot demand for anyone to make us happy. The person that thinks only of their own happiness, will never find it!

Individualitibleness

Most successful singles develop an over-powering sense of self-worth and individuality, which may have been virtually non-existent in a previous marriage. This phenomenal feeling is so fantastic that it's worth hanging onto at almost any price. As a result, many of us have a horror of losing it in the course of becoming recommitted.

In truth, we usually do have to sacrifice some of our freedoms as a result of a commitment, however, a good love not   only fulfills our individuality, it can increase our self-esteem. There will never be anyone, more prejudiced of you, than someone who really loves you. If the love is right, we can retain the identities and emotions that make us, us, and feel even better about ourselves in the process.

Other people also fight for being right as well, and our attempts to try and change another is usually about as successful as nailing jello to the wall.   If we can't accept someone for who they are, it's best to move on and look for someone else whom we can love for who and what they really are.

Communication

<u>Honest</u> communication is the backbone of any relationship. One of the main problems in communicating, however, is not communicating!   Another is translation!

One reason for this is because we often hear only what we want to hear or expect to hear.   Another reason is manipulation.   When communication is filled with manipulation, it usually creates an emotional-type of earwax that prevents hearing.   No matter how subtle we are in trying to manipulate another through "honest" communication, there exists a certain deficiency of credibility.

Communication also helps to reduce our tendency to emotionally hallucinate.   What is an emotional hallucination?   It's when something enters our ears as an honest statement of fact and somewhere in the one-inch gap between our ears and our brain, it turns into an insult or threat!   It's like when she says, "I'm too tired tonight," and he hears her say, "I'm getting bored with your lovemaking."   Or, when he says, "C'mon, the exercise will do you good," and she hears, "You're really getting fat and lazy."

This illustrates yet another point in the self-honesty philosophy -- those who search for acceptance are usually pleased to find it, but those who search for rejection are seldom disappointed either.

In order to make a relationship work it's important to understand where we are in relation to those with whom we become related and honest commmunication is the best circuit to use.   The problem with emotional circuitry, however, is maintaining verbal continuity.   If one and/or the other simply doesn't feel like being verbal or honest, the circuit is broken and communication is terminated.   The other person can keep talking but no one hears.

(297)

It's like talking into a dead phone. The humorous aspect of this communication occurs when both parties have a dead circuit and each is screaming into their own phone in an attempt to make the other hear. In an argument like this, no one ever hears you until you screw up anyway so outside of exercising your adrenal glands, it's just a waste of time!

The best way to interrupt a circuit and break the communication is criticism. Criticism is somewhat like the way Mom used to spit on her handkerchief and wash my face with it. Sometimes criticism can be just a little TOO personal!

The best way to establish a circuit of communication is by telling the communicate something that they want to hear, such as "I realize that I'm at fault too." Now this may be hard to do because, when in an argument, our world is sometimes divided into only two groups -- us and those who are wrong! The fact remains, however, that if the relationship is worth saving, someone is going to have to establish the circuit and both are going to have to be honest, not only in the communication but also the translation.

Now some singles seem to believe that any problem worth discussing is worth avoiding altogether, and this theory is substantiated somewhat by the <u>Single's First Law of Debate,</u> which states -- "No matter how much trouble you have winning an argument, your rival will seek to discredit your victory anyway!" If this is the case, the cause is probably due to the fact that the rival is not "honestly" trying to find a solution to the existing problem or that the one avoiding the discussion is afraid of "honestly" being wrong!

Again, honest communication is the backbone of any relationship and without it, the relationship will definitely collapse. Our ability to achieve honest communication is usually proportional to our desire to make a relationship work, but sometimes mind games become more important and as the result our relationship fails. Singles who are infatuated with mind games and the subversive distaste for truth, generally put the complete blame squarely on the shoulders of their past partners, and then they run back out into the single world looking for yet another relationship so they can repeat the same old mistakes.

This theory of honest communication does have one main fallacy and is revealed in <u>The Single's Second Law of Debate</u>, which states -- "Any simple argument can be made insurmountable if the debate lasts long enough." Consistent with the average single's tendency to overdo anything good, a relationship <u>can</u> be communicated to death. This is usually accomplished through --

1. The reluctance of one to communicate and the obsession of the other to communicate anyway;
2. The tendency some have to search for problems which don't even exist;
3. The desire that some have to always be right and the resulting failure of ever coming to terms;
   and
4. The subconscious desire to destroy a relationship and still stay "the good guy."

<u>Termination</u>

If I were smart, I would conveniently forget this portion of the book as I have <u>never</u> enjoyed any degree of success in an unsuccessful relationship. I have been in four relationships in the past six years and as a result I have ended up with twojust plain old conventional enemies, one chronically crazy and one who merely hates my guts! In every case, we have agreed to be the best of friends, always but within a month after our super profound relationship is reduced to plain old friends, a spontaneous, emotional reaction occurs and our platonic love for one another is blown into oblivion. If, in each case, we would have let go <u>completely</u> until after the pain of passion had passed, we might have remained good friends. But no! In our incessant desire to get all we can out of this experience, we usually keep the fires of our passionate discord smoldering until it completely burns up all trace of friendship whatsoever.

Previously, we have compared dating again to experiencing an incredibly horrible itch but the profoundness of an itch doesn't stop here. An itch is also like love! Have you ever noticed that the severity of an itch is in direct proportion to its inaccessibility? In each case, the harder it is to reach that inaccessible goal, the worse it itches. Love, an emotional itch, can become excruciating the second we realize that we can't scratch it!

This is due in part to the pure human trait that singles often have, which makes us desire the things we can't have. But this is only part of it. The real prickly heat of this itch industry has to be...hurt pride!

Have you ever had your pride hurt by someone who broke things off with you! It can feel just like a broken heart. I once broke up (nicely) with a girl over social incompatibilities. She wanted desperately to achieve socially and survive in luxury, while I wanted desperately to simply survive. As a result we were making one another miserable. Shortly after we agreed to always be friends, etc., etc., etc.; she told me that it was best comparing herself to Saks Fifth Avenue and me to a cut-rate bargain store.

I instantly broke into a massive case of emotional hives. I fantasized for months about getting even. "Sorry, sweetcakes, you had your chance! Now let go of my foot, I'm late for a date with a beautiful redhead who owns upper Manhattan!" "Let go," I say, "my Lear jet is waiting!"

I allowed my hurt pride to turn the thankful failure of this gross mismatch into one of the most traumatic experiences of my life. How else could one handle it? Simply by not making it so important. I have found that nothing is quite as inevitable as an insult from a disgruntled lover. In this case, I had let a simple statement of fact, regarding where we bought our clothes, govern my very existence for months. Now it does go somewhat beyond the simple case of hurt pride. I did love this girl very much (the price of not watching my warning lights) and the emotional withdrawal was very traumatic. The thing that made my trauma reach critical proportions, however, was my hurt pride and the resulting fantasy of getting even was what perpetuated my misery. So whatever happened to her? Has fate evened the score for me?   I don't know, because I haven't heard from her since she married and moved to the islands!

Before I learned how to watch my warning lights, I became involved with a gal who conned me out of a great deal of money, time and work. During the process, she tried to ruin other relationships I had with friends and family and then beat my son black and blue. When I broke things off, she couldn't understand why, and as a result she stole my Nikon camera and started spreading false rumors about me that made Adolf Hitler look like a boy scout. Now the _really_ sad part of this story has to do with her overwhelming desire for love and acceptance. This desire, however, will remain elusive so long as she feeds her dislike and distrust for the opposite sex -- the product of some programming or experience she endured long before she met me.

There is a very valuable point to all of this. The point is that grief from bad experiences can affect us to any degree that we let it. We can turn our experience into an asset by learning from it and being (somewhat) grateful for it or if we are big on self-inflicted torture, we can take the easy way out by hating the enemies that we create and blame them for our self-induced grief.

Why the hate and anger? I think one reason is that, after a month or so of painful emotional withdrawal, and the accompanying itch, it sometimes seems that if we could learn to hate this person, it would be much easier to stop loving them. As a result, many people start looking diligently for reasons to hate.

If no reasons exist, outside the fact that it just wouldn't have worked, then some people create reasons. Those with a vivid imagination can make up reasons for hating that are so bizarre they would have made Hitchcock green with envy. Those without a vivid imagination can always look to their friends for help. When there is something as exciting as hate at hand, you can get all of the help you could ever want! The <u>Single's First Rule of Decision</u> is -- "If you consult enough friends, you can confirm any conclusion." This is because friends generally tell us what we want to hear. They listen diligently to our five minute dissertation on circumstances that have helped to form our entire life and suddenly, being overwhelmed with this dose of "instant experience" they begin to tell us exactly what went wrong and what we should do.

Not only that, our very own friends and family often feed the fires of our grief by confirming our suspicions that this degenerated ex-lover was indeed sired by some dog food machine and has managed to con us, abuse us, and use us all in the name of love. Our obsession to hate instead of love is often perpetuated by the single's <u>First Law of Romantic Termination</u> which states -- "Regardless of the reason for termination, it's best to do it in such a way as to make the other person the bad guy!"

The pain of unrequited love can be very consuming, especially when it combines forces with hurt pride and the emotion of hate. In fact, the more adverse emotions that we can pile on it, the more we can hurt and the worse the other person looks to us.

Now many singles have learned how to view their broken relationships with honesty and these are the ones who usually heal the fastest. The fact remains, however, that a great deal of pain can still exist, even though we refuse to amplify it and time seems to be the only antidote. It helps somewhat to realize that everyone goes through this painful process at times, and as long as relationships remain more pleasant to <u>get into</u> than <u>out of,</u> this pure human pain will continue to continue.

I have found that it helps to view these past relationships as an educational experience, that was for the most part, pleasant but which simply didn't make it all the way, rather than a bad investment or a waste of time.

When we discover that the pain which we experience through the termination of a relationship is not there simply because of our loss, it can make the whole thing a lot easier to deal with.   In other words, this type of pain is comprised not only of the affects of emotional withdrawal, it is comprised of a number of less significant emotions such as hurt pride, loss of self-esteem, anger, hate, jealousy, revenge and so forth.   When we learn to see things in an honest light and control the less significant emotions, we heal of love's pain much faster.

These, with many of the other antidotes and concepts listed here, are the product of years of soul searching and an obsession for finding certain truths.   If you can follow the advice in these pages, I really believe that most of your single problems will be over.

If you can't, don't feel bad.   Each time I come out of another one of the excruciating experiences that I am so good at getting myself into, I ponder over these pages and say: "Man, if I had just listened to this book...!"

un-inhibited
single
party
single
single
lover
single
lover
single
Hunk
Extremely Good
single
Ski
single
tennis
single
supurb, brilliant & humble
single

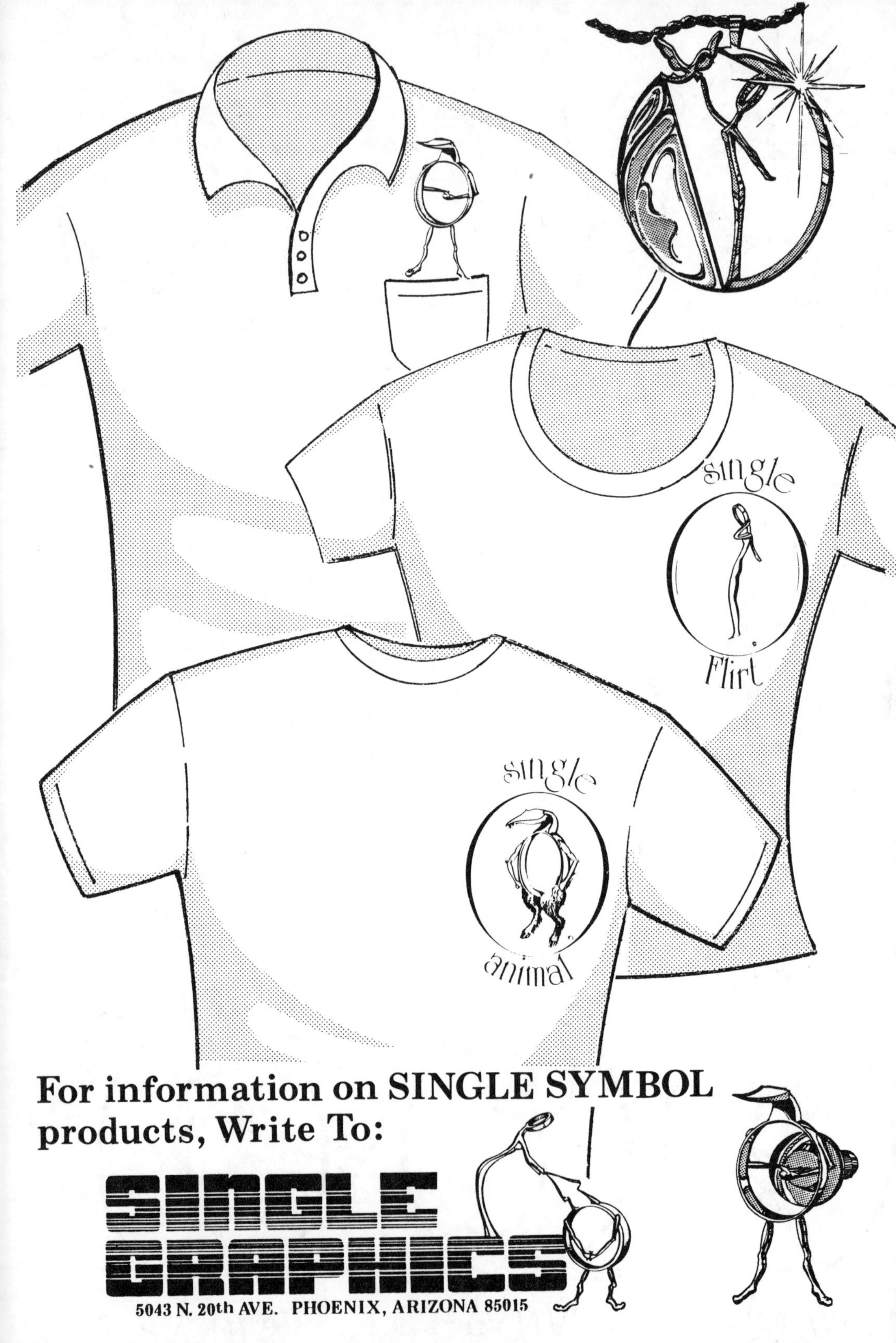

single
Flirt
single
animal
For information on SINGLE SYMBOL products, Write To:
SINGLE GRAPHICS
5043 N. 20th AVE.   PHOENIX, ARIZONA 85015